PRAISE FOR MATT FITZGERALD

"In *Iron War*, Fitzgerald recounts in gripping detail the show-down between Mark Allen and Dave Scott. *Iron War* delves into the vastly different personalities and psyches of these two iconic athletes and presents an anatomy of mental toughness that both men shared."

—*Triathlete* magazine

"A true page-turner about a too-little-known great moment in sports."

—*Booklist* on *Iron War*

"To be a great athlete, you need more than natural ability; you need mental strength to keep going when your body wants to quit. In his new book, writer Matt Fitzgerald dives into the research behind these coping skills and highlights the top athletes who use them. Anyone, whether pro or everyday exercisers, can use these tactics to push further."

—*Men's Journal* on *How Bad Do You Want It?*

"A crucial resource for anyone who wants to run their best marathon. I highly recommend it."

—Ryan Hall, American record-holder, half marathon and 20k, and Olympian on *The New Rules of Marathon and Half Marathon Nutrition*

"In his latest book, Matt Fitzgerald successfully explains the mind-body method of running. Anyone trying to improve and realize their true running potential should read *Run*."

—**Kara Goucher, 2008 Olympian and world championship medalist**

"Fitzgerald has been writing about the psychology of endurance performance for more than a decade now and is really one of the pioneers in terms of trying to take this body of research out of the laboratory and into the field for everyone to try. His latest book examines a series of notable races through the lens of Samuele Marcora's 'psychobiological' theory of endurance. The races make it a fun read, and the psychology is thought-provoking."

—***Runner's World***

"Being a three-time Olympian, I thought I knew all there was to know about diet and training, but Matt blew me away. I can't wait to start implementing all his knowledge into my running."

—**Shalane Flanagan, Olympic bronze medalist and American record-holder**

"Reaching an ideal weight for endurance sports is important, but doing it the right way is even more important. Matt Fitzgerald provides scientific and sound advice for anyone trying to achieve their racing weight."

—**Scott Jurek, 7-time winner of the Western States Endurance Run and 2-time winner of the Badwater 135**

LIFE IS A MARATHON

Also by Matt Fitzgerald

80/20 Triathlon

The Endurance Diet

80/20 Running

Iron War

How Bad Do You Want It?

Racing Weight Cookbook

The New Rules of Marathon and Half-Marathon Nutrition

Racing Weight

Iron War

Maximum Strength

Brain Training for Runners

LIFE

IS A MARATHON

A Memoir of Love and Endurance

MATT FITZGERALD

Da Capo

LIFE
LONG

Da Capo Press
Hachette Book Group
1290 Avenue of the Americas, New York, NY 10104
www.dacapopress.com
@DaCapoPress

Printed in the United States of America
First Edition: March 2019

Published by Da Capo Press, an imprint of Perseus Books, LLC, a subsidiary of Hachette Book Group, Inc. The Da Capo Press name and logo is a trademark of the Hachette Book Group.

The Hachette Speakers Bureau provides a wide range of authors for speaking events. To find out more, go to www.hachettespeakersbureau.com or call (866) 376-6591.

The publisher is not responsible for websites (or their content) that are not owned by the publisher.

Print book interior design by Jeff Williams

Library of Congress Cataloging-in-Publication Data has been applied for.

ISBNs: 978-0-7382-8477-4 (hardcover), 978-0-7382-8478-1 (ebook)

LSC-C

10 9 8 7 6 5 4 3 2 1

Success rests with having the courage and endurance and above all the will to become the person you are, however peculiar that may be. Then you will be able to say, "I have found my hero and he is me."

—George Sheehan, *Wisdom for the Soul*

I believe deeply in the idea of two. Two people. It's the only sanity. The only richness.

—Don Delillo, *The Names*

Author's Note

All of the events described in this book, many of which were recorded contemporaneously with their happening, are faithful to the author's recollections. In a few instances, time has been compressed for the sake of narrative flow. Some names have been changed.

CONTENTS

CHAPTER 1

HEAD CASE

RUNNERS OFTEN SAY that a marathon doesn't really begin until you're twenty miles in. What they mean is that, unless you've completely blown it, only the last 6.2 miles of the race are truly testing and determinative. If the essence of a marathon's challenge is running on tired legs (and it is), the first twenty miles are prologue, not the thing itself.

Something similar can be said of life. If a human life begins *factually* at birth, it does not begin *symbolically* until sometime later, when events transform a mere existence into a story. Take me, for example. I was born on May 5, 1971. But the story of my life, as I tell it, does not begin until seventeen years later, on May 21, 1988, which is the day I discovered I was a coward.

The scene of this unfortunate revelation was Hanover, New Hampshire, a bosky little college town in the western part of my home state. I was there with my fellow Bobcats of Oyster River High School to compete in the Ninth Annual Hanover Invitational, a big regional track meet. Around three o'clock on a mild but overcast afternoon, after most of the other events had been

1

contested, an official raised a megaphone to his lips and, in a strong Yankee accent—all nasal *A*s and silent *R*s—spoke the words that precipitated my undoing as a young athlete.

> First call, boys' thirty-two hundred meters. First call, boys' thirty-two hundred. Competitors should warm up and make their way to the start line for check-in.

A colony of bats took wing in my gut as I rose from my seat on a grassy area outside turn three of the host school's state-of-the-art, eight-lane, rubberized track, half hearing muttered wishes of good luck from a couple of teammates. My legs went noodly and my tongue turned to cotton.

Running competitively over long distances is a lot like dangling by your fingertips from a cliff's edge with certain death below, except it's your entire body that feels as though it's losing its grip. No runner finds pleasure in this doomed sense of strained weakening, but some young runners handle it better than others. Those who possess what exercise scientists refer to as a "low tolerance for perceived effort" tend to quit the cross country team after the shock of their first hard interval workout or race. At the other extreme, a special few runners seem not to problematize these unpleasant feelings at all but instead just accept them, operating under the attitude that, as legendary Australian running coach Percy Cerutty put it, "It's only pain." And then there are those who neither flee to another sport nor shrug off the pain but instead, for whatever reason (and there's really no way to tell if one is predisposed), develop an immoderate dread of this unique brand of suck, a fear so intense that it leads eventually to avoidance behaviors ranging from reduced effort (your coach might not notice the difference between 95 and 100 percent, but *you* sure as hell do) to faked injuries. These runners are known within the sport as head cases, and I was one of them.

I hadn't always been. The previous year's Hanover Invitational had been an occasion of personal triumph. As a tenth grader I'd placed sixth in the 3200 meters, crossing the finish line a few ticks under ten minutes, a huge personal best. While this performance did not quite mark me as a future Olympian, it impressed coach Bob Rothenberg at Brown University (my first-choice college) enough to tell me when I visited the campus in the fall of '87 that if I was able to lower my time in the same event by fifteen or twenty seconds before I applied, he could all but guarantee admission (my grades and SAT scores were solid).

Rothenberg had intended these words as an encouragement, but they signaled the beginning of the end of my sporting aspirations. It wasn't the pressure they imposed that did me in; so-called chokers, who fear failure and cave under pressure, are an entirely different breed of head case. The true seed of my athletic demise, rather, was what my prospective future coach's articulated standard required of me. To meet it, I had to not only mature physically (which was a given) and step up my training (which was doable, as I ran just thirty-five miles per week as a sophomore) but also *try even harder* and *suffer still more* in races, and these demands turned out to be deal breakers.

Where the running / cliff dangling analogy falls apart is at the fact that, in a race, the alternative to hanging on is *not* certain death. It's relief. The suffering you endure in a race like the 3200-meter run that I had just been called to check in for is self-imposed. You choose it. But the choice is not binary: to suffer or not to suffer. There are infinite degrees of trying and suffering. At no point during such a race, except in the final sprint to the finish, are you trying as hard as you can. You're pacing yourself, saving a little something for that final sprint. You have to. And so, no matter how great your present torment may be, you always retain the physical capacity to increase your pace to match the surge of a competitor, however briefly, or to hold on just a bit longer to a rival who's setting the pace. The question is, *can you bear to?*

Most runners, beginners especially, don't recognize this freedom. When they choose to let a competitor go, they don't think they're choosing. I myself did not discover that I could try harder and suffer more until I rose to the level of high stakes, where the decision to hang on or let go became a choice between winning and not winning, between getting into Brown and not getting in. Only then did I learn that I had the capacity to dig deeper, but with each succeeding race I found it harder to take the plunge, or even face its prospect.

My panic at the announcement of first call for my event ascended swiftly from my noodly legs to my roiling stomach to my cotton tongue to my vulnerable brain, where an idea hatched with the jolting suddenness of an epiphany: I would sneak away from the track and conduct my prerace strides on a soccer pitch hidden behind a small grandstand, killing time there until the race started, at which point I would dash back to the track in phony alarm, pretending I hadn't heard the announcements.

No sooner had this craven escape plan come to me than I began to carry it out, as though some outside force were controlling my body. A variety of emotions wrestled within me as I ran from end line to end line on the freshly mowed playing surface. Strongest among them was exhilaration—the thrill of the illicit risk. Almost as powerful was relief—a bosomy comfort that came from knowing I would be spared the suffering of racing today. But then there was the spoiler: shame.

A part of me (a part I would come to know later as The Person I Want to Be) looked on in utter disgust as the rest of me perpetrated this gutless charade. All the other boys who had committed to race the 3200 would show up and take their medicine. I alone lacked the balls. Compounding my shame was the fact that I felt terrific physically—light and bouncy and bursting with well-earned fitness. No doubt about it: I had a Brown-worthy performance in my legs today, if not in my head.

This is the second and final call for the boys' thirty-two hundred meters. Final call, boys' thirty-two hundred. All competitors should come to the start line immediately for check-in.

Jeepers, that sound sure carried! I had counted on *not* being able to hear the race official's last summons from my bleacher-protected hidey-hole. Both my alibi and my resolve depended on it. In an instant, my head emptied of exhilaration and relief and shame expanded to fill the vacuum. I felt as if I had woken from a trance to find myself doing something appallingly out of character, like dancing.

What the hell were you thinking? said The Person I Want to Be to the rest of me. *You have to race! It's not too late!*

Breaking from the line of my current stride, I sprinted toward the track, all too aware that the most absurdly self-sabotaging thing a runner can do immediately before a long-distance race is sprint to the start line. As I tore around the edge of the grandstand, the other runners in my event appeared in the near distance, a nervous cluster of skinny boys responding one by one to the clipboard-holding race official's roll call. It was then that I remembered why I'd chickened out in the first place—and I chickened out a second time. When the starter's pistol cracked, I was again striding to and fro on the soccer pitch in solitary dishonor.

Now came the hard part. Donning a mask of stunned disbelief, I made a second urgent beeline toward the track, tingling with a liar's apprehension.

"What the hell happened?"

Coach Bronson (not his real name, but an uncanny resemblance to the *Death Wish* actor made it impossible for us to call him anything else) spoke these words in a shrill, almost unhinged voice I'd never heard from him. He was standing at the start line with his arms spread wide and his palms turned skyward.

"I was warming up!" I answered in almost the same voice as I crossed over to the infield side of the track. "I didn't hear the announcements!"

Bronson filled my ears with a few choice words, his face purpling and his neck tendons popping out. I dropped my head, not only to show contrition but also to hide my smile, amazed that

I was actually getting away with my half-baked ploy. When my coach had said his piece, I took up right where he'd left off, lashing myself with abuse for my unforgivable screwup, playing the part of a brave warrior denied a chance to do battle by the stupid accident of tardiness.

These histrionics were interrupted by the passing of the runners I should have been vying against. Their strung-out single-file formation indicated a fast tempo, unsurprising given the favorable conditions. Bronson watched them flash by in silence before spinning around to address the meet official.

"Can you let him run a time trial by himself after this race finishes?" he asked, jabbing a thumb at me like a shiftless horse trader talking up a diseased pony.

Before the official could open his mouth to quash this unwonted request, Coach Bronson hurriedly explained that I was one of the state's top runners, but I hadn't yet run the 3200 this season, so I still needed a qualifying time for the state championship, which was only a week away. Now was my only chance.

I hadn't thought of this. Indeed, teenager that I was, I hadn't planned a single step beyond the present moment. Yet I did not dislike my coach's proposal. With minimal discomfort, I realized, I could pace myself to a time just under the state championship qualifying standard of 10:40. But what would that get me? A free ticket to *maximal* discomfort in the state championship itself, which would then be my very last opportunity to meet the mark that Coach Rothenberg had set for me. Unless—

"We can't delay the relays for just one kid," the official said, not without compassion, referring to the final events of the day. "I'm sorry."

Bronson turned back to me and shrugged hopelessly, and with a pang of guilt I saw real remorse in his eyes, an empathetic mirroring of the heartbreak he assumed I felt. My conscience burst into flame, and for about three-tenths of a second I was sorely tempted to come clean.

"It's okay," I said consolingly. "I'll just run the sixteen." I had already qualified for states in the 1600 meters.

It was during the three-hour bus trip back to Oyster River, interrupted by a ritual stop at McDonald's, that the real regret hit. I sat with my forehead planted against the cushy high-backed seat in front of me, consumed by self-loathing. At seventeen, I had only the vaguest ideas about what sort of man I wished to become, but one thing I knew for sure was that I wanted to be like my dad, a three-time marathon finisher who had introduced me to running at age eleven and whom I regarded as the personification of mental strength. Tom Fitzgerald served as a Navy SEAL in Vietnam, trained to deploy atomic bombs underwater on his back. Before that he undertook a series of audacious solo long-distance swims across frigid Lake Ontario, the longest of which he completed in twenty-two hours with a collapsed lung and severe hypothermia. And before that he overcame a traumatic childhood in a wildly dysfunctional family to eventually become a successful novelist and a husband and father willing to make himself truly vulnerable—for example by hiring a psychotherapist—in his earnest pursuit of personal growth. Never had I felt more unlike this towering role model, more incapable of ever matching his capacity to face the fight, hang in there, and endure, than I did on that long ride home.

Deepening my inner despair was the happy chatter and screechy pubescent laughter of my surrounding teammates, all of whom had given their best effort in their various events, or close enough. My only consolation was knowing I could pass off my uncharacteristic muteness and my inability to ingest more than a few swallows of my Big Mac, Filet-O-Fish, french fries, and vanilla shake (same order every time) as swallows of disappointment at having missed my race. No one would ever know.

Approaching Concord, my bleak meditations were interrupted by the concerned voice of my seatmate and best friend, Mike.

"Are you okay?"

Mike and I were evenly matched as runners. Sometimes he beat me, other times I beat him. Our distaste for pain was about equal as well. The previous year, before a cross country meet, Mike and I had been warming up together when a siren loud enough to wake the entire city of Manchester began to wail. After listening to it in silence for several strides, I turned to Mike and said, "I have to admit, my first thought was, *Maybe it's a nuclear attack and we won't have to race!*"

"Mine too!" Mike said.

And yet, unlike me, Mike did not become literally sick with fear before races, and, when the horn sounded, he flipped a switch and left it all out there, every time. Unlike me, Mike was not a coward. He was brave. Normal.

"I'm just disappointed I didn't get to race," I told him.

"There'll be other chances," Mike said.

Well, yes and no. A heat wave struck on the day of the state championship, and I used the inclement weather as an excuse to run a half-assed 1600. The following autumn, still unable to shake my terror of racing's appalling hurt, I mailed in my cross country season, which ended with my being kicked off the team after I goaded Mike and another teammate into showing up at the start line of the New England championship dressed as Batman and Robin. I skipped the indoor track season, and in the spring I was kicked off the outdoor track team when I showed up at the first workout weighing thirty-four pounds more than I had in my last race and refused Coach Bronson's order to run penalty laps after failing to hit my times.

The very next day, I wrote to Coach Tom Donnelly at tiny Haverford College, a Division III school where I was to matriculate in the fall, and informed him, with apologies, that I had decided to quit the sport. (I hadn't even bothered applying to Brown.) I knew with absolute certainty I would never run again.

CHAPTER 2

WE'RE ON TO CINCINNATI

(Modesto Marathon)

TWENTY-EIGHT YEARS AFTER I quit running forever—at 6:55 A.M. on March 19, 2017, to be precise—I pointed an iPhone at my face and pressed a virtual button on the screen labeled "Go Live." My few friends around the world who were awake and on Facebook at the time, and who chose to tune in, saw me standing under a gray sky in dawn light with a mild case of bed head, not alone but in a crowd of men and women, many sporting running caps, all facing the same way. Eddie Money's "Shakin'" blared from unseen outdoor speakers.

"I'm on the start line of the Modesto Marathon with my brother Josh," I said, shouting hoarsely above the din.

I panned the phone until Josh entered the frame, sporting a red Nike running top and a three-day beard.

"Heeeeere we go!" he said, teetering toward me until his nose was almost touching the lens.

"The weather is good," I continued, swinging the camera back to me. "The mood is jolly. For me this is the first of eight marathons in eight weeks. I'm going cross-country in search of the magic of the marathon. More to come."

Four minutes later, we were running.

....

What can I say? I was wrong. I did run again. Lots. Since 1998, when I returned to the sport of my youth, I have completed more than forty marathons plus countless shorter running events, a few ultramarathons, and more than a dozen triathlons, including one Ironman. In a typical day, I spend two hours working out and several more hours writing about running and other endurance sports, which is my job. If a palm reader had shared a vision of this future with the eighteen-year-old me who quit running forever, I would have demanded a refund. Nothing could have seemed more unlikely at the time. Except this: that I would one day grow to accept, embrace, savor, and even crave the very suffering that ruined running for me in high school.

Over the past twenty years I have become a connoisseur, of sorts, of this unique brand of suffering. The pain of endurance racing is to me now as wine is to the oenophile. What seemed a featureless monolith of unpleasantness in my adolescence has evolved into a universe of many dimensions (perceptual, emotional, cognitive) that combine in novel ways in every race. Just as no two wines taste the same to the master sommelier, whose palate also never stops gaining in sensitivity and refinement, I could run a marathon a week for the next one hundred years and never suffer in precisely the same way twice, nor fail to come out unaltered.

When I got back into running as an adult, I wanted two things. One was to realize the athletic potential I had failed to realize in my youth—to run the best race I was capable of. The other was to defeat the coward inside me, whose fault it was that I had not run more successfully the first time around. Progress toward these goals did not come easily, especially in the marathon, a race that thwarted me again and again and thereby became something of a personal white whale—a concrete symbol of what I wished to conquer. I gave extraordinary quantities of time and energy in this cause, more than any mere hobbyist could easily justify, but I did not see my training and racing as a hobby. A coward on the racecourse is a coward off it. My pursuit of the perfect race was nothing less than a quest to become The Person I Want to Be. Twenty years into this journey, I can say without hesitation that I wouldn't take back a single minute I've invested in it. To the extent that my relationship with the suffering of endurance racing has changed, *I* have changed.

There's nothing unique about my experience; every longtime marathoner can tell a similar story. In the middle of the twentieth century, the great Czech runner Emil Zátopek said, "If you want to run, run a mile. If you want to experience a different life, run a marathon." To anyone who hasn't run a marathon, this statement must seem a little over the top. *A different life? Really?* But those who have crossed one or more marathon finish lines receive Zátopek's promise with a nod of recognition.

Even non-runners understand something about the marathon. "Life is a marathon" has become such a commonplace that rappers have been known to use it. Most people take it to mean that life is long and difficult. But anyone who has actually gone the distance knows this equation can also be flipped around: *A marathon is life*—a simplified, compressed, and intensified copy of life. And therein lies its power. To run a marathon is to *practice* life and to practice *for* life. Marathons serve humans in much the same way flight simulators, which assault trainees with every possible crisis, one after the other, serve aircraft pilots. Because life truly is long and difficult, it demands endurance, fortitude, patience, resilience, and long-suffering. The marathon develops all these fundamental human coping skills.

Other types of endurance races also have the power to change people into better versions of themselves, but the marathon has a special magnetism, a singular mystique stemming from its deep history. With origins in a legendary battle fought in Greece in 490 B.C., the marathon has become a byword for testing one's mental or physical endurance. "Life is an Olympic-distance tri-athlon" might be equally true, but it just doesn't have the same sparkle.

In 2016, Sheree Henderson, a runner from California, described in a personal essay for *Women's Running* how running helped her overcome the lingering trauma of childhood sexual abuse, conclud-ing, "When you see how you can physically turn around due to consistency and hard work, it's confirmation that you . . . can turn around emotionally, mentally, and spiritually as well."

Holocaust survivor Sylvia Weiner overcame the psychic wounds of her horrendous wartime ordeal by running marathons. "Running saved my life," she has said. "Without running, my life would have slipped into some bad times."

Through running, Mike Brannigan defied doctors' prognostica-tions for his life with severe autism, becoming a high school grad-uate and a popular teammate (not to mention a sub-four-minute miler) rather than a ward of the state.

Marshall Mathers, better known as the rapper Eminem, used run-ning (fourteen miles a day on a treadmill!) to beat a drug addiction.

Countless amputee war veterans have used running to feel whole again, often with assistance from organizations such as the Challenged Athletes Foundation that serve as a pipeline from the front line to the start line.

The Students Run LA program steers at-risk teens away from the usual fates by training them to run the Los Angeles Marathon. It works.

Girls on the Run harnesses the transformative potential of run-ning to build self-confidence in young girls. Ditto.

Psychiatrists are increasingly prescribing running and other forms of aerobic exercise instead of drugs to treat clinical depression.

The Back on My Feet program lifts men and women out of homelessness—*homelessness*—by turning them into runners.

Whatever it is a person looks for in the marathon, he or she usually finds it. Biased though I may be, I believe running marathons is possibly the single most reliable way to stimulate personal growth in the modern world. And if I'm right, does this not say something profound about the human condition? Our very best scientists and thinkers—whether or not they are runners themselves or have any interest in running—ought to be studying the magic of the marathon.

In the meantime, there's me. I've been fascinated by the marathon ever since I failed spectacularly in my debut, after which, instead of vowing "never again," I vowed to master the distance, seeing in it a way to move past the wimpiness that marred my high school running experience and that continued to tarnish my self-image long afterward. It took me the better part of two decades to complete this mission, but even that hard-won fulfillment did not end my fascination. And so, at the age of forty-five, on the very day in November 2016 when I finally ran the race I had always hoped and believed I had in me, the race that harpooned my personal white whale and redeemed the act of cowardice I committed on a soccer pitch in Hanover, New Hampshire, almost thirty years earlier, I decided to travel America in search of the magic of the marathon—not the science of it so much as its human essence.

The whole thing came together very quickly. In the four months that followed my decision, I came up with a name (the Life Is a Marathon Project), found a sponsor (Hyland's, a Boston-based maker of homeopathic products), created a Facebook page, chose a charity partner (the Treatment Advocacy Center, which works to remove obstacles to the treatment of serious mental illness), signed up for eight marathons scattered throughout the United States on successive weekends, scheduled book signings between marathons to help pay the bills, and, of course, ran a lot.

The Life Is a Marathon Project kicked off with the Modesto Marathon in north central California, a race I had completed twice before, not because I love Modesto so much but rather because I happen to live two towns over in Oakdale and can sleep in my own bed the night before. I persuaded my brother Josh to do it with me, confident the fraternal bonding experience would supply an interesting angle on the marathon's magic. Three years my senior, Josh was my approximate equal as a runner when we were young, but he had taken a different path in life and was struggling against a host of challenges to pull off a middle-age comeback. These included his job as a nurse practitioner serving the underserved in Salem, Oregon, his responsibilities as a husband and a father to two preternaturally energetic young boys, susceptibility to injury and illness, and a nebulous mélange of health issues—chronic fatigue, moderate depression, insomnia, and food sensitivities—that seem to be common in people who had difficult childhoods. (An intense and sensitive boy, not to mention the firstborn, Josh had needed a kind of nurturing that our father, who carried demons from his own painful boyhood, just wasn't ready to give him at twenty-five. Tom did much better with me and our younger brother, Sean.)

Josh's long-term goal was to qualify for the Boston Marathon. He made great progress toward this objective in the latter part of 2016, doing his most consistent training in ages and ripping off a 1:39 half marathon. If he'd been able to sustain the trajectory he was on, he would have stood a good chance of running a sub-3:25 marathon five months later in Modesto and punching his ticket to Boston. But a double whammy of bronchitis and Achilles tendonitis over the winter dashed these hopes, forcing him to dial back his goal to merely finishing the Modesto Marathon and to defer his qualifying bid for another time.

Prior to these setbacks, Josh had wisely planned to take the week of the race off from work (and from his zoo-like home life) and hang out at my quiet house in the country to rest up for his first marathon in thirty years. He flew from Portland to San Francisco and from there took a train to the East Bay, where I picked him up. When I spotted Josh amid the crush of passengers approaching the station exit from the platform, my mouth fell open.

He looked not exactly fat but *fattened*, as though he'd spent the twelve weeks since I'd last seen him on a foie gras farm rather than training for a marathon. And since when was his hair so gray?

"I seem to have picked up some kind of bug," he announced cheerfully as I took the backpack off his hands. "I feel a little off."

"Remember that time you *didn't* feel a little off?" I said. "Yeah, me neither."

The next morning, after a breakfast of eggs and turkey sausage (Josh doesn't do well with carbs), we stepped out my front door to tackle our last long training run before the marathon, an easy ten miler. Within three strides I was two strides ahead. When I looked back at Josh I pictured an old diesel locomotive, straining against rust and inertia to build momentum. Unable to resist the opportunity to indulge in a bit of brotherly hazing, I transitioned from running to Groucho Marx–style speed walking, making a show of being able to keep up with him in this absurd fashion. The stung look in his eyes made me regret the joke, and I switched back to running, pledging inwardly to do nothing more in the days ahead to rattle my brother's confidence.

Our route consisted of four laps around my neighborhood, each lap ending with a short climb up a gentle hill that rose forty feet over a quarter mile. On our last ascent of this glorified speed bump, Josh began to unravel. I watched in rising alarm as the color drained from his face and neck. Near the top, he lurched abruptly off the sidewalk, dropped to all fours on a patch of grass, and vomited copiously. I stood over him in silence, shaking my head. How the hell was this man going to run 26.2 miles six days from now if he couldn't even run half the distance today?

Stomach emptied, Josh wiped his mouth with his shirt and hauled himself back up onto his feet. Our eyes met. I knew exactly what he was remembering, and I knew he knew I was remembering the same thing.

The Chocolate Cake Incident.

It happened in the summer of 1987. Josh had recently completed his freshman year at Hobart College and had even more recently completed his first marathon, the Lake Ontario Distance Classic, easily qualifying for the Boston Marathon with a time just under three hours despite modest preparation. I was a rising junior at Oyster River High School, having earned All-State honors in cross country and track as a sophomore. On the weekend of July Fourth, the whole Fitzgerald family—Mom, Dad, Josh, Sean, and I—trooped down to North Kingstown, Rhode Island, to visit our mother's parents, Stewart and Dorothy Sandeman. Per tradition, Grandma baked a chocolate cake for the occasion. For some reason, Josh and I thought it would be a good idea to go for an evening shakeout immediately after devouring a hearty dinner plus dessert. Midway through the run, as we were cresting a hill not unlike the one in my Oakdale neighborhood, a horrid chicken-and-chocolate chowder blasted into the day through his gaping piehole.

That fall, instead of signing up and training for Boston, Josh put running on the back burner to focus on his studies, a 4.0 grade point average at Hobart having enabled him to transfer to the Ivy League, where he could no longer count on being the smartest person in the classroom to turn in the finest essays and the most flawless exams. At Penn, Josh's reduced activity level conspired with a newly discovered weakness for Philly cheesesteaks to bring out a previously hidden potential for corpulence that, once unleashed, proved forevermore resistant to re-leashing. Although his best days as a runner lay ahead of him, specifically in his midthirties, when a rare confluence of motivation and good health carried him to success at race distances ranging from 5K to the half marathon, the comeback was cut short by a sudden swerve into marriage, nursing school, and child-rearing. I couldn't argue with my brother's priorities, but I yearned to see him run again, knowing how hard he fought for physical and mental well-being, and knowing what running can do for a person.

"Are you okay?" I asked Josh as he steadied himself after his spectacular reprise of the Chocolate Cake Incident (or the Eggs and Turkey Sausage Incident, as I suppose we'll call it), thinking, *Well, at least he's running again.*

"We're on to Cincinnati," Josh said.

Another person in my place might have heard this statement as a baffling non sequitur, but I did not. Three years before, our beloved New England Patriots suffered a devastating loss to the Kansas City Chiefs on a Monday night, a rare drubbing that dropped the Pats' record to two wins and two losses in the early part of the 2014–2015 season. At the postgame press conference, the team's famously surly head coach, Bill Belichick, answered nearly every question he got with a mumbled, "We're on to Cincinnati," New England's next opponent. Belichick's point was that he wasn't interested in dwelling on a bad game, believing as he did that a short memory for failure is essential to ultimate success. Subsequent events proved him right, the Patriots winning ten of their next twelve games, including the 2015 Super Bowl, and ever since then Belichick's prickly deflection has been a refrain in my family, repeated anytime the need arises to shrug off a loss in life. What do you say when you back your car into your own mailbox or when your second grader gets the whole household sick for the third time this winter or when you show up at the wrong airport for an international flight—or indeed, when you throw up your breakfast 9.75 miles into a 10-mile run six days before a marathon? *We're on to Cincinnati.*

"Well played," I laughed, relieved to see Josh's color returning. "Let's both just pretend this didn't happen."

After dinner that evening, Josh and I sat down in the family room to "solve the universe," as we like to say.

"What does running the Boston Marathon mean to you?" I asked, gulping from a bottle of IPA as Josh nursed a glass of water.

"Well, it goes back to what I wrote about in the first post in my journal," he said. "Do you remember it?"

I did. Eleven months before, Josh had created a Facebook page to document his crusade for Boston qualification. In the introductory post, he wrote, "It feels like there's a bit of unfinished business in our family, one last journey that needs to be completed. I'm still running, but my health is not what it used to be, my body not so young anymore. Yet I feel like I need to rally, to get myself back on track, to finish the journey."

The journey Josh needed to finish started thirty-four years earlier, on April 18, 1983, when Josh was fourteen, I eleven, and Sean ten. The sun rose unseen in Madbury, New Hampshire, on that drizzly Monday. Despite the weather, the whole household was up early, and by seven o'clock the five of us were buckling seatbelts in a van driven by Mr. Marshall from up the street. Two hours later, in the sleepy colonial village of Hopkinton, Massachusetts, Dad leapt out the front passenger door to take his place at the very back of a crowd of runners awaiting the noon start of the Boston Marathon, among the other numberless "bandits." The author of three published novels, he was working on a new fiction about a man haunted by demons from a rough childhood (much like him), whose response to learning he has Lou Gehrig's disease is to train for the Boston Marathon—his way of finishing life on his terms. People run Boston for many reasons; my father's was research.

After leaving Hopkinton we rendezvoused with a family friend, Dori, who lived locally and was able to direct Mr. Marshall to a few good viewing spots. When we saw Dad at the halfway point in Wellesley—impossible to miss in red shorts, a red cotton T-shirt, and a red headband—he was all smiles. Six miles down the road in Newton, no longer smiling, he stopped to chat, a choice he seemed to regret when he tried to start moving again. At Cleveland Circle, just over a mile from the finish line, Josh and Sean and I (by prior arrangement) broke from the curb and ran with our father, now shockingly altered, his size 14 New Balance 990s sticking to the road like combat boots in battlefield muck, his gaze cast yearningly ahead in the manner of a lost navigator squinting for land.

Many years would pass before I understood what Dad was going through. In the moment it was all I could do to keep my head from exploding. Seventy-two hours earlier I was calculating fractions in Mr. Emerson's room at Oyster River Elementary School. Now here I was striding freely down the middle of a major urban boulevard, watched and applauded by thousands of spectators, many of whom mistakenly assumed my brothers and I had gone the whole distance ("Oh, look at the kids!"). From my youthful perspective it seemed as if I had blinked and become Elvis, above the law and able to cause mass hysteria just by showing up. But what I felt most powerfully during those enchanted ten minutes was pride in my pops, who had been a hero to me even before this day. Unlike his war service and the other great feats on which his legend was built, however, this one was happening before my very eyes. It didn't matter that he weighed close to two hundred pounds and would complete the marathon more than ninety minutes behind the winner and that he didn't even have a number on his belly. As far as my brothers and I were concerned, our father was the toughest man alive, and his marathon proved it.

Despite the friction between them, Josh looked up to Dad no less than Sean and I did. So I shouldn't have been surprised when, at the breakfast table the next morning, he declared that he was going to start running. Surprised I was, though, and not exactly thrilled, having intended to make the same declaration. I now had to think of a way to second it without sounding like a copycat little brother.

"Me too!" I said.

After school that day, Josh and I ran six miles together on the narrow roads, paved and unpaved, that snaked through the piney forests surrounding our home. Two days later, we did it again, and so on. Neither of us thought about running the Boston Marathon ourselves, however, until many years later—in Josh's case not until 2013, when the bombing occurred. In the wake of this tragedy Josh vowed to run the race the following year in defense of the spirit of the event that meant so much to our family (Dad having run it twice more, in 1987 and 1988, and I once, in 2009). But he forgot to start training, and the next Fitzgerald to run Boston was not Josh but Sean, who came to running much later than we had but proved to have his own knack for it. Inspired by Sean's achievement, Josh renewed his pledge, but again he made no effort to fulfill it. Then, in 2016, I ran Boston a second time, and after that Josh finally got serious, going public with his intentions on Facebook and hitting me up for a training plan.

"I get all that," I told him in our solving-the-universe session on the eve of the 2017 Modesto Marathon, "but isn't there also a more personal significance to this goal for you—something that has nothing to do with the rest of the family?"

"Yes, definitely," Josh said. "To be brutally honest, I've felt like a complete fuckup my whole life. I've had a really hard time finding my place in the world. Like a lot of people who had an unhappy childhood, I've never really grown up in certain ways. I have trouble sticking with things. But there are a few things I *am* sure about, and one of them is that I'm a runner. For me, qualifying for Boston is partly about just that—qualifying for Boston— and partly about breaking patterns I've been mired in for way too long. The true goal is to stick with this thing and not quit, no matter what. I may not be able to control certain factors that could prevent me from ever getting to Boston, but I can control this much. I know I'm not where I wanted to be physically right now, but it doesn't even matter. In Modesto on Sunday, I don't care how ugly it is or how long it takes—I'm going to finish that fucking marathon."

....

It got ugly around mile eighteen, on a farm road hedged on either side by budding almond trees. I'd known what was coming for some time, having become a little uneasy when I noticed that Josh hadn't said anything in a while, then a little more uneasy when he refused a gel packet I offered him, and finally resigned to disaster when he ran his slowest mile on the fastest part of the course. I waged an internal debate about whether to acknowledge openly what was now so plainly happening or to just let it happen. When we came to a big yellow sandwich board at the side of the road with a bold red 18 painted on it, I decided to speak.

"The way I figure it," I said, "if you can run eighteen miles, you can run a marathon."

These words hung in the air for several awkward seconds before Josh mustered a reply.

"I hate to say it," he said, "but I think I'm hitting a wall."

I knew the feeling all too well. This was my thirtieth marathon, give or take, and although I was cruising it, running not to achieve a personal goal but to help Josh achieve his goal, I had hit the wall in many past marathons.

"Just manage it the best you can," I said.

Josh's pace continued to slow. I forced myself to stop looking at my watch, fearful of adding a layer of self-consciousness to my brother's misery by appearing to mark his decline. I considered suggesting that he try to make it to twenty miles without walking—knowing I would have done just that in his place—but refrained. It's easy to say the wrong thing to a struggling marathoner.

At precisely the twenty-mile mark, Josh began to walk. Runners all think alike.

"I just need to gather myself a bit," he said.

My heart went out to my brother. I felt as powerless to help him now as I had when Josh was nine years old and I was six and a neighborhood bully pinned him to the ground and pummeled him (undersized and undisguisably brilliant, Josh was a magnet for bullies) and Sean and Mom and I stood on the opposite side of the street protesting impotently until something in me snapped and I charged the bully and leapt on his back and pummeled *him*, wailing in frustration at the inability of my kindergarten haymakers to halt the humiliation. The last thing Josh needed was another blow to his pride.

"You know what I'm craving?" he said out of the blue during a second walk break in mile twenty-three. "A great big milkshake."

"What flavor?" I asked, privately elated by what Josh's remark revealed about his state of mind.

"Chocolate!"

We crossed the finish line at 4:12:54, a number that exceeded by seventy-three minutes Josh's previous marathon time and fell more than fifty minutes short of the Boston Marathon qualifying standard for his age group. Feeling faint, he stopped abruptly and folded in half, hands on knees. A member of the medical staff approached him.

"Are you okay?" she asked.

"Yeah, I'm just old," he said, erecting himself.

We shuffled our way to the finish festival, where Josh suffered a second bout of lightheadedness and took a seat on the pavement with his back against a security fence. When he was ready, I hoisted him upright and told him about a nearby burger joint I knew that made killer milkshakes. Our eyes met again.

"We're on to Cincinnati," he said.

I realized then that I had greatly overestimated the effect that Josh's unspectacular race would have on his psyche, and in so doing I had greatly underestimated Josh. Perhaps, too, I had misjudged the power of running to teach human beings the invaluable skill of failing with poise. Everyone fears failure, and many of us fear it so much we seldom risk it. This is a sure path to regret and bitterness. Happier are those who aren't afraid to fail.

The marathon tames our fear of failure in much the same way antibodies prevent viruses from striking us twice: exposure. If you run marathons, *you will fail*. The marathon is no respecter of persons. It humbles everyone sooner or later—and I mean everyone. I'll never forget the strained smile of raw mortification I saw on the face of Haile Gebrselassie, widely considered the greatest runner ever, as he limped along a London sidewalk in April 2007, having just dropped out of a marathon he was supposed to win, miles from the finish line. All marathoners get their turn on the struggle bus. What matters is what happens next. Will the runner have a long memory, dwelling on his failure and taking no further risks, or will he have a short memory and try again? Most runners try again. When Haile Gebrselassie ran his next marathon, he broke the world record.

Josh had already shown considerable willingness to risk failure in changing careers at age thirty-seven, on the heels of his previous running renaissance, abandoning his job in computer programming to start nursing school. Eleven years later, in the midst of a second comeback, he seemed unflappable. So it was only to be expected that, the following morning, as I chauffeured him to the same train station I'd picked him up at a week earlier, he told me he wanted to get right back on the horse and run the Eugene Marathon, which was seven weeks away and would be the eighth and final event in my search for the magic of the marathon, an aspect of which my brother had already revealed to me. We spent the rest of the drive discussing what he could do to improve in the meantime. Losing weight and going on sleep meds topped our list.

"See you in Cincinnati—er, Eugene," I said as we embraced at the passenger drop-off area.

Less than twenty-four hours later, I loaded up my Mazda CX-5 (nicknamed the Fun Mobile) with two large suitcases, a duffel bag, a fluffy white bichon frise named Queenie, a bucket of dog food, a cooler, one hundred boxed copies of my latest book, a cache of healthy snacks (cashews, tinned anchovies, apples), and a pair of thirty-five-pound dumbbells and hit the road for Clayton, New Mexico, site of marathon number two in my search. Beside me, then as always, was Nataki, my wife, the person for whom I have most needed the courage I wasn't born with and the person for whose sake I have most needed to run marathons.

CHAPTER 3

BLIND DATE

I GAINED SIXTY-EIGHT pounds in four years at Haverford College, where I routinely ate an entire large cheese pizza on a Friday night after pounding several beers and made zero use of the lovely 2.2-mile jogging trail that limned the small campus. When I graduated with a bachelor's degree in English in 1993, I couldn't climb the fifteen steps to my room on the second floor of Leeds Hall without getting winded. Two years later, still fat and out of shape, I decided to relocate to San Francisco to pursue a career in writing, becoming even fatter and more out of shape during a four-week, fast-food-fueled crossing of the lower forty-eight.

Accompanying me on this journey were my two brothers, both of whom were at transition points in their own lives. Josh was to fly home afterward to start a PhD program in computational neuroscience at the University of Rochester. Sean would remain with me in California, having just graduated from Kenyon College and figuring Frisco was as good a place as any to look for something to do with the rest of his life. We took a northerly route, passing through Cincinnati and St. Paul and Bozeman before hitting the

West Coast at Seattle and dropping south on Route 1 to our final destination. I didn't know it was possible to have so much fun. My brothers are my best friends, and in our monthlong road trip we discovered a bonding experience nonpareil and a perfectly timed shared rite of passage, an interlude of absolute freedom made possible by the singular confluence of youth's lack of responsibility and adulthood's competencies. Through the better half of a steamy American summer we created each day's agenda on the fly, pitching a tent some nights, crashing other nights with friends or friends of friends or friends of friends of friends, staying in motels only twice. We smoked an ounce of weed, played our favorite CDs until we couldn't stand the sound of them, ordered from drive-thrus at least once a day, nearly died in a whitewater rafting adventure gone wrong, laughed to the point of vomiting (okay, that was me) in the flickering light of campfires, visited a former family home in Illinois that we hadn't seen in eighteen years, and managed to limit ourselves to just one speeding ticket and a single shoving match.

We crossed the Golden Gate Bridge in what was left of our '86 Volkswagen Golf on the afternoon of August 12, 1995, a sparkling Saturday that did nothing to dispel the East Coaster's stereotype of California weather. We gawked like visiting aliens from a dim desert planet at the flawless sky hanging high above us, an indigo hint of outer space lurking behind the familiar pale blue. Below us, jagged waters shot blinding sparks of reflected sunlight. An intricate jumble of pastel architecture—the city—beckoned ahead.

The bridge spat us out onto Lombard Street. Following directions I had received on a pay phone at an Oregon convenience store from Mike, my old high school running pal who now lived in San Francisco, we took a right on Van Ness and a left on Bush and parked outside a narrow apartment building on Dashiell Hammett Street, a one-block alley on Nob Hill.

Sean, who'd run the anchor leg for us, so to speak, yanked the parking brake lever and killed the ignition. A brief silence ensued as we shared a common thought: *it's over.* Life's transitions are always brutally abrupt and appear smooth only later, through the warping lens of memory.

The next morning, we woke up stiff and sore on the hard floor of Mike's apartment, a studio so tiny it had a Murphy bed. Josh dressed in musty clothes he'd worn half a dozen times since their last laundering, shouldered his bag, and left for the airport. Sean and I stepped out together to grab coffee and a copy of the *San Francisco Chronicle*, our elder sibling's sudden absence making us oddly shy with each other.

Back at Mike's place, we took turns scouring the classifieds for leads on jobs and more permanent accommodations. The few opportunities I saw for writers were either dull-seeming or beyond my reach, and I was beginning to regret the whole foolish endeavor when the sound of my name drew my attention outward. I looked up and just then Sean snapped a photo with the pocket camera we'd brought along to record our adventure. I still have it (the photo, I mean). It shows me peeking over the top of the paper with eyes that seem to me now to betray an almost haunted presentiment of hard times ahead. I'm just glad I didn't know how hard.

We'd chosen an interesting time to move to Fog City. The Bush recession had ended some eighteen months earlier, and the dotcom boom was just around the corner, Generation X culture in full flower, and the city in the thick of its worst housing crunch since the great fire. Despite being new in town, Sean and I had no trouble finding the dozens of apartment showings we went to in every part of the peninsula over the next two and a half months. All we had to do was look for a line of twentysomethings extending from a certain building entrance to the nearest corner and around the block. Lacking employment, savings, and references, we just couldn't compete with the more stable homeseekers we queued up with again and again, less hopeful each time, like serial casting-call rejects slowly getting the message that they can't act.

While our search dragged on, we stayed in a seedy residence hotel in a neighborhood known as the Tenderloin. Our fellow boarders included wild-eyed dipsomaniacs, broken war veterans, twitchy drug addicts, and men in rumpled suits failing in all manner of gray-market enterprises involving hushed conversations on the lobby pay phone. All these people were clearly on their way down in life. Sean and I alone were on our way up—or so we hoped.

Our room was a stale-smelling cell barely big enough to accommodate the two twin beds we slept on. We moved into it a couple of days after arriving in town and escaped just before Thanksgiving without ever having unpacked our luggage. It seemed important to maintain the illusion that we were short-timers. Plus, there was no closet, so our suitcases served as footlockers, making entrance to, egress from, and movement within the room akin to a game of Twister. I wish I had a dime for every time I tripped over the damn things in the middle of the night as I made my reluctant way toward our floor's foul communal lavatory, which was the sort of bathroom that you leave after a shower feeling like you need a shower.

The building superintendent was a beady-eyed simperer who spooked us with sly suggestions of a sixth sense. Every time we tried to tiptoe past the reception desk and out the front door unmolested, he floated in ghostlike from the back office and roped us into one-sided conversations in which he never failed to drop hints that he overheard every word we spoke in our room. ("North Beach is a nice area, don't you think?" he might say as we left the hotel for an apartment showing in North Beach.)

Most of the other residents took it for granted that Sean and I were lovers. In the early days, we hastened to correct this misapprehension, but we stopped caring what other people thought when we realized other people didn't care who we did or didn't sleep with. As it turned out, the Bay Area's laissez faire sexual culture became the very thing that brought our domestic purgatory to an end when, on a day of apartment hunting that seemed as unpromising as any other, the manager of a building in the Haight-Ashbury District accepted our application for a two-bedroom apartment that at least two hundred better-qualified parties had also applied for, freely admitting that he did so because he found us attractive. This was almost certainly illegal, but we weren't about to look a gift horse in the mouth.

Finding steady work proved no less difficult than finding a home. Sean's poli-sci degree wasn't much older than his last haircut, a reality that inclined him to take the first respectable job that came his way, which turned out to be an eight-dollar-an-hour gig fetching lunches for the stock traders at Montgomery Securities in the Prudential Tower downtown. After three fruitless weeks of combing the Bay Area for writing work, I panicked and registered for an accelerated course in bartending (or mixology, as our instructor insisted on calling it). Lacking the cash to cover the eight-hundred-dollar tuition, I put it on a credit card, telling myself it was an investment in my future, a one-time exception to my rule against carrying plastic debt. In fact, it proved to be the first step in a long descent into negative net worth. I never worked a single night as a bartender.

Throughout this ill-conceived foray into the service industry, my search for writing work continued, and my perseverance was rewarded when, around Christmas, I discovered a job posting in the *Chronicle* that stood out from the usual mix of dull and out-of-reach opportunities for journalists. *Multisport*, a soon-to-launch endurance sports magazine based in Sausalito, was looking for an assistant editor. Though I had no present interest in long-distance racing, I figured my past interest might give me a leg up on other applicants for the position, and indeed it did, when I correctly identified Dave Scott as the only six-time winner of the Ironman World Championship during my interview with the publication's founder, Bill Katovsky, who previously had founded *Triathlete*. Then again, maybe it was my willingness to work for under-the-table wages and no benefits that separated me from the other candidates. In any case, I got the job.

Inspired by the conspicuous fitness of my new coworkers, I started running again, but only casually; my goal was not to compete but to lose a bit of weight and improve my fortunes with women. The job paid just enough to keep the cupboards of Sean's and my new place stocked with boxed mac-n-cheese, but what it lacked in remuneration it made up for in opportunity. A literary savant who could (and did) make a defensible claim to having discovered David Foster Wallace, Bill helped me develop my voice as a writer, and before long I was composing half the magazine's content. It was a short ride, though. As bad with money as he was good with words, Bill was soon handing me IOUs instead of paychecks every other Friday. After publishing its second issue (on credit from a too-trusting printer), *Multisport* folded.

My job hunt resumed. Five weeks of anxious bush-beating led to an invitation to interview with an explosively growing Oakland-based multilevel marketing start-up called Destiny Telecomm. The company traded mainly in prepaid phone cards, but the real money was made off so-called independent associates (or IAs), who wittingly paid many times what the phone cards were worth in exchange for the chance to turn around and sign up other IAs, who did the same, ad infinitum. Destiny Telecomm had its own propaganda organ, the *Destiny*, whose mission was to keep the IAs profitably brainwashed, and I was up for its senior editor position. On the morning of my interview, I rose early and caught a bus and a train and another bus to the firm's headquarters on Hegenberger Road, near the airport. I located the media department and was shown into a small room that had the thrown-together look of a fake office in a hidden-camera TV prank show. On the other side of a cheap particleboard desk sat a mousy Kansan with a hairstyle from another time, who introduced herself as Lori, managing editor of the *Destiny*.

"Are you familiar with multilevel marketing?" she asked.

Something was wrong with her eyes. There was a desperation in them that did not match the chipper tone of her voice but instead seemed to communicate a secret plea, as though Lori were being held captive and her office was bugged. Ignoring this red flag as best I could, I assured Lori that I was not only familiar with multilevel marketing but had an abiding interest in the industry and would feel privileged to use my talents on behalf of one of its most dynamic businesses.

Few experiences in life are more demoralizing than that of acting like you really want a job you know you'll hate if you get it. I was hired on the spot.

On my first day, I arrived at my new workplace a few minutes early, ahead of Lori and the rest of the media department, and as I poked around the offices I got an uneasy feeling, a gut inkling of impending disaster, and I was just heeding it, just turning to flee the building, never to return, when Lori walked in and I was stuck.

A few months later, I arrived at Destiny to find dozens of my coworkers loitering in the parking lot, speaking in hushed tones while FBI agents filed out of the building, arms wrapped around cardboard boxes and computers. To the surprise of no one, it turned out our employer was operating an illegal pyramid scheme.

The thing I liked most about Destiny, while it lasted, was the diversity of its staff. The company employed a veritable rainbow of young men and women—Latinos, whites, blacks, Asians, and Filipinos—among whom there was a goodly amount of after-hours fraternization, to which I happily contributed. About midway through my tenure with Destiny I befriended Teisha, a Spanish-speaking Afro-Panamanian woman with a zillion-watt smile who worked in customer service and who was involved in a strained long-distance relationship with a white guy named Anthony. The handful of times we went out together—to Crown Memorial Beach in Alameda for a picnic, to Lake Merritt in Oakland for a jog, to a low-key gay bar near my place in the Haight for a cocktail—I couldn't discern whether Teisha's intention was to collect relationship advice from another white guy's perspective or to vet me as a possible replacement for Anthony. Nor did I really care. I just liked hanging out with Teisha, platonically or otherwise.

We were discussing the usual topics (men, women, dating) on a picnic blanket in Yerba Buena Gardens one Thursday when, out of nowhere, Teisha said, "I gotta be honest, Matt: I really don't see you with a white woman." Surprised as I was by this declaration, I sensed it was intended as a compliment, and that's how I chose to take it, little knowing what it would lead to.

The very next week Teisha called me and announced that she was setting me up on a blind date with a new friend of hers, Nataki, whose sister, Tayna, had also worked at Destiny. By now the business had fully imploded, its founder had fled the country, and I was working for *Triathlete* in the city, having been hired there by none other than Bill Katovsky, who in the wake of *Multisport*'s demise had gone crawling back to the magazine he'd sold ten years earlier. I learned sometime later that Teisha had been inspired to pair us up by something Nataki had told her when she was doing Teisha's hair at her home in Oakland. As the story went, the two of them were taking turns complaining about men when Nataki said, only half in jest, "I'm tired of brothas. Too much drama. I'm gonna get me a white boy." Teisha, who perhaps had decided by then that she was tired of white boys, immediately thought of me and stepped into the role of matchmaker, wasting little time in arranging a Saturday dinner rendezvous at Oakland's trendy Jack London Square on the waterfront.

In the days leading up to the event, I pumped Teisha for information about Nataki.

"Is she pretty?" I asked.

"No, I'm setting you up with a total hag just to spite you," she said.

"What's she like?" I pressed.

"Well," Teisha said, smiling as though recalling something specific, "let's just say she likes to have a good time."

"She's not slutty, is she?" I said. Teisha glared at me.

"You'll probably marry her," she said.

Saturday came. Teisha had instructed me to meet my future wife outside T.G.I. Friday's at six o'clock. Arriving at Jack London Square a little early, I killed time by shopping for a small icebreaker gift, settling eventually on a cheap box of chocolates. At 6:01, I strolled with conscious nonchalance toward the restaurant,

candies in hand. The square was swarming with men and women
of all ages and races dressed for a night out, and I was chagrined to
discover a large throng lingering near the entrance that seemed at
first to contain a few possible Natakis, but my eyes quickly zeroed
in on a graceful figure standing expectantly before a big wooden
sign identifying the establishment. She had medium-brown skin
and long, auburn hair that was tied up in a French roll. High cheek-
bones, plush lips, and sloe eyes added up to a striking, double-take
sort of facial beauty. She wore flowing satin pants that knotted at
the front and a close-fitting sparkly top with three-quarter-length
sleeves. This was a conservative look by her standards, I would
discover, yet it did little to hide the lean athleticism of its wear-
er's limbs, the feline suppleness of her neck and shoulders, and
(I couldn't help but notice) a nice butt.

Please let it be her, please let it be her, please let it be her.

"Are you Nataki?" I asked.

"That's me!" she said brightly, looking me dead in the eyes. "You
must be the guy I'm supposed to meet."

If Nataki was embarrassed at having forgotten my name, she
didn't show it. I refreshed her memory and presented the chocolates.

"Teisha didn't tell me anything about you except you was
white," Nataki offered matter-of-factly. "I saw a guy with a ponytail before you came. I asked him if he was here to meet me and
he said, 'No, but I wish I was!'"

"I don't blame him," I said, blushing.

"You don't want to eat *here*, do you?" Nataki said, gesturing
toward the restaurant and wrinkling her cute little button nose.

"Heck, no!" I said, wondering what was wrong with T.G.I.
Friday's.

We made an impromptu plan to cross the square to Kincaid's,
an upscale seafood restaurant, for cocktails, and then move one
block down the square to Scott's, another upscale seafood restaurant (what was the point?), for dinner.

"I don't really drink," Nataki asserted as we claimed a table with
a good view of the bay in the bar area of Kincaid's. I felt a pinch of

disappointment. *Strike one.* My date ordered a virgin daiquiri, and I requested a whiskey sour. No reason I couldn't still tie one on.

We talked comfortably for ten or twelve minutes before hitting our first awkward lull. My mind raced for something to say, but Nataki beat me to it.

"So, what do you think of me so far?" she asked.

In that very instant, I began to like her a lot. She seemed almost incapable of discomposure, a woman who had nothing to prove to anyone.

"You look nice," Nataki said later, as I paid our tab. "Very GQ. We need to do something with the hair, though." I was wearing it close cropped with a neat side part, à la Mr. Rogers.

At Scott's, Nataki ordered lobster, which I couldn't afford. I didn't care. She did most of the talking as we ate, sharing the Cliff's Notes version of her life story. Born in Oakland ("in the 'hood," as she put it), she went to high school in the mostly white suburb of Antioch. When Nataki was eighteen (she was now twenty-two), her parents divorced and her father quickly remarried—interracially. Nataki had since returned to Oakland, where she lived with her mother and sister and Tayna's five-year-old son, Devante, in the same cramped two-bedroom house Nataki came home to on the day she was born.

Having recently earned her cosmetology license, Nataki "did heads" on the side while working a full-time gig with Chrysler, for whom she traveled to malls throughout the Bay Area to show off cars and beguile men who had no interest in buying a new Chrysler into signing up for test drives at the nearest dealership. She dreamed of making it big as a singer or fashion model and had already danced in a few music videos and taken second place in the 1996 Most Beautiful Girl in the World pageant.

"Sing something for me," I said.

Dispensing with the standard phony demurral, Nataki set down her fork and belted out a verse from an unfamiliar R&B tune. It had a staccato rhythm, the words coming too quickly for me to catch all of them, but the theme of womanly independence was clear enough, unfolding through lines about being true to oneself and not trying to please others.

When she finished, in lieu of a curtsy, Nataki picked her fork back up and popped a hunk of butter-dipped lobster meat into her mouth. I dropped my own utensils and clapped, drawing looks from our neighboring diners. This wasn't flattery. The voice I'd just heard was a bona fide original, its soulful, world-weary timbre textured with a sultry hint of raspiness.

"Erykah Badu," Nataki said, as if I were praising the songwriter.

"You have a gift," I said.

Nataki regarded me uncertainly.

"My dad says every black girl in the ghetto can sing," she said. "He thinks I should join the army."

"I have a hard time picturing you in the army," I laughed.

"My dad works for the army," Nataki said seriously. Her eyes dropped to her plate, then returned to my face. "I think every generation should do better than their parents."

When the check came, Nataki proposed an agenda for the rest of the evening. We would travel in separate cars to her mom's place, where she would change into something a little more flattering. From there we would drive together into San Francisco, my turf, and hit the clubs.

"You're lucky," she said. "I date some brothas for weeks and don't ever let 'em know where I live!"

"I'm honored," I said.

"You seem pretty harmless," Nataki said, shooting a glance at my hair.

"We're just the ones you need to watch out for," I said.

I walked Nataki to her black Ford Mustang, and she waited while I retrieved my white Honda Civic. I was then led on what amounted to a high-speed chase into West Oakland, Nataki barreling through stale yellow lights at more than one intersection, testing me it seemed.

The pursuit ended in a neighborhood of flat-roofed, one-story houses painted in vibrant hues. Its narrow streets were choked to the point of near impassibility by parked cars, a plurality of which were barge-like old-model Cadillacs, Pontiacs, and Oldsmobiles. Foot-high speed bumps were spaced at one-hundred-yard intervals on every block. Clusters of teenage boys dressed in sagging jeans and sports jerseys hung out on stoops and curbs with girls half-clad in Daisy Dukes and baby-doll tops, shouting laughter-filled conversations as though for an audience. Here and there a ragged tweeker lurched along the crumbling sidewalks.

We parked in front of a house that looked like all the others except in color: bright blue with maroon trim. Nataki guided me through a chain-link gate at the side of the property and into a small backyard where a low-key celebration of Nataki's mother's forty-fourth birthday was taking place. Eight or nine guests, all black, sat around a patio table sipping from Solo cups. A single porch light provided faint illumination. The Isley Brothers were playing on an eighties-vintage boom box.

"Mom, check out who Teisha set me up with," Nataki said, addressing a smiling woman who bore a striking resemblance to Aretha Franklin.

Eight or nine pairs of eyes looked me up and down.

"Not bad, girl!" said the woman, her speech suggesting that her cup had been refilled more than once this evening.

"Matt, this is my mom, Lorene," Nataki said.

"Happy birthday," I said with a stiff bow that, I realized a half second too late, probably came off as a bit much.

Nataki left me with the revelers and went inside the house to change. I was offered a seat and a beer and accepted both.

The man on my left gave me his right hand and introduced himself as Uncle Eli. I assumed he was Nataki's uncle, because he looked to be about Lorene's age, but in fact he was Lorene's uncle (and her elder by two years). Having learned from experience that sports are usually a safe topic with men of all races, I took a shot at starting a conversation with him.

"So, are you a Raiders guy?" I asked.

"Yeah, unfortunately," Eli grumbled.

"I like the 'Niners," I volunteered.

Remembering suddenly that most fans of the struggling local NFL franchise despised their cross-bay rivals *and* their fans, I felt compelled to explain my allegiance.

"My first big sports hero was O. J. Simpson," I said. "When the Buffalo Bills traded him away in '79, my loyalties went with him."

This remark was met by absolute silence from the entire gathering. Realizing my mistake, I turned scarlet. The O. J. Simpson murder trial was a recent event, and still an active wedge in America's widening black-white racial divide. It was Eli who rescued me.

"Man, that dude's guilty as shit!" he said, cackling.

When Nataki returned, now wearing a long, knitted skirt in pale yellow and a matching halter top, she found her great uncle and her date doubled over in hysterics, slapping each other's backs.

Not much of a raver, I took Nataki to the only dance club I knew in the city. At the velvet rope, my wallet was lightened by a heart-stopping forty dollars. Inside we found a dance floor fire-coded for hundreds but peopled tonight by three or four grave-faced couples swaying like seafloor vegetation in a high surf. Robotic techno music thumped from the sound system. A bored bartender reposed chin-in-palm before a massive display of neglected bottles. At dinner, Nataki had told me she loved to dance and spent much of her free time at the hottest East Bay clubs. My heart sank as I took in the pitiful scene I'd lured her into, certain I'd blown it. But Nataki didn't seem to care.

"Let's sit down," she said.

We plopped ourselves onto a huge, marshmallow-soft chair that sank in the middle, causing our bodies to press together. It was our first physical contact (the handover of chocolates having precluded a handshake earlier) and, for me, almost too intense, too sudden. I felt an urgent need to create a distraction.

"Teisha said you and I would probably get married," I blurted.

"Maybe," Nataki said offhandedly. "But no kids. I don't want no babies."

Strike two. Maybe.

We didn't stay long. When I delivered Nataki back to her place, we exchanged chaste pecks on the cheek.

"I had fun with you," I said. "I'd like to go out with you again."

"Hold on a second," Nataki said.

She left the car and raced inside the house. A minute later, she appeared at my open window bearing an item in each hand.

"This is my phone number," she said, passing me a slip of paper. "And this is Mr. Pajamas," she added, handing over a worn old pajama-clad pink stuffed bunny. "He'll keep an eye on you."

As I drove home, I tried to make sense of this gift, which was stunningly intimate in an odd sort of way. Although my desire to see Nataki again was genuine, I couldn't help but imagine myself in the awkward position of returning Mr. Pajamas to his rightful owner in the likely event that things didn't work out between us. But when, seven years later, I did in fact give him back, the circumstances were much worse than either of us could ever have imagined.

CHAPTER 4

THE FINISH LINE FIX

(Dust Bowl Marathon)

NATAKI AND I (and Queenie) rolled into Clayton, New Mexico, at 4:02 p.m. on the eve of event number two in my search for the magic of the marathon. I note the exact time because it was a bit of a disappointment. Like many runners, I approach road trips with a marathon mind-set, setting time goals and going to great lengths (such as enduring extreme bladder discomfort) to achieve them, even keeping track of personal records for long drives I repeat often (Oakland to San Diego: six hours and forty minutes). During the 270-mile drive from Albuquerque, where we'd spent the previous night, I'd set an utterly arbitrary goal of reaching our destination by four o'clock sharp, and it pained me to miss by two minutes.

Clayton is a hardscrabble high-plains whistle-stop whose best days as a livestock shipping center are long behind it. Every second restaurant we passed on our final approach to the Kokopelli Lodge had a "Help Wanted" sign posted outside. I did not actually see tumbleweeds blow across the road, but I pictured them.

The lobby of the Kokopelli featured the rustic southwestern interior design style I had expected and vaguely hoped for. In keeping with this aesthetic, the man behind the reception desk spoke in a basso cowboy drawl that sounded uncannily similar to the voice of Sam Elliott. As he looked up my reservation on the computer, I asked the gentleman (who looked absolutely nothing like Sam Elliott) for a noon checkout.

"A lot of people have been asking for those today," he said as though remarking on an unseasonal turn in the weather.

It was within my power to explain the anomaly, but I chose not to, confident of the innkeeper's indifference to the fact that his hotel was infested with runners, my fellow participants in the next day's Dust Bowl Marathon, who, like me, would be unable to complete the race, return to the hotel, clean up, and clear out before the standard 11:00 A.M. checkout time. My stomach fluttered reflexively at the thought of all these as-yet-unseen rivals, but then I remembered that I had no intention of actually trying to defeat them.

The official name of the race, actually, was Dust Bowl Series Marathon #5, the number denoting its position as the final event in a five-day series that passes through the states most affected by the great drought of the 1930s. A majority of participants do all five. Knowing this, I felt sheepish about dropping in for just one, and the last one at that. Staged annually, the series is organized by a New Mexico–based outfit called Mainly Marathons, which caters to serial marathoners—men and women who try to run marathons in as many states or countries as possible or who just try to run as many marathons as possible wherever. I had no such goal, but my present mission would be incomplete, I believed, if I did not expose myself to this flowering subculture within the broader marathon community. I was especially keen to meet the series' marquee entrant, Jim Simpson, a seventy-five-year-old Californian who had completed more than 1,660 official marathons and had run as many as 181 in a single year.

After settling into our room, Nataki and I went out for an early dinner at the Rabbit Ear Café, a restaurant specializing in the local cuisine. The words "Help Wanted" scrolled by on an electric billboard outside. Inside we encountered a big square dining room occupied by seven or eight even earlier eaters, four, of whom I pegged immediately as runners, tipped off by their T-shirts, caps, and footwear. A pair of hatted old-timers sat together near the back, empty plates between them. Two younger runners sat alone at adjacent tables near the one Nataki and I had taken. As we studied our menus, the old-timers stood and began to make their way toward the exit, but when they passed between the younger guys and recognized their kind, they paused for a quick chat.

In the name of research, I eavesdropped. The conversation began with an exchange of marathon credentials that sounded casual enough, but my inner ethnographer recognized it as a serious ritual effort to establish relative status, as when two tech guys meet for the first time.

"Once I got my fiftieth state," said one of the old-timers, "I needed another goal, so I decided to do fifty in one year."

The younger guys, who were facing me, exchanged looks that said, *Can you top that? No? Me neither.*

"I'm doing half marathons, though, not marathons," the old-timer confessed. "They're more manageable."

He might as well have said he was doing 5Ks. The younger guys could not conceal their smiles, nor did they really try.

Back at the hotel, the day's exertions caught up with me suddenly, and I scotched my plan to scout the race venue at Clayton Lake State Park. It seemed a reasonable decision at the time. Siri had assured me the park lay just 1.2 miles from the hotel, and in all likelihood there would be a veritable motorcade of runners heading that way from the hotel in the morning. But when I crept out of the room at 5:15 A.M., careful not to disturb a still-sleeping Nataki, I found the parking lot emptied of every vehicle but mine. Neither did Clayton Lake State Park lie 1.2 miles from the Kokopelli Lodge. Siri's directions led me into a literal ditch, in which stood a road sign that read, "Clayton Lake 12 Miles," like some kind of satellite-assisted practical joke. Tossing my phone into the backseat, I sped on through the dark, determined to catch up to others seeking the same destination, but the road was as desolate as Neptune. Only after I turned onto the park's access road did I spy taillights ahead and relax.

A man wearing a reflective vest and brandishing an industrial-size flashlight pointed me to a parking area where another man, sporting a Merlin beard, guided me to an open spot. As he back-pedaled in front of me I noticed that he walked with a pronounced limp. My immediate assumption was that he had acquired it by running too many marathons.

I stepped out of the Fun Mobile into refrigerator-temperature air and hustled toward the staging area, having glimpsed it on the way in. Ahead of me I saw the wavering lights of headlamps moving right to left through the blackness. Only then did I remember that the race organizer had offered slower runners the option to start at five thirty. This explained the empty parking lot at the hotel. I had dismissed the early-start option as masochistic. Was I the only one?

After several minutes of humping I stepped into a lighted space where I found hot food and drinks set out on large folding tables and a second table for check-in. I gave my name to one of the women stationed there and received in return my number bib and a finisher's medal. Seeing my puzzled expression, she explained, "You get the medal now. When you finish, you get this." *This* was a little brass New Mexico state flag hanging from an earring-style hook. She inserted the hook through an eye at the bottom of the medal and dangled it in front of me in the manner of a QVC host demonstrating product features. I made sounds of approval, but in truth the thing looked absurdly incomplete, like a one-trophy trophy case. With all five state flags, though, it would have looked really cool.

I walked back to the car to keep warm and kill time. At 6:20, ten minutes before the "late" start time, I reemerged and began to strip off my outer layer, reluctantly. The guy with the Merlin beard, still on parking duty, looked me up and down and spoke.

"What are you doing today?" he asked.

"I'm doing the marathon," I said. There were half-marathon and 5K options on the menu as well.

"How many do you have?"

"I don't really know," I said. "Thirty, maybe, thirty-two. Almost all of them have been in California."

Merlin looked at me queerly—confounded by the notion of a person who ran lots of marathons without counting them.

"Are you injured?" I asked, pointing at his gimpy knee.

"It's a little stiff," he said, reaching for it. "I'm just doing the 5K today."

Someone else in my place might have pointed out that even walking 3.1 miles in his condition was probably a bad idea. I did not. Either Merlin knew this already and didn't care or he would never know.

Picking up on my reference to California, my new friend told me a longwinded story about a marathon he had run on the rim of the volcano at Mt. Shasta. I made a show of checking my watch. Seven minutes to start time. Merlin took the hint and let me go.

When I returned to the staging area, Clint Burleson, the founder and director of Mainly Marathons, was halfway through his pre-race announcements. Concerned that I might have missed some important information, I concentrated intently on his voice, trying to orient myself. The first phrase I caught was "dinosaur tracks." I kept listening, and it soon became evident that we were being encouraged to stray from the official racecourse at a certain point for the purpose of checking out a set of dinosaur tracks that were a featured attraction at Clayton Lake State Park. I wondered what the event's insurer would think of this idea.

Clint concluded his announcements with a series of shout-outs to runners who were achieving milestones ("Vincent Ma, who's out on the course already, is doing his one hundredth event with us!"), to long-serving staff members ("George Rose, who will lead you out on his bike, has been with us since the beginning!"), and finally to runners celebrating birthdays. He then ushered us behind a long divot in the dirt that appeared to have been made with the heel of a boot and sent us off like a pack of third-graders with the words, "On your mark. . . . Get set. . . . Go!"

The rest of the racecourse was as eccentric as the start. Shaped like a flattened figure eight, it had turnaround points at both ends and was a mere five kilometers in length. I and my fellow marathoners would complete eight and a half laps, snatching a wrist band (actually just a rubber band) off a table each time we passed through the staging area at the figure-eight's center to keep from losing count. We started out on what Clint had described as the Camp Loop because it penetrated the park's camping areas. The field quickly separated into pairs and small groups, becoming a sort of movable mixer. I took part fully in the mingling, trading marathon credentials with a series of strangers, all of whom were running their fifth marathon or half marathon in as many days.

It was during lap two that the genius of Clint Burleson's compact course design became apparent, as I met again—and exchanged greetings, high-fives, and words of encouragement with—the folks I'd met in lap one. But when a runner I hadn't yet spoken to called out, "Hi, Matt!" I had a moment of confusion. My best guess was that he recognized me from the cover of one of my books. Then another total stranger hailed me by name, and another. I was beginning to feel like a real big shot when a less self-flattering explanation came to me. Glancing down at my bib, I saw that, sure enough, my first name had been hand-printed below my number.

As I made my third foray through the Dam Loop (so named because it crossed a dam on the west end of the lake), I met a pair of walkers, both elderly and both dressed in red and black. I recognized them from my Internet sleuthing as the aforementioned

Jim Simpson, who holds the distinction of being the first American to complete more than 1,000 marathons, and Betty Wailes, also an accomplished serial marathoner and Jim's "sweetheart" (as he referred to her in interviews). I hotfooted it to the turnaround at the far end of the loop and caught the couple from behind. When I drew even with them I slowed to their pace and introduced myself.

"Do you mind if I visit with you for a few minutes?" I asked.

"I've got all day," Jim said in a pleasing accent that reminded me of . . . who was it?

"How are you holding up?" I asked.

Jim and Betty had already collected four flags for their finisher's medal and were earning their fifth with a mix of walking and running.

"Nothing to it," Jim said. (Jimmy Carter! That's who he sounded like!) "As you can see, we're not going for speed. It's all about conserving energy. Imagine waking up on January 1 and knowing you have one hundred or two hundred marathons ahead of you that year. You want to get to the other end in one piece. That's your goal: not to run fast but to just get through it."

Over the next mile and a half, I learned enough about Jim to have written his Wikipedia page, had I been so inclined. He grew up "dirt poor" on a small farm in Douglasville, Georgia (which explained the Carteresque accent). After high school, he joined the navy and was shipped to San Diego for boot camp, put in his four years of service, and then went back to civilian life, finding work in Huntington Beach, California, as a plastic injection mold maker. The next twenty years of Jim's life were what every American is supposed to want: he got married, bought a house, raised a couple of kids, saved money, and retired at age forty-three. What I most desired to know, though, was how Jim had managed to leap from the utterly typical existence he described to his present oddball lifestyle of crisscrossing the continent year-round in a camper, sleeping in Walmart parking lots, and running three or four marathons a week—and also what the heck he got out of it.

"It's just something to do," he said, deadpan. "We all have to have something to pass the time when we retire. For the first two days that I was retired I watched *Get Smart* on daytime TV. I figured, 'There's got to be something better than this.' So I started a little training program. I ran three miles three days a week. I did that for a little over a year. One Saturday, I took the family to see a movie and they had an entry form for a 5K at the ticket counter. My son and I ran it and had a good time. A little later, we started running 5Ks and 10Ks regularly and worked up to the half marathon."

"Ah, the slippery slope," I interjected.

"My first marathon was Los Angeles in 1988," Jim continued. "Six months later, I ran the Portland Marathon. So I did two that first year. It took me ten years to do the first one hundred marathons. That seems kind of quaint nowadays, when people run a hundred in one year."

Having also learned from my Internet sleuthing that Jim and his wife were divorced in 1998, which was the very year his rate of marathon participation exploded, I asked (rather indelicately) whether his running had been the cause of the split.

"We just found that we were different people," he said. "I wanted to go out and run marathons, climb mountains, and jump out of airplanes, and she was more of a homebody. She wouldn't have minded going to Las Vegas every weekend. We just grew apart. So we decided to go our separate ways and be friends and it worked out. On holidays we still got together with all the kids and her new husband and we were like one big happy family."

Although divorce freed Jim to run as many marathons as he pleased, this freedom came at a price. As much as he enjoyed the quixotic way of living he'd chosen, there was an empty space at the center of it. At races, Jim often saw couples holding hands and hugging each other to keep warm before the start, and his stomach twisted in envy.

What Jim did not know was that the older women on the serial marathoning circuit considered him a prime catch. At the

2009 Martian Marathon in Dearborn, Michigan, a group of these women—a group that included Betty Wailes—voted him the nicest person they knew during a late-night gossip session. In the morning, Betty informed Jim of the flattering designation that had been bestowed upon him while he slept, but Jim was a little slow on the romantic uptake and did not immediately recognize the flirtation for what it was. Even so, a seed was planted.

Jim and Betty continued to bump into each other often at events, yet more than three years passed before Jim worked up the courage to make a move. It happened finally at the 2013 Potomac River Run Marathon, where Jim arrived with a plan—an odd one, but a plan all the same. The race offered two separate start lines, one in the District of Columbia and the other in Maryland. Jim, who had chosen the DC start, asked a mutual friend to tell Betty, who had chosen the Maryland start, that he wanted to talk to her when the two courses merged. Betty was understandably intrigued, but, when they met up, all he did was complain about how cold his hands were.

"Will you hold my hand?" he asked.

Betty took Jim's right hand in her left.

"Boy, it *is* cold!" she exclaimed.

Betty was still holding Jim's hand when the pair came upon an aid station staffed by a couple of women of roughly her own age.

"How cute!" one of them said. "They're holding hands!"

Betty's heart began to thrash inside her chest. Had she and Jim just become a couple without her even realizing it? The next moment would reveal the answer—and might also determine the course of the rest of her life. If Jim withdrew his hand in embarrassment, as she feared he would, then the nicest person she knew would remain nothing more to her than an acquaintance with a shared hobby. But if—

Jim squeezed Betty's hand tighter, and they've been together ever since, an inseparable fixture on the circuit.

"Finally," Jim said to me, "after three and a half years of keeping my eye on Betty, I found somebody to fall in love with. We are compatible in every way you can think of. We are so fortunate to have found each other and to be so much in love and to be able to participate together in what we both love to do."

Betty cast a tender look at her boyfriend as he spoke these words. I swallowed my last question, said farewell to the couple, and resumed running, pulling out my phone and FaceTiming Nataki as I went.

"Good morning!" she answered, projecting a bright morning smile that quickly turned into a confused squint. "Wait—are you still running?"

"Yes," I said. "I've got a little ways to go. But I wanted to tell you about these people I just met." And so I did.

"Aw, that's beautiful!" Nataki said when I finished the story, as I'd known she would. Happy older couples give us hope.

I ran the next several miles alone, absorbing impressions. Several runners, I noticed, were wearing shirts, hats, and jackets branded with the Marathon Maniacs logo. Founded in 2003 as a club for serial marathoners, Maniacs doesn't admit just anyone. I had qualified for a bronze-level membership by completing three marathons and a fifty-mile ultramarathon in the span of thirty-eight days the prior year. To attain the highest level, titanium, a runner must complete fifty-two or more marathons in a single year; thirty or more marathons in any combination of thirty American states, Canadian provinces, or other countries in one year; or marathons in twenty or more countries in the same time span. Visitors to the club's website are presented with a quiz they can use to determine whether they are "addicted to running marathons," hence likely to feel at home as members. "When asked about your racing from non running [sic] people," goes a typical question, "do you find yourself talking with great passion to the point that the person that asked the question regrets ever asking?"

On the Camp Loop section of my fourth lap, I passed two men, one short, the other tall, engrossed in conversation. I could tell they had just met because they were exchanging credentials.

"I have a record," I heard the short one say to the tall one in a Spanish-speaker's accent.

"You have a record?" echoed the tall one, shouting instead of enunciating.

"In Guatemala, not here," the short one hedged.

"What is it?" asked the tall one encouragingly.

"Thirty marathons in one year," the short one confessed.

"Wow, that's good!" said the tall one, his tone now that of a parent praising a child's inscrutable finger painting.

"Not really," the short one said, wishing he'd never brought up the whole record thing.

Halfway through lap five, having just slipped a ninth rubber band onto my forearm, I was addressed by a hippie-looking race staffer standing behind a kind of mini–buffet table.

"Come again?" I said, still running.

"I said, 'Would you like a hotdog?'" he repeated, lifting the lid off a warming tray that contained a jumble of dogs in buns, cut into thirds.

Hell, no! I thought. I find hotdogs repulsive and hadn't eaten one in ages. But then I caught a whiff of the steaming wieners and my stomach overruled. I captured one, buried it in mustard and diced red onions, and ate it on the fly. It was freaking delicious.

Approaching seventeen miles, I caught up with Clint Burleson, who speed-walks most of his own events. As I'd done already with Jim Simpson, I slowed down, introduced myself, and requested an interview.

"Oh, okay!" Clint said good-naturedly. "Sure!"

"So, what's your story?" I asked. "The running version, I mean."

"Let's see," he began, searching his brain. "I ran my first marathon in 1982 . . ."

A second marathon soon followed, and a third, and so on. By the mid-1990s, Clint was on a mission to run a marathon in every state, a rarer but by no means unheard-of ambition in those days. Upon retiring from his job as a computer science professor at New

Mexico's Alamogordo Community College in 2008, Clint, then fifty-seven, went all in, driving east to knock out seven states in seven weeks. Having spent the bulk of this period waiting around between Sundays and wasting money, he returned home with an idea for a business, one that would enable folks like him to run a lot of marathons in a lot of different states more efficiently. After all, there was no law against staging a marathon on a Wednesday.

Five years later, the Dust Bowl Marathon Series was born. Clint reckoned he needed to attract twenty to twenty-five runners to each event of the five-state, five-day series to make it work. He got more than a hundred.

"And it just kind of grew from there," he told me.

By the time I met Clint, Mainly Marathons was rapidly becoming the Starbucks of event organizers in the serial marathoning space, with plans to host eighty events in 2018, covering all fifty states.

"Is there a certain type of customer you tend to attract?" I asked him.

"Well, I think that people who are doing lots of long-distance running probably have an addictive personality," he said. "And I'm not the only one who has said that. This conversation happens a lot. If these people weren't addicted to running, they might be addicted to something not so good for them."

"What do you get out of this?" I asked, repeating a question I'd asked Jim Simpson earlier.

"I like these people," Clint said. "They're the best customers you could possibly have. Runners are a good bunch. I mean, sure, they're out here to abuse themselves, but the ones we get like to have a good time. We've got people who follow us for every series, so we're seeing our friends over and over. If my wife were here she would tell you she'd like to spend a little more time at home. We'll be on the road probably one hundred and thirty days this year. But when we get a little break, I start missing these folks. It's a pretty good life."

I thanked Clint for his time and forged on, full of thought. *Can people really be addicted to something as challenging and uncomfortable as running marathons?* I wondered. The answer to this question was all around me—and within me too, for here I was running eight marathons in eight weeks.

Too much is made of human laziness. Yes, we are lazy. That's why 75 percent of us don't exercise at all. But we're also *not* lazy. That's how we peopled every habitable inch of the planet within 85,000 years of first venturing out of Africa and how we landed on the moon a mere 15,000 years after that. George Mallory famously said that he climbed Mt. Everest "because it's there." It would have been more accurate of him to say he climbed the mountain because he's human. There is an instinct within us—as irresistible as our instinct to take the path of least resistance—to set and achieve goals, to complete tasks, to test our limits and discover what we are capable of. A person can become addicted to anything that brings pleasure, and achievement is one of life's most transcendent pleasures, because it is attainable only by passing through pain and struggle, pleasure's antipodes. The marathon is a Mt. Everest for everyone—a healthy challenge, universally respected, that rewards its conqueror with a sense of earned pride that, on the spectrum of life's satisfactions, falls somewhere between splitting the last log in a pile of cordwood and being the first human to set foot on the moon.

My reflections on this aspect of the marathon's magic were interrupted here by an abrupt change in the weather. Clouds rolled in from the west and a ferocious wind kicked up. Many of the runners I had befriended in earlier laps began to look a tad miserable. Within another thirty minutes, only two or three other participants were still running; the rest had been reduced to the Jim Simpson Shuffle. More than ever, I felt like a cheater for not having run four marathons in the preceding four days.

A stop sign—a real one, propped against a sawhorse in front of the rubber band table—marked the finish. The moment I crossed it a familiar bliss rose up inside me. I felt expansive and all-loving, as after a third glass of wine. I approached the hotdog guy, pumped his arm as though *he* had just completed a marathon, and over-praised his frankfurters. Another race staffer then came up to me, and, despite the fact that I'd had no prior interaction with him, I liked him very much.

"Are you done?" he asked.

"Huh?" I said. "Oh, yes. Just finished."

"Well, you need to tell *them*," he said, pointing at a pair of women who sat with clipboards and papers spread before them on a folding table.

I did as instructed. One of the two women looked at my race number, then looked at her watch, and wrote "3:56:40" next to my name on the official results sheet. I looked at my own watch, which I'd stopped back at the stop sign, and saw 3:55:25. *Whatever.*

Moving on, I came to a table laden with munchies, and all of a sudden there was nothing I wanted more than to eat all of them. Like a broke stoner crashing a picnic I wolfed down apple slices, hardboiled eggs, and small squares of PB&J on raisin bread as the ladies who'd prepared the spread congratulated me on my appetite.

At the next table, I stopped to thank two more race workers, Shaquita and Brenda, for keeping me well supplied with Gatorade and repartee all morning. I felt a mad urge to tell them that my wife was black just like them, as if this created some sort of soul bond between me and all black women, but I managed to resist it, thank goodness, channeling my euphoria instead into one last bit of banter.

"You're all bundled up," I said, pointing at their long coats. "Is it cold or something?"

"You'll find out in a minute," Shaquita retorted.

On my way back to the Fun Mobile I encountered my dear, dear blood brother Merlin, whose real name, I now learned, was Emery. I asked for permission to take his picture, and he nodded like someone who got this sort of request all the time. While I set up my phone, Emery removed his jacket and adopted what looked at first like some kind of gangsta pose, but when I had him in focus I saw he was just pointing at a string of letters on the chest of his club shirt: SWFTR.

"It stands for Southwest Fun Time Runners," he said. "Fun is our middle name."

"Literally!" I said, like an idiot.

Continuing toward the car (and indeed beginning to feel rather chilly), I remembered something Josh had told me seven days earlier, after we finished the Modesto Marathon.

"I've been high all day," he confided in a tone of spaced-out wonder. "Not just in a good mood. *High*."

When Josh crept downstairs the next morning, Nataki asked him how he was feeling. She'd had to help me out of bed more than once on the day after a marathon and was prepared to fetch the Advil bottle if necessary.

"Still high," he said.

"I meant your body," Nataki said, amused.

That's how I felt as I settled gingerly into the driver's seat, my thirty-second marathon (give or take) having induced the same state of lucid insobriety as Josh's second marathon. I started the engine, cranked up the heat, and laughed, realizing I couldn't wait for the next one.

CHAPTER 5

MY WORLD OR YOURS?

MY FIRST DATE with Nataki was followed in short order by a second date, a third, and a fourth. Each time we got together, we did so either in my environment or in hers, which is to say—with only slight exaggeration—that either she was the only black person in a restaurant, theater, or home full of white people, or I was the lone representative of my race in a gathering of her family or friends.

On the increasingly rare nights when Nataki and I did not see each other, we had hours-long telephone conversations. During one of these calls, she mentioned that her best friend, Antwan, had invited us to a dance party being hosted the following weekend at the headquarters of the East Bay Dragons, a black motorcycle club.

"We don't have to go if you don't want to," Nataki said.

"Oh, but I want to!" I said. "It sounds like an adventure."

This statement was true as far as it went, but it disguised the main reason I accepted the invitation: that I didn't want Nataki to think I was afraid to go. When the call ended, I went right on trying to convince *myself* I wasn't afraid. The tacit psychic backdrop for this internal pep talk was the act of cowardice I had committed nine years earlier at the Hanover Invitational, which, although I seldom thought about it anymore, continued to challenge my self-regard, heightening the stakes of subsequent scenarios in which I was tempted to chicken out. There was, in fact, a pretty good argument to be made for not worrying in this case. After all, how often do you hear about a white guy with a Mr. Rogers haircut getting his ass kicked at a black biker bar? But this argument was undercut somewhat by what I remembered reading about the East Bay Dragons in Hunter S. Thompson's *The Great Shark Hunt*, where they came off as a bunch of bad motherfuckers.

On the appointed evening, I met up with Nataki and Antwan at Nataki's place. When we were introduced, Antwan gave me an exaggeratedly limp handshake and leered at me in bald defiance of accepted social norms. Nataki had warned me about her friend. She'd met him in cosmetology school a couple of years before, at which time he'd been in the closet, though not really fooling anyone. But whereas others whispered behind his back, Nataki gently coaxed him out, and now he was *way* out.

"Oh, my, what do we have here?" Antwan cooed, putting a finger to his lips. "You don't by chance have any brothers, do you?"

"Two, but they're quite straight," I said.

"Well, do you have any friends? Cousins? Uncles? Dads? Stepdads? Male pets?"

Antwan threw his head back and laughed like Popeye the Sailor Man, only four octaves higher. Nataki had described him to me as "kind of a human cartoon," and he seemed exactly that.

On the drive over to the club, which was located on a sketchy stretch of East Fourteenth Street, Antwan talked nonstop, as manic as Robin Williams in his cocaine phase, and at times I could barely understand him.

"I'm hell bent for leather!" he hollered as we neared our destination. "Call me Harley! Get on and ride, boy! Vroom! Vroom!"

Again Antwan cackled like Popeye on helium. If anyone was going to get his ass kicked tonight, I figured, it was this guy.

At least two dozen Harley-Davidsons were lined up in front of the Dragons' hangout when we parked Nataki's Mustang in an adjoining lot with the other four-wheeled vehicles. A massive leather-clad dude with long sideburns stood at the entrance enforcing strict admission standards. Antwan dropped the name of Monique, who worked on an assembly line with Antwan and was dating a club member. The oversized bouncer turned aside and asked another scary-big hog rider to fetch her. Moments later, Monique came to the doorway and waved us in.

It was well past ten o'clock and the place was jumping. A booming hip-hop beat (I hear Tupac's "California Love" in my memory) pummeled my chest as our party struggled through a dense mob of suited and booted groovers in search of a bit of open real estate. Instinctively, I scanned the crowd in search of other white faces. There were none.

Nataki, Monique, and I tried gamely to make small talk (Antwan having already gone on the prowl), but the thunderous music made it a hopeless exercise. Hankering for a tipple, I asked the ladies if I could buy them drinks, communicating the offer with a bottoms-up hand gesture in lieu of words.

"Juice!" Nataki commanded in a petulant little girl's voice that had become a sort of inside joke between us. She could make me do anything with that voice. Monique requested a beer.

I elbowed my way to the bar, attracting curious looks from left, right, and center as I went. I bought Budweisers for Monique and myself and a cranberry juice for Nataki, who, after receiving the glass, took two quick sips and declared, "Let's dance!"

I enjoy dancing about as much as I enjoy having my teeth cleaned, but there was no escaping it now, so I began to lift my feet and put them back down alternately in approximate synchronization with the music while Nataki broke into a funk-style boogie that looked like something straight out of the *Soul Train* line. There wasn't a man in the building I would have traded partners with.

Alas, not everyone in the building was equally content. Just when I'd begun to loosen up a little, taking a chance here and there with my technique, a wiry young man who looked barely old enough to drive approached Nataki from the rear, tapped her shoulder, and spoke. Despite our proximity, I failed to hear either his line or Nataki's response, but their body language made it clear enough to me that he was trying to persuade her to ditch me and dance with him and she was refusing. He persisted. Anger rose up in me. Without thinking, I stepped forward and put a hand on the teen's shoulder.

"You heard the lady," I said, channeling my inner Jimmy Stewart. "She doesn't want to dance with you."

Where I come from, putting a hand on a man's shoulder in this type of showdown is not necessarily crossing a line. Where this young fellow came from, evidently, it was. Raising his arms, he delivered a violent shove to my chest, launching me backward.

"Yo, don't touch me!" he shouted, revealing a grill of gold-capped teeth. "I don't play!"

It was game-on now no matter where you're from. I responded in kind, slamming my palms against my challenger's pecs with all the force I could muster, knocking him into yet another leather-clad giant, who whipped around ready to crack heads. The boy rushed at me and was suddenly flanked by two more lean high schoolers, fists at the ready. A wide circle of empty dance floor opened around us.

My eyes shifted left and right in search of Antwan, who, cartoonish or not, came from the streets and was no stranger to fisticuffs. No sign of him. My challenger had just cocked his arm back in preparation to launch a knockout punch at my nose when the guy he'd collided with grabbed him by the scruff and yanked him away from me. In the same instant I felt strong hands grip my biceps from behind, and a couple more Dragons stepped between us.

"Cool it!" barked the older of the two. "Keep this shit up and I'll toss both your asses outta here. You can settle your beef on the curb."

The three young troublemakers dropped their hands and melted into the crowd. My savior then addressed me singly.

"You a'ight?"

"I'm fine," I croaked, my heart still skittering.

Shaken and mortified, Nataki apologized desperately for the contretemps, but I waved away her sorries.

"A random asshole can show up anywhere," I said.

"Do you want to leave?" she asked.

"Heck, no!" I shouted. "We just got here!"

Of course I wanted to leave. But I still didn't want Nataki to think I was scared, even if I now had every right to be. Something about her—something to do with her frank and unapologetic *realness*—challenged me to face this particular fear with a degree of backbone I hadn't shown often enough in life.

We started dancing again. The DJ picked a slow jam, wisely taking the adrenaline level down a notch, and Nataki and I joined the other couples in pressing our bodies together and rocking in a loose embrace. After five or six rotations one of my earlier antagonist's partners approached us, again from Nataki's blind side. The hairs of my forearms stood up. *Not again!* But instead of balling his right hand to strike, he extended it toward me, open. I broke away from Nataki and took it.

"Respect," he said, as we performed the three-position soul handshake that I'd hurriedly mastered during my brief courtship of Nataki. I nodded and said nothing. With a two-finger salute and nothing more out of his own mouth, the youngster turned and walked away.

"What did he say?" Nataki asked.

"We can go now," I said.

....

When Nataki and I first met, I had existing plans to visit my parents—who still lived in the house in Madbury, New Hampshire, that I grew up in—for Thanksgiving. But it wasn't until after the Dragons incident that I got around to booking flights, and, when I did, I purchased tickets for both myself and Nataki. According to census data, my home state was the whitest in America at the time. It was Nataki's turn in the barrel.

"You don't have to go if you don't want to," I told her, consciously parroting her earlier words to me, after it was already sort of too late.

Nataki, assuming the role I had taken on that prior occasion, assured me she wanted very much to go, and she meant it, I could tell, rightly interpreting the invitation as proof of my seriousness about our relationship. But I could also tell that she was as nervous about meeting my parents as I'd been about partying with the black bikers. Indicators of anxiety kept poking through the veneer of calmness she tried gamely to project, like when she started packing three weeks before our departure day—controlling what she could, I suppose. Of course, any young woman might fret about traveling to a distant and unfamiliar place to stay in the home of a new beau's parents, wondering, *Will they like me?* But Nataki had a deeper question to brood on: *Will they even give me a chance?*

I did my best to assure her that neither of my parents was at all "funny style," as Nataki put it. Though I knew better than to tell her that some of their best friends were black, this wasn't even an option, because *there were no black people* in Madbury, New Hampshire. So instead I offered what little evidence I could, mentioning that the hero of my dad's first and second novels was a young black boy, and recounting a story from my mom's childhood about her sharing packed lunches with the hungry Price kids—Herman, Barbara, and Martha—who were among the only African American students at the elementary school they attended together in coastal Rhode Island. These admittedly weak examples, though clearly appreciated, did little to calm Nataki, whose one past relationship with a white man, John, fizzled after he failed to introduce her to his family on a visit to his hometown of St. Louis.

Nataki spent at least two hours of the five-hour flight from San Francisco to Boston retouching her makeup, again controlling what she could. My folks met us at the gate, as was customary in those last days of pre-9/11 innocence. As I made the introductions, everyone tried hard to act casual, but a painful awkwardness bubbled through the relaxed façade. There was on both sides, it appeared to me, a gap between expectation and reality, my parents having expected Clair Huxtable and gotten something closer to Jackée, while Nataki had expected who knows what and gotten Santa and Mrs. Claus. Everyone found their footing, however, during the succeeding drive north, Nataki fielding one softball question after another from my eager-to-soothe mom and dad. I could feel the tension dissipate from the hand I held in the backseat.

"What did I tell you?" I said later as we lay squished together on my old twin bed, my mother having placed us in the same bedroom without fuss despite our unmarried status.

In the morning, I borrowed my dad's car and took Nataki to the nursing home where my mom's mom, widowed ten years, had been installed three months earlier after locking herself out of her home at night. Too proud to seek help, she'd spent hours shivering in the dark before being discovered by a neighbor. On learning of the incident, my mom and her sister, Lorna, decided Dorothy's dementia had reached the point that she could no longer safely live alone. I had come home not just to remake *Look Who's Coming to Dinner* but also to say goodbye.

We located Grandma's hall on the second floor and began to wander it in search of the room number Mom had given me. Along the way, we were met by an apple-cheeked nun who pegged us as first-time visitors and asked whom we sought. I gave her the name, in response to which the sister, cooing encomiums about my dying relative, led us not to my grandmother's room but to a common room where she sat us down to wait while Grandma was awakened and prepared for her guests. All around us, milky-eyed

nonagenarians drooped like cut flowers, sadly disregarding their
puzzles, mugs of cooling tea, a blaring television, and one another.
Boiling in self-consciousness, Nataki and I put on fixed smiles of
apology for our radiant youth. After a very long four minutes, the
nun returned and led us into the spotless, cheerless quarters that
had been my grandmother's home for the past thirteen weeks.

When I saw her the previous Christmas, not long after her brain
exhibited the first worrisome signs of decline, she was more or less
the same Grandma I had always known. The intervening months
had destroyed her. We found her propped shallowly upright in a
metal-framed hospital bed, her wasted body scarcely displacing
the bedclothes that enshrouded her. The heavy eyeglasses she'd
always worn seemed doubled in size and weight, an oppressive
burden on her shrunken face, her eyes looking out frightened and
febrile through goggle-like lenses. Her hands lay limp in her lap,
all veins and liver spots. Even her hair looked frail. As I drew a
hard chair up beside her bed and sat, I saw a mental picture of a
gorgeous young woman smiling like a silver-screen ingenue from
a lost world trapped inside an antique frame in my parents' home.

Nataki crossed to the back of the room and sat in the other
available chair, several feet farther away from Grandma but directly
in her line of sight, whereas I had her three-quarters right profile.

"Hi, Grandma," I ventured, unintentionally using the same
high-pitched voice I might use with a toddler or a pet.

Grandma shifted her eyes toward me and grunted softly. That
was it. Mom had counseled me to expect a one-sided conversation. After a two-beat silence, I continued speaking, somewhat
desperately, uttering whatever came into my head. I first told my
grandmother who I was, just in case. I then introduced Nataki,
spoke about my life in California, and reminded Grandma of the
family's plan to transport her to the house for Thanksgiving if she
felt up to it. While I spoke I studied Dorothy's minimal responses,
trying to evaluate her mental state, and concluded from her rep-
tilian eye blinks and subtle lip movements that she was perhaps
following the general contours of my soliloquy but no more. What

I noticed also, though I pretended not to, was that her attention was directed not at me but elsewhere. Specifically, at Nataki.

Nataki, of course, noticed this as well, but it was not in her nature to feign obliviousness. As I continued to stave off silence with my one-on-one filibuster, she stood abruptly, approached the bed, and plopped herself down on the thin mattress at about the level of Grandma's brittle shinbone. I felt my lungs clench, my mind's eye picturing the bed collapsing beneath the two women, Nataki's sturdy young body crushing the last bit of life out of my eggshell-fragile grandmother.

"Careful!" I said lamely.

"It's okay," Nataki said, a hint of disappointment in her voice. She then turned to my grandmother and leaned in.

"Have you ever been to California?" she asked.

"No, never," Grandma replied in a weak but perfectly intelligible whisper.

"Really? You can come visit us there when you get better. We'll go to the beach and you can sit in the sun with a nice hat."

Grandma smiled. I exhaled. All was well.

"So," Nataki resumed, "what do you think of your grandson being with a girl like me?"

Time stopped. My head filled with sudden heat and pressure, as though I'd been caught in an egregious lie. My eyes darted to Grandma, then back to Nataki, and then back to Grandma. I had absolutely no idea what Dorothy, born in 1917 in another of the whitest states in America, would think of my being with a girl like Nataki. Not once had the topic of race ever come up between us. What I did know, however, was that John had blown it big-time in keeping Nataki away from his bigoted kin in St. Louis, a measure that he considered protective but Nataki judged cowardly. I couldn't make the same mistake; I had to let this play out.

Seconds passed, and I began to worry that Nataki had managed to kill Grandma after all. Then, at last, she spoke. The words came haltingly, but they came, a last burst of eloquence that would have no sequel.

"I have to say," she rasped, "I'm not surprised. But, having met you, I'm pleased."

I closed my eyes and bit down hard, fighting to control the emotional upwelling released by these few phrases, which revealed so much: that Grandma was *still there*, still her kindhearted self inside the desiccated carapace; that she was *not* a racist; that she *understood* me, "got" me, appreciated me as the kind of person who goes where his heart leads him, wherever it may lead. I hadn't known any of this until Nataki drew it out of her, and if not for Nataki, I would never have known.

I leapt back into the conversation, my tongue freed by the intimacy of the women's exchange. Only now was I able to say what I should have said already. I told Grandma I loved her. I thanked her for having always been so good to me and I vowed that I would forever treasure my memories of her, like the time we watched a Frank Sinatra concert on television together, just the two us, when I stopped to visit her on the way home from Haverford.

"You were so surprised I liked Old Blue Eyes too!" I said, half-laughing, half-crying.

I left the hospital feeling as if I might float away. The very last thing I had expected from the visit was to connect with Grandma more deeply than I ever had. I'd just wanted to get through it—to check the box and move on—not because I didn't care but because I did. And that's all I would have done if Nataki hadn't been there with me. What did this say about me? What did it say about her? Us?

Two days later, Dorothy's caretakers judged her well enough to leave the nursing home for turkey dinner. She was placed in a wheelchair, loaded into a van, and delivered to our doorstep like freight. My parents had invited three others to the feast, among them Dori, the longtime family friend who had squired Mr. Marshall and my mother and brothers and me around Boston in 1983 while my dad ran his first marathon. Dad now wheeled Grandma from the doorway to a small gap in a loose circle of chairs in the living room. Nataki and I and the rest were already seated and plucking hors d'oeuvres from a tray that had been set on a coffee table within reach of all. Nataki was positioned at my left side and again directly in Grandma's line of sight.

A fog of embarrassment settled over the gathering in the conversational vacuum that followed the bustle of Grandma's entrance. It was evident that the guest of honor was not present enough mentally to be included in any kind of normal conversation. This left us with two options, neither of them agreeable. One was to collectively interview Grandma, treating her like some kind of clan celebrity renowned for her nearness to the grave, which would be a strain on both sides. The alternative was to carry on as if she didn't exist, and that felt just plain heartless. Unable to hold a vote, we went by instinct, trying briefly to have it both ways before drifting down the path of least resistance, heartless though it did feel. True to form, I pretended not to notice how utterly lost Grandma looked as we nattered on without her.

Nataki, also true to form, noticed too but refused to pretend otherwise. Instead she rose quietly from her seat and shimmied around the circle until she came to an empty chair next to Dorothy, where she sat down as familiarly as she had on Grandma's bed two days before.

"Are you hungry?" Nataki asked.

Another hush fell upon us as all eyes turned toward Nataki and Grandma. Construing whatever slight reaction my grandmother gave her as affirmative, Nataki began to point at items on the food tray, naming each in turn.

"This is crab dip," she said. "Do you want some crab dip on a cracker?"

I had no idea if Grandma was even eating real food still. For all I knew, she was back on baby food, or getting her nutrition intravenously. Nataki, however, had no such doubts. Stalled only for a moment by Grandma's inscrutable reply, a breathy murmur that could have meant anything from "I thought you'd never ask!" to "I'm deathly allergic to crab," Nataki made her own decision. Betraying not a hint of self-consciousness despite the five pallid faces following her every move, she spread some dip across a Triscuit with careful strokes, brought the cracker to Dorothy's lips, and fed her nibble by tedious nibble until the morsel had vanished. By then, the rest of us had gone back to talking amongst ourselves. But I kept one eye fixed on the feeding ritual. For the second time in seventy-two hours, emotion squeezed my throat.

Later, after pumpkin pie and coffee, I took Nataki aside and thanked her for showing such kindness to my mother's mother.

"She looked hungry," Nataki shrugged.

This is the moment I think of whenever Nataki asks me why I chose her (and she asks not infrequently these days). There were many reasons, I suppose, but the clincher was finding in her, despite our obvious differences, a living model for The Person I Want to Be—an everyday hero who casts fear aside and does the hard thing when the hard thing is the right thing.

CHAPTER 6

WE'RE ALL IN THIS TOGETHER

(Rockin' K Trail Marathon)

A LOW RUMBLE roused me from a dreamless sleep, my eyes opening to total darkness. I reached out blindly and plucked my cell phone off the night table. Four twenty. My alarm was set to go off in ten minutes. I dropped back onto the pillow open eyed, listening. The rumble came again, louder, unmistakable. *Uh-oh.*

The Rockin' K Trail Marathon—the third event in my eight-week quest—is a challenging race even in the best conditions, with its 3,500 feet of elevation change (in Kansas!), multiple water crossings, and outrageous diversity of surfaces (ranging from crushed brick to "orange sand" according to one past participant's online review), but on this thunderous April Fool's Day it promised to be tougher than usual—and quite possibly treacherous.

After taking a highly conflicted Queenie outside to poop in an icy downpour, I breakfasted on instant oatmeal, a banana, and orange juice, gathered my gear together, and headed out, feeling a pinch of guilt about leaving Nataki (whom I'd once again managed not to wake) stranded for the next several hours in a drab room in a dingy hotel in the blighted city of Salina, where, judging by what we'd seen of it since rolling into town the previous afternoon, there was absolutely nothing to do. But Nataki always assures me that she doesn't mind these brief abandonments, being no longer as easily bored as she once was. She's been through a lot over the past, oh, fourteen years, and she prefers—needs—a quiet existence now. At home Nataki often watches game shows while I work or exercise because, she tells me, "I like to see people win."

Thirty-two miles of tense driving through near zero visibility brought me to Kanopolis State Park, where I left the Fun Mobile in a line of vehicles mired on the muddy shoulder of a dead-end road and hiked the last three hundred yards to the Corral Shelter, a one-room stone hut in which Nataki and I had eaten a prerace meal of spaghetti and meatballs with about twenty others the evening before. The same space now held several times that number, wet-faced men and women in foul-weather garb packed together like civilians in a bomb shelter, their anxious chatter producing a happy-hour-like din. A fire blazed in the hearth, but its heat failed to penetrate beyond the ring of people huddled around it. Laughter erupted each time the walls were set aglow by refracted lightning. *We're all gonna die! Ha-ha!*

I checked in with a race official at the back of the room and then jostled my way to an open spot against the near wall. No sooner had I rested my shoulders against its cool surface than race director Elden Galano, a sturdily built man of middle age with a ropelike braid hanging down to his L2 vertebra, stepped up onto a picnic table bench with a clipboard in his hand and read off the names of the runners who hadn't shown up.

"Mike Bannen?"

No response.

"Donald Baldank?"

Crickets.

Name after name (about thirty in all) received no answer. I kept expecting some joker to say "Bueller" and was on the verge of doing it myself when a young woman standing to my immediate right spoke up in reply to her name, but only to say, "I'm here but I'm not running." More laughter. Elden concluded his remarks by informing those of us who *were* willing to risk our lives for a finisher's medal that the start of the race would be delayed "a few minutes" on account of the threat of electrocution.

The moment Elden descended from his perch, I stepped up onto another bench and scanned the faces in the room, looking for a certain beard—a simple task made difficult by a surprising pervasion of facial hair in the gathering. (If I had only gotten the memo I wouldn't have shaved.) Eventually, though, I spied the beard I sought. It belonged to James, who'd made an impression on Nataki and me at the prerace dinner. I caught his eye and waved. He smiled with a mix of recognition and surprised delight and began to wrestle his way toward me through the crowd.

Twelve hours before, James had rolled up to the Corral Shelter in a metallic purple Honda Insight that looked like a 1950s vision of 2006 personal spacecraft. Unfolding his rangy frame from the three-cylinder machine, he made his way with purposeful strides toward a circle of runners, I among them, who were drinking Bud Lights outside the shelter while the noodles boiled. Guessing he was probably the only person present besides us who knew nobody else, I took it upon myself to welcome him.

"Are you running the fifty?" I asked.

The Rockin' K Trail Run, as it was officially named, offered marathon and fifty-mile options. Only one in five entrants had chosen the longer distance, but my gut told me this late arriver was an ultra guy.

"Yeah," James said. "How about you?"

"Marathon," I said. "Do you do a lot of these?"

"I do obstacle races mostly. A lot of Spartans."

Noting a southern accent, I asked James what brought him to Kansas.

"I messed up my shoulder in the warehouse where I work," he said, "so I've been traveling around the last couple weeks, finding different races to do. I did a fifty miler last weekend. The weekend before that, I did a 15K and two Spartan Races on Saturday and another 15K and two more Spartan Races on Sunday."

It was more than an accent. There was something just a tiny bit off in the way James enunciated, a not-quite-lisp that caused me to imagine him as a hermit who'd recently come down off the mountain and wasn't used to talking. His appearance, too, was curious. He wore an old hoodie, a frayed pair of hiking shorts, knee-high compression sleeves, and sandals. His curly hair was snarled and matted, his scraggly beard just beginning to gray, his right central incisor slightly chipped. It was the eyes, though, that stood out: pinhole pupils floating in the palest blue irises I'd ever seen. I could look into them only so long before I began to feel as though I were succumbing to hypnosis.

James told us he was from South Carolina. I told him I was searching for the magic of the marathon.

"Food's ready!" Elden shouted.

I hustled shamelessly to the head of the line, leading Nataki by the hand. We loaded up our plates and carried them inside the shelter, where we sat down at the first picnic table to the right—the same one I stood on the next morning. James trailed behind as though by unspoken agreement and took a seat facing us.

"I know what you mean about magic," he said, continuing our interrupted conversation. "That's what I love about obstacle racing. Everyone has a story. Everybody's ailing in different ways, and racing is the remedy. We're all out there together working out our issues. I'm no different. I've been through some hard times."

A brief silence ensued as I waited for James to offer details and he withheld them. I didn't press. Something told me this would not be my only chance to learn my new friend's backstory.

When we met again, James having slept on-site in his non–flying saucer, James was costumed in a secondhand air force–issue track suit and two hats, one thermal, one trucker.

"Is that all you're wearing?" he asked me, resting his back on the wall I had recently abandoned in favor of the picnic table.

I nodded gravely. Forgetting that California weather exists only in California, I'd failed to pack any proper rain gear for the trip. All I had on was a pair of half-tights and a thin long-sleeve top worn over a sleeveless base layer, the whole ensemble soaked through already. The outside air temperature was forty-seven degrees.

"I hate the cold," James said. "It hurts me. I've got a metal rod here [he pointed at his left forearm], and another one here [right wrist], and an artificial shoulder [right]."

Again I waited for a fuller explanation that never came.

"You're shivering," James said. "Here, take my jacket."

I laughed, assuring James he needed the jacket more than I did.

"We're starting in two minutes!" Elden called out from behind my back. "Everyone outside!"

An urgent need to piss hit me suddenly. I squeezed out the door and darted inside a men's room located at one end of the shelter, where I encountered a three-deep line at the only urinal. My turn had just come when I heard a hubbub outside. Scrambling back into the elements, I saw my fellow racers charging away, the leader already beyond where I'd parked. I took off after them and soon caught up with the rearguard. Remembering that I was there to learn, not to race, I picked my way patiently toward the front. At the head of the main pack was none other than James, running with his fists jammed into his jacket pockets.

"Keep warm, James!" I said as I passed.

After half a mile, the course veered off the road and onto a single-track trail submerged in ankle-deep water. I kept to the grassy edges as best I could, but when a large puddle appeared in my path I saw the futility of trying to keep my feet dry and splashed straight through the stinging-cold slop. No further efforts were made to avoid water.

Within another half-mile I reeled in a couple of runners who, judging by their talk, knew each other.

"Have you guys done this race before?" I asked.

The Rockin' K's course was famously complex, and I hadn't bothered to study the online map, so I was keen to run with people who were unlikely to take a wrong turn.

"Jeff won this race last year," said the tall guy behind me in reference to the short guy ahead of me.

"And Mike was fifth," said the short guy in reference to the tall. *Perfect.*

The three of us snaked along together in easy harmony, speaking in snatches as we rotated positions according to a tacit logic based on our relative uphill and downhill running abilities, who among us chose the better line, and who did or didn't stub his toe on a root. We hit the first major stream crossing just past two miles. I followed my companions into the frigid torrent and felt my balls clench. Halfway across, I lost my footing and cried out involuntarily as the turgid flow began to carry me off. Mike, who had just gained the far bank, whipped around and shot out an arm, grasping my flailing hand and pulling me to safety.

Approaching six miles, we were confronted with one of several horse gates punctuating the racecourse, another wrinkle in its devilish design. The first to reach it, I stared at the latch as though it were an unsolvable riddle.

"Here, let me do it," Jeff said, stepping forward. He pulled on a rod I hadn't seen and the gate swung open. Instead of passing through it, though, Jeff turned his back to me. "Gotta pee," he said, beginning to spray a wooden post. "Go on ahead; we'll catch you."

I had to pee again too, but I took care of my business on the fly, pale urine soaking through the crotch of my half-tights and cascading oh-so-warmly down my left leg as I cruised along a relatively smooth stretch of gravel. A bone-chilling rain continued to fall.

For the next mile or two, I could hear Mike's and Jeff's voices behind me, but they faded steadily until distance silenced them outright. I was on my own.

Beyond the next water crossing the trail forked. Pink ribbons tied to twigs at approximate eye level led in one direction, orange ribbons the other way. I had no clue what the different colors meant. Knowing the smart move was to wait for Jeff and Mike, I went left, a decision that the superstitious side of me took as a sure sign I was supposed to have gone right.

Ten minutes later I tumbled out of the woods and into a clearing, where I saw what appeared to be an aid station—five or six race staffers milling in front of a popup tent shading water coolers set out on folding tables.

"There's a runner coming!" I heard a woman say excitedly.

"Yeah, but he's going the wrong way," said a familiar male voice.

It was Elden, who repeated more or less the same words to my face when I got to the aid station.

"Can't I just do the loop in reverse?" I asked.

"No way," Elden said. "You have to go back."

I looked at my GPS watch and did some mental math.

"I'll end up running thirty miles!" I protested.

Elden shrugged. I knew not to push any further. When I'd met Elden at the prerace dinner, we had the following exchange:

ME: What time does the race start?

ELDEN: Seven.

ME: What time should I plan to arrive here?

ELDEN: Before seven.

I ran back to the fork and went right this time, only to meet a line of eight or nine runners head-on.

"Am I going the wrong way?" I asked their leader.

"Well, you're going the same way I was a minute ago," he said. "But these guys are saying something else."

I reversed my direction a second time and followed the group. We quickly found ourselves stopped at a multidirectional divide in the trail, a kaleidoscope of ribbons beckoning us every which way. The alpha males present immediately fell into bickering about what to do. I hung back and observed, trying to identify the Magellan of the bunch. Unable to come to a consensus, the disputants scattered, each would-be captain taking a loyalist or two with him along a different path. I stayed put with a couple of other ditherers.

"We found a checkered flag!" called one of the guys (invisible now behind thick foliage) who'd taken the path I'd had the least confidence in. "Come this way!"

"Okay, thanks!" shouted one of the guys he'd been arguing with not thirty seconds ago.

Faster than my companions, I was soon alone again. The course began to ascend, the terrain becoming more arid and rugged. Eventually the trail disappeared altogether, and I was left orienteering, scrabbling from ribbon to ribbon. I came to the base of a muddy promontory atop which a lone pink ribbon flitted tauntingly. Between it and me stood a good thirty yards of slick muck slanted at the angle of a playground slide. I charged up on my hands and feet, slipped, and slid back down. A second attempt netted the same result.

I stood with my hands on my hips and studied the crude puzzle before me, searching for a better way. Finding none, I chose a new line at random, speed-crawling to the peak like a starving predator. Lungs billowing, I returned to standing in several slow stages, wiped my filthy palms on my filthy shirt, and lumbered on. Just then my watch beeped, letting me know I had completed mile eighteen in 14:59. Had I ever "run" a slower mile in my life? Unlikely.

The course bent downward now, and I was beginning to feel better about my prospects for surviving the day when a mucky precipice appeared suddenly before me and I hit the brakes, trying to buy an extra half second to judge the safest path forward. Too late. My legs vanished from under me and I dropped like I'd been brained with a tire iron. Twisting as I fell, I landed in a plank position and glided feet first to the base of the declivity as smoothly as if I'd intended it. This time I didn't bother wiping my hands.

Just past twenty miles I felt a dip in energy, so I pulled a gel flask out of a hip pocket and took a sip. It tasted like dirt. I checked the nozzle and found it caked in grit. I took another sip.

When my watch showed I had covered 26.2 miles—the distance I'd signed up for—I was still almost four miles from the finish line. Having just peed on myself again, I hoped to encounter one more waist-high water crossing, lest I arrive back at the Corral Shelter smelling like a wet diaper. What I got was a chest-high water crossing.

Squishing away from the river, I noticed what felt like a nettle in my right shoe, underneath the arch. I knew from experience that such things are best nipped in the bud, so I stopped and removed both shoe and sock, raking the bottom of the latter with numb fingertips in a clumsy effort to dislodge whatever sharp something was stuck in there before reshoeing and continuing. One painful step was all it took to confirm that the nettle remained.

I arrived next at a T-junction marked by a pair of yard signs. The one on the left read, "Outbound Runners / Big Bluff Loop." The other read, "Inbound Runners / Finish Line." I knew which way to go—that wasn't the problem. The problem was that I had come to an unnervingly similar T-junction marked by identical signs twenty minutes earlier. Was I running in circles? I wouldn't have bet against it. All I could do was press on and pray I didn't see the same thing a third time. I just about whooped with relief when, a few hundred yards farther on, I realized I was now running on a fire road, whereas previously I had been on singletrack.

At the finish line, a race official patted me on the back and handed me a trophy in the shape of a horseshoe.

"Congratulations!" he said. "You got second place!"

Ignoring the trophy and its presenter, I stared hungrily at the fresh hamburger that Elden—who'd somehow made it back to the shelter ahead of me—was chomping on.

"That looks really good," I said.

Elden squinted at the sandwich as if considering whether to hand it over, then shook his head, dismissing the idea. "There's a bunch of them inside," he said, motioning toward the shelter.

Inside I found my former confederates Mike (who had won the marathon) and Jeff (who was entered in the fifty and was taking a break between laps—a break that, as it turned out, never ended), stuffing their faces. One or two more marathon finishers soon joined us, and we all stood around trading war stories, united by the madness we'd just gone through together. The few spouses present looked on with expressions of helpless exclusion, as though we were sharing inside jokes in a language they didn't speak. Observing this, I thought of my own spouse and tried to picture what she might be doing at this very moment, but the images that came to me—Nataki singing to old recordings of the music she made in times when her energy was better, Nataki meditating on the back patio with the water fountain burbling and Queenie on her lap, Nataki turning the kitchen upside down to prepare a feast for us, as she enjoys doing when she feels up to it—represented the things I was most likely to find her doing when I returned from a run back home, not out here on the road.

When the opportunity presented itself, I buttonholed Jeff and asked whether I might interview him for Postcards from the Finish Line, a social media project I was helping my sponsor with. Each subject got the same three questions, the last of which was, simply, "Why do you keep running?"

"My favorite thing about running is the friendships," Jeff said in answer to this one. "The camaraderie we have is awesome."

I nodded knowingly, recalling the competitive/cooperative gestalt that Jeff and Mike and I had achieved together for a few miles earlier in the day.

Shared suffering forges human bonds like nothing else. Psychologists have demonstrated that people tend to behave more altruistically after experiencing pain. Soldiers exhibit less severe symptoms of posttraumatic stress when they are deployed with their brothers-in-arms than they do when separated from them back home. Boxers embrace in genuine love after the final bell puts an end to their efforts to flatten each other. And marathons use the same alchemy to transform strangers into comrades faster than you can say, "Man, this sucks!"

During the long drive back to the hotel in Salina, I thought of that well-known line of uncertain origin, "Be kind, for everyone you meet is fighting a hard battle." No one would deny the wisdom of this counsel. In everyday life, though, it's all too easy to fail to see the hard battle others are fighting. But in a marathon, *you can't miss it*, and seeing your own suffering mirrored in the faces of those around you kindles a feeling of solidarity that transcends the moment, creating a kind of empathetic community that, for folks like Mike, makes running much more than a sport.

By the time I got back to the hotel, these deep thoughts were far from my mind, thrust aside by more material concerns. I burst into the room screaming, scaring the daylights out of Nataki, who was napping on the bed.

"What's wrong?" she asked, leaping up. "What happened?"

"My feet!" I said, darting into the bathroom and beginning to fill the tub with hot water. "They're burning!"

"Burning?" Nataki asked, pressing her fingers to her temples.

"*Cold* burning," I said.

Some kind of delayed reaction to my numerous soakings had occurred out on the road, a pins-and-needles sort of pain radiating from toe to heel and intensifying rapidly, forcing me to take urgent relief measures that included taking off my shoes and socks as I drove and venting the heater downward on full blast.

"Is it frostbite?" Nataki asked as I tested the water temperature with a finger, stepped in, and screamed anew. "Should I call someone?"

"Let's see if this works first," I said through gritted teeth.

Our eyes met, and in hers I recognized a look that once upon a time portended a question: "Why do you do this to yourself?" But not this time. We'd been together almost twenty years, and within this span each of us had changed for the other and had also, for each other, accepted what would never change.

The bath worked, and after a quick snack and a change into dry clothes I returned to the park with Nataki to watch James complete his fifty miles. The sun set, and the temperature plummeted as we waited at the edge of the road terminating at the Corral Shelter. Having had my fill of feeling cold for one day, I was on the verge of saying, "Forget it," when James emerged from the gloaming. Nataki and I clapped and cheered, celebrating our own imminent escape from the chill as much as James's success. Hearing his name, James smiled the same smile of surprised delight I'd seen when I spotted him from the picnic table in the morning.

An hour later, the three of us were seated together in a booth at the Iron Skillet, a restaurant located across the street from our hotel, where James had tailed us at my invitation, his retro space car threatening to come apart at sixty miles per hour on the freeway. Nataki ordered the Salisbury steak, James went for the meat-lover's omelet, and I chose the fish and chips. The time had come to satisfy my curiosity.

"Last night you said something about going through hard times," I said to James, who again sat across from us. "I'd like to hear more about that, if you're comfortable telling me."

"Sure," he said. "My dad died when I was less than a year old. After that it was just me, my mom, and an older brother, Michael. We didn't have a lot but we made do. My brother and I made our own toys, used sticks as swords, that sort of thing. After my dad passed away, we moved to San Diego and stayed there until I was eight, then we moved back to South Carolina to be near my dad's family, so they could help my mom here and there."

"That's a pretty rough start," I said.

"By the time I was twelve or thirteen I was already working," James went on. "On the way to school I would cut grass, and on the way home I would do another lawn. I left the money at the house for my mom to spend on groceries or whatever. If I needed clothes or something like that I had to come up with the funds, because we didn't have them. When I was fourteen or fifteen years old I moved out of my mom's house. There were some issues."

"What kinds of issues?" I prodded.

"She was manic depressive," James said after a moment's hesitation. "She was in and out of the hospital, and it was hard for me to stay home by myself and go to school."

"Nataki's bipolar too," I said.

"So I understand," Nataki chimed in matter-of-factly, her eyes not straying from the slab of overcooked beef she was sawing at.

James eyed her expectantly, but she said nothing more.

"How did that affect you?" I asked.

"It was hard," he said. "I was very young and I didn't really understand. My brother kind of understood, but I didn't. I was a loner. A lot of people knew me, but I didn't really care to hang out with them. I liked to build stuff. I would get a bunch of cardboard boxes together and make some kind of weird robot or something out of them. Some people might have said I was wild, but it was just because my mom was in and out, so I had a lot of free time. I had this little twenty-inch bike that I rode a lot. I went for rides that were fifteen, twenty miles each way. I wanted to go places."

James was interrupted here by the reappearance of our waitress, who asked how the food was tasting and refilled my mug of hot cider.

"I wasn't what you would call a typical kid," James resumed. "Most people thought I was weird. I had long hair. I didn't really fit in in South Carolina. My mom accepted me for who I was, and I didn't care what other people thought. I didn't want to fit into a certain clique or try to be a certain way so people would like me."

James's alienation deepened when he joined the high school cheerleading squad, but his willingness to endure the predicable taunting paid off when the University of Southern California offered him a full-ride cheerleading scholarship. Eager for escape, James drove 2,400 miles with Michael to visit the school. On the way home, his brother fell asleep at the wheel and drove off a twenty-five-foot cliff. That's how James got the metal rod in his left forearm—and how he ended up going to work as a heating and air conditioning installer instead of earning a bachelor's degree in sunny Los Angeles.

Despite this unwanted change of course, James stayed determined to escape the poverty of his youth and worked with superhuman tenacity to get ahead. He took a loading job at a warehouse where he logged as many as 120 hours per week. He opened a CrossFit gym and a shop that built custom cars. He bought a house, then bought another house and rented out the first one, and eventually bought four more houses.

Somewhere in the midst of all this toil and acquisition, James discovered that his single-minded devotion to making money created more problems than it solved. He wrecked two motorcycles, both accidents associated with sleep deprivation and both resulting in major injuries (hence the other metal parts in his body). Then his six-year marriage to a woman who owned a local automobile dealership fell apart. Only then did James begin to understand what was really missing from his life.

"When I was married," he told us, "I saw that obstacle races were becoming popular and I wanted to try them. My wife wasn't really hot on the whole idea. She was a second-degree black belt in karate and not into the whole running thing. When I got divorced I said, 'I'm gonna try this.'"

I smiled at these last words, remembering Jim Simpson, whose serial marathoning habit exploded after his own divorce.

"My first obstacle race was a short one, just three miles," James continued. "I took my ex-wife with me. She hated it. Then I signed up for a Spartan race. It was five miles, thirty obstacles. I went there and I was so stoked on the community. It was a real race. People wanted to push themselves, and yet they would stop and sacrifice their own time to help you get over a wall. They would put everything out there just to help you accomplish something."

Before the year was out, James had completed obstacle races of up to thirty-one miles plus a fifty-mile ultramarathon. The following year, he purchased a Spartan Pass, which enabled him to do an unlimited number of races, and he got his money's worth, competing in events all over the country and "doing laps" at each of them—repeating the same course multiple times by entering every division from beginner to elite.

"I would do whatever was available," he said. "Sometimes I would do forty or fifty miles in a day. I would start off with the elites because I had to start early in order to run more laps. The pros don't really talk all that much, but in the open heats you get these people who are from different backgrounds. They've all got a story and I loved listening to them. When I ran multiple laps, I wore my medals from previous laps. Sometimes I had four medals on me because I'd already run four laps and I was on my fifth. I wanted to inspire people. Someone might be on his first lap and really struggling and he would see me with a bunch of medals and he'd stop struggling. It was still hard for them, but they didn't feel they had the right to complain because I had done so much more. I told them, 'We all have our own journeys. We all have our own goals.' At one time I was where they were."

"Have any of these connections turned into lasting friendships?" I asked.

"Yes!" James said, pleased with the question. "I met so many people that we formed a community. Now, when we go to races, we all pool together and get rooms. Next week we're going to New Jersey. We rented a fifteen-passenger van and a house and we're going to stay there all weekend. That's very typical. It makes races so much better and so much cheaper. You get to spend time with friends, and you don't have to spend a ton of money to do what you want to do."

I opened my mouth to ask another question, but James wasn't done.

"Since I messed up my shoulder and started traveling," he said, "I've stayed at people's houses all over the US. In Colorado the other day I stayed at a friend's house. I got a warm shower and crashed there, and we went and hiked the next day. This is just a guy I met on the racecourse. We don't really know each other."

"You're like Paul from the Bible," Nataki said.

James nodded, whether in understanding of the reference to the apostle's peripatetic, alms-dependent lifestyle or out of politeness I couldn't tell.

"In December," he said, "when I was traveling in Pennsylvania, I had some problems with my car. I put out a call for help. An athlete I know from Virginia drove all the way up and towed my car back to his garage and took care of it. I compensated him, but he didn't want it. He just did it because that's the bond we have."

"Paul, definitely," Nataki affirmed.

"A lot of times," James said, "if there's someone who can't afford to go to a race, we'll pool together and cover their expenses so they can come hang out. There's a few people who take advantage, but for the most part they're going to turn around and do the same thing for someone else."

"Let me get this straight," I broke in. "You were a loner your whole life. Then you discovered this obstacle racing community and suddenly you're the life of the party. That's a pretty radical transformation. How do you explain it?"

"I've always been a giving person," James said. "But when you're that type of person, you find yourself around a lot of takers. They don't appreciate what you do for them, they just want you to do it. Joining this community enabled me to be who I am and support other people because they're supporting me. It really changed me for the better."

"What's different about obstacle racers?" I asked.

"They're just so open," James said. "I've never really been a people person. Buying and selling cars and having rentals and dealing with tenants—that was just business. But the people in this community want to see you achieve a goal. They have nothing to gain from helping you get over a wall or complete a course. But they do it anyway. When you're in a mud hole and you can't get out, they're going to pull you out. For no reason. Just because they're there, suffering with you. Because we're all in this together."

CHAPTER 7

UNFINISHED BUSINESS

MY JOB WITH *Triathlete*, which I'd held for three months when I met Nataki, did not pay very well. Scraping by on twenty-eight grand a year bothered me little as an unattached single, but when I fell in love my meager bank balance became an intolerable burden, a vexing drag on efforts to court my newfound soul mate with the extravagance she deserved. Financial lack had denied Nataki much in her twenty-two years, most recently a long-held aspiration to pursue a college degree at the Fashion Institute of Design and Merchandizing in San Francisco. She was, by dint of both her life experience and her essential nature, the furthest thing from spoiled, as she proved to me on one of our early dates by removing her stilettos and walking several city blocks barefoot on rain-soaked pavement to spare me the cost of hiring a cab. But Nataki's queenly bearing fairly demanded a queen's appurtenances, for which she had no lack of appreciation ("That's my dream car," she told me on another date, pointing at a passing Mercedes-Benz CLK350 convertible), and I would have given her the world if I'd only had it to give.

Working for a magazine did offer some advantages to compensate for the low salary, perks I exploited at every opportunity in a no-holds-barred campaign to sweep Nataki off her feet. I wrote a monthly column called Doctor Jock's Product Lab, a parody of the traditional consumer publication product review, that I abused frequently for this purpose. When a puffy orange mountain climbing suit arrived at the office, inspiration struck; I engaged one of the publication's regular photographers and then called Nataki and requested, without explanation, that she put on her sexiest dress (a black lace number that showed her tush) and meet me at Harry Denton's, an upscale bar on Nob Hill, where the two of us were photographed sipping champagne in our head-turning attire. I reviewed the mountain climbing suit as a "$500 power suit" in my next column, and Nataki got another clip for her modeling portfolio.

The next opportunity landed on my desk a few weeks later in the form of a press release announcing that Porsche, the automaker, had licensed its brand to a company that manufactured mountain bikes. Doctor Jock had another great idea, and within fifteen minutes I had arranged to test ride a Porsche mountain bike and review it in *Triathlete*. My next step was to phone Porsche Cars North America and tell the gentleman in charge of arranging test drives for members of the press that I wanted to kick the tires of a Boxster and compare it to the mountain bike in my magazine review. The concept made absolutely no sense and both of us knew it. But I got the car.

The following Saturday, I drove across the Bay Bridge in a brand-new carmine-red Porsche Boxster with two tickets to a Patti Labelle concert at Oakland's Paramount Theater stashed inside the breast pocket of my tweed sport coat and a bouquet of Casablanca lilies (Nataki's favorite) on the passenger seat next to me. I'd told Nataki about the tickets but not about the car.

Uncle Eli answered my knock. Spying the wheels I'd rolled up in, he opened his mouth to say "Holy shit!" but I shushed him with a quick finger to my lips. Inside the house I found Nataki primping in front of the bathroom mirror.

"You might want to put on a hat for the convertible," I told her casually.

"Okay," she said, distracted by her efforts to perfect the arch of an eyebrow.

Two beats of silence followed. Nataki then turned to me and narrowed her eyes. I smiled. She ran to the front door and flung it open.

"Oh, Booby!" she said.

Nataki started calling me Booby around the time we began sleeping together. It probably goes without saying it was not the pet name I would have chosen for myself. And yet, in its very corniness, it was among the purer signs that Nataki (or Kitty, as I'd taken to calling her) loved me as wide-openly as I loved her. (But still: *Booby?*)

We drove back across the bridge to San Francisco to dine at a hip fondue restaurant on Van Ness Avenue. As our meal neared its conclusion, the melted chocolate cooling and the number of un-eaten fresh strawberries dwindling, I broached a subject I'd been dreading.

"So, this is kind of embarrassing," I said, "but can I borrow twenty bucks for parking?"

Nataki stared at me stone-faced, as though her brain had blown a circuit, fried by the notion that a man who had just picked her up in a $40,000 sports car could not afford to valet it. I swallowed hard, convinced I had blown it for real this time, hating myself for lacking the foresight to borrow cash from Sean. But Nataki's expression softened.

"Let me tell you a story," she said. "When I was a little girl, I wanted a pink remote control Barbie Corvette for Christmas. Oh, I wanted it so bad! But my parents couldn't afford it. So my mom got me something else. It looked like a Corvette, and it was pink, but it wasn't no Barbie Corvette and it wasn't remote control. I'd seen it before. They sold them in bins at the supermarket for ten dollars."

"What did you do?" I asked.

"I tied a string to the bumper and pulled my Barbie around in it," Nataki said, handing me a twenty-dollar bill.

....

In July 1998, a full year into our relationship, my blitzkrieg on Nataki's heart was continuing apace when I received a call at work from a representative of the St. Maarten tourism office, a bubbly woman with a fetching French Caribbean accent who offered me an all-expenses junket to cover the debut of a triathlon that the local chamber of commerce had cooked up as a way to attract adventure travelers and their dollars. This time I needed no help from Doctor Jock. I told the woman that the trip sounded great but, alas, it coincided with my girlfriend's birthday and therefore I would not be able to make it . . . unless my girlfriend was permitted to come along. I was lying, of course, and both of us knew it. But I got the second ticket.

Five weeks later, a Boeing 737 packed with American fun-seekers glided into Princess Juliana International Airport at the precise moment of sunset, the windows on our side of the cabin perfectly framing a luminous pink orb melting into aftershave-blue water. We passed through customs in less time than it takes to floss your teeth and were greeted outside by a pair of white folks with the same accent I'd heard on the phone. The male half of the pair piled our bags into a van and took the wheel. Nataki and I goggled like the first-timers we were at our passing surroundings—an alien twilight teeming with flamboyant trees (their actual name), miniature cars, and lots of brown bodies in bright clothes—as we rumbled from the Dutch side of the island to the French, stopping eventually at a four-star resort where we were to spend the next three nights in a palatial suite.

The evening was balmy and Nataki and I were wired, so rather than settle in we immediately threw on our swimsuits and went down to the beach.

"Do you think it's warm?" Nataki asked, regarding the gently lapping surf.

I dipped a toe into the foam. It felt like bathwater.

"It feels like bathwater," I said.

We waded in hand in hand until we were waist deep. Nataki couldn't swim, so I made a hammock of my arms and rocked her. Back on the beach, she challenged me to a race.

"I used to be the fastest girl on my block," she said.

"Well, I was an All-State cross country runner," I countered.

Nataki made a surprise start. I gave chase at three-quarters speed, confident I could run her down without going all-out. Not so. Nataki pulled away from me as though I were walking. I got up on my toes and pumped my arms, charging after her with everything I had. When I began to nose ahead, Nataki burst into laughter, and I did the same. We collapsed breathless onto the sand, where we remained for some time.

"I wish we could live here," Nataki said, as we lay on our backs admiring familiar constellations from an unfamiliar angle.

That one word—*we*—made my heart glow.

At breakfast the next morning we met several other journalists who had accepted the same invitation I had. Among them were Greg, an editor with *Men's Health*; Miles, who published a New York–based endurance monthly; Kendra, an editor with *Body & Soul*, a health magazine for black women; and her colleague Kim. While we sipped mimosas and forked eggs Benedict, our hosts laid out the day's agenda: a tour of the island in the morning followed by an outdoor lunch at a different resort, free time in the afternoon, dinner at a celebrated seafood restaurant overlooking the ocean, and finally an evening of club hopping. I gave Nataki's hand a conspiratorial squeeze under the table, as if to say, *Can you believe we're actually pulling this off?*

The island tour ended at a nude beach, where a local photographer who'd been hired to document our fun tried to convince me to disrobe for a few "tasteful" R-rated pictures. Nataki flashed a glare of warning at the woman, and that was the end of that. During afternoon free time, Nataki and I split off from the others, rented a car, and drove to Marigot Beach, where we ripped through glassy waters aboard a Jet Ski, Nataki's lithe arms wrapped trustingly around my life jacket from behind. Between the hours of 6:00 and 8:00 P.M. our party succeeded in racking up a four-figure bill at the celebrated seafood restaurant, and afterward Greg and I propped up the bar at a series of nightspots while the ladies dominated their dance floors. Years later, I was both surprised and not surprised when Greg, whose quick wit brought out my falsetto laugh at frequent intervals, turned up on my television screen as a wisecracking political pundit on Fox News.

In the morning Nataki and I walked into town to purchase souvenirs. She wore a canary yellow thong bikini with a matching fishnet sarong that showed a lot more than it hid. As we strolled together along the busy sidewalk, a man driving a car the size of a riding mower became mesmerized by Nataki's backside, his head whipping around like a fish on a line as he buzzed past. Seconds later, we heard a sound similar to dishes crashing to a tile floor. Turning around, we discovered that, in his distraction, my girlfriend's admirer had driven into a pole. For the second time in three days, we fell to the ground laughing.

As we resumed our stroll, I was seized by a sudden certainty that I would remember the present moment for the rest of my life. *Savor this,* I told myself. *You're twenty-seven years old. You're getting paid to frolic in the Caribbean. The woman beside you is beautiful enough to cause traffic accidents. Savor this—because it won't last forever.*

On our final day on the island, at precisely 5:00 A.M., the bedside phone in our suite rang shrilly, shooting sonic arrows into my throbbing brain. Greg, Kim, Kendra, Nataki, and I had spent the previous evening at a club called Boo-boo-jam, hidden deep in the jungle and little known to tourists and white people, where again I had been scandalously overserved. I fumbled for the receiver and pressed it to my ear.

"Hello?" I rasped. My mouth tasted like the floor of a frat house on Sunday morning.

"Hello, Mr. Fitzgerald!" piped an overcaffeinated male voice on the other end. "This is your wakeup call."

The inaugural St. Maarten International Triathlon, my official reason for being on the island, was scheduled to start in two hours at Great Bay Beach, on the Dutch side. My original plan had been to arrive there just in time to watch the start and then hang out with a cup of coffee while the action took place, perhaps writing down a few notes for appearance's sake. But that plan went out the window two days earlier, when, in a fit of gratitude to our unstinting hosts, I'd decided to write about the race as a participant. It had seemed like a good idea at the time, despite my having never done a triathlon. Now, after forty-eight hours of indulgence, I wanted to cry.

I pried myself off the mattress and shuffled into the bathroom, where an unexpected eagerness began to devour my dread as I teetered over a toilet bowl of decidedly foreign shape. The feeling baffled me momentarily, and yet there was also something spine-tinglingly familiar about it, like a scent from the distant past. Then I knew: A part of me that I'd given up for dead was stirring from a decade-long slumber, a part that relished competition and the testing of bodily limitations. It was this part of me that had lobbied for doing the triathlon in the first place, tantalized by recent glimpses of the runner I had once been. In the month before the trip, bending to the influence of my fitness-crazed professional milieu, I had consistently logged twenty to twenty-five miles a week, and those miles were beginning to have an effect. Just days before Nataki and I flew out, on a lark, I found a high school track and ran an all-out mile in 5:12—not a time that would have impressed my teenage self but a damn sight better than I'd been capable of doing when I moved west in 1995.

A triathlon is not a straight running event, however. The one I had signed up for was an Olympic-distance race, comprising a 0.93-mile ocean swim, a 24.8-mile bike ride, and a 6.2-mile run. I hadn't owned a bike since before college and the only swimming

I'd done recently was a quick splash in the resort's waist-deep pool, which I undertook for the sole purpose of assessing my chances of surviving the first leg of the race, lasting all of five minutes before my shoulders cried uncle. My confidence should have been shattered by the experience, but it was not. With the sanguinity of the young, I assured myself that adrenaline would get me through the swim on race day, and that my renewed terrestrial fitness would carry me the rest of the way. I pictured myself gobbling up other competitors like Pac-Man during the 10K run.

Head still pulsing, I drove toward the race venue through inky darkness, searching left and right for a place to grab a few quick calories. (Nataki, still sleeping, would hitch a ride later with Greg.) Eventually, I spotted an open gas station and popped inside the food mart to purchase a Snickers bar and a bottle of Gatorade.

Dawn was breaking when I arrived at the beach, but the sun itself was obscured by a thick layer of clouds—the first I'd seen since landing on the island—giving the changeover from night to day the feel of house lights on a dimmer switch being turned up very slowly. I parked and opened the back hatch and hauled out an ancient, rusted, forty-pound mountain bike I had rented from a local shop less than twenty-four hours before. All around me were my fellow racers, mostly members of the island's wealthier white minority. I followed a stream of them to the transition area, where I racked the bike, spread a towel on the ground, and laid out my running gear. Only then did I realize I had no swim goggles.

Catching sight of the race director, an elderly gentleman I had met at dinner earlier in the visit, I flagged him down and explained my problem. He fixed me with a look that said, "How the hell does the editor of a triathlon magazine show up for a triathlon without goggles?" before advising me to borrow from another athlete and hurrying off to fry bigger fish. Suddenly embarrassed of my American accent, as if the islanders might attribute my unpreparedness to my nationality, I put the race director's advice into action, whiffing twice before scoring a pair of swim specs that fit so poorly on my pinhead that I just knew they would leak. Compared to my hangover and my lack of training, though, this was a minor concern.

At seven o'clock I found myself at the water's edge amid a throng of one hundred and fifty racers, give or take. I felt a little nervous but not nearly as worked up as I used to get before races in high school. After all, it wasn't as if I had Ivy League college admission on the line. But the bigger reason was that I had no idea what I was in for.

Glancing to either side, I noticed that almost everyone, men and women alike, had smoothly shaved legs. My own hairy shanks suddenly seemed a monstrous deformity. At the office I liked to mock my male coworkers for shaving their legs, but at that moment I would have given anything for an Epilady and some time to use it.

An air horn blasted and we dashed into the tepid sea. My goggles flooded instantly, and I was left behind by all save the oldest and heaviest participants. Before I'd even reached the first turn buoy my deltoids were boiling in lactic acid. Knowing it was only a matter of time before I would have to transition to breast-stroking, I challenged myself to put off this surrender as long as possible. When it came, I challenged myself to return to the front crawl as soon as I'd recovered sufficiently. And so it went.

My return to shore was greeted by halfhearted applause from a smattering of bored onlookers who had seen the leader of the race dash past more than a quarter of an hour earlier. I shambled into the transition area with sand-caked feet to find the racks nearly emptied of bikes. This was another embarrassment, but on the positive side it made my own machine easy to find. I threw on some baggy mountain biking shorts I'd cadged from an advertiser, wrestled a cotton T-shirt over my wet torso, and completed my beginner's costume with tube socks, a pair of broken-down Nikes, and a way-too-big helmet. My right thigh cramped viciously as I bent over to tie my left shoe. No problem. I straightened up, massaged the muscle briefly, and tried again, cramping again. *To hell with it*, I thought, and proceeded to wheel the bike to the mounting line at the edge of the transition area with one shoe laced, one not, keys jangling in my left pocket.

It had rained overnight, and the road was still damp. I've always had a special phobia of breaking my collarbone, so when I came to a sharp bend in the road about a mile into the bike course I squeezed the brakes, only to find that the front brake pad was worn to the point of uselessness. It hadn't crossed my mind to test the loaner before I left the store. After the bend came a hill. I tried to shift into a lower gear, but nothing happened. I then tried to shift up, just to see, and got the same result. Diagnosis: busted derailleur.

With the bike stuck in its highest gear, I was forced to stand up and mash the pedals in arduous slow motion to get up the steep grade, a test that felt more like lifting weights than riding a bicycle. As I came over the top, a Jeep cruised by in the opposite direction. Behind it was the race leader, the locomotive to my caboose: hard-bodied, hairless, slicing through the air at twenty-five miles per hour on a space-age Quintana Roo. I hated him.

On the second lap (of six) I heard someone shout my name just as I was approaching the sharp bend before the hill. It was Miles, standing curbside with the local photographer who'd tried to convince me to drop trou at the nude beach. Wanting to put on a good show for them, I took the curve at full speed, leaning hard into the turn. The next thing I remember is lying in a tangle of flesh and metal on the pavement, conscious of nothing but pain up and down the right side of my body and a terrifying absence of air in my lungs.

Miles and the photographer rushed to me. More mortified than hurt (although I was bleeding from nasty scrapes on my upper arm and thigh), I scrambled to my feet like a fallen cat, as though by doing so I could make the crash seem intentional, just a bit of goofing, no different than popping a wheelie.

"I'm fine," I said, shooing away my helpers and remounting the worthless piece of shit I was stuck with for another sixteen miles.

Minutes later, as I was grinding my way back up the big hill, the Jeep I'd seen before passed me again, this time from behind, followed still by the guaranteed winner of the inaugural St. Maarten International Triathlon. I felt secretly grateful for the garish wounds I had acquired when I went down. Let the hard-bodied stud on his $3,000 bike—and everyone else, for that matter— believe my spectacular wipeout, not my woeful inadequacy, was the true reason I was bringing up the rear.

By lap four my road rash no longer bothered me, but that was only because an escalating soreness in my nether region had stolen all my attention. The obvious (and only) solution to this new difficulty was to finish the bike ride and get my ass off the saddle, and I thought about nothing else, giving no consideration whatsoever to the suffering that awaited me in the third and most challenging segment of the race, where even now I pictured myself gobbling up other competitors like Pac-Man.

At last my rolling perdition came to an end. I racked the mutinous two-wheeler that had caused me so much grief and broke into a herky-jerky trot, my legs feeling like I'd just returned to earth after six weeks in space, barely able to support my body weight, much less churn out the six-and-a-half-minute miles of my fantasies.

Pressing on, I began to notice that the day had turned rather soupy, assaulting my broken body with a one-two punch of temperature and humidity that I never had to deal with back home. It felt like running inside a hot towel wrap. My goal shifted from passing competitors by the dozens to sparing myself the final indignity of being reduced to walking. *No matter what*, I told myself, *you will not be seen walking in a running race.*

I began to walk just after I completed the first lap of the two-lap run course. No sooner had I done so than I was overtaken by one of the few athletes still behind me, a hoary-headed geezer tilted forward at a precarious angle, as though leaning on an invisible walker.

"Hang in there, Matt," he wheezed.

Only then did I recognize him: the race director, competing in his own event. An emotion I hadn't felt since the eighth grade, when I lost an arm-wrestling match to my classmate Julie, a kind of incredulous abasement, froze my brain as the old man drifted away from me. When the mind cramp eased, I spurred my body back into an ugly canter, plunging headlong into a new and unimagined realm of suffering as I strained to reel in my superannuated challenger. Ever so slowly, I closed the gap between us and then clawed ahead. This effort came at a cost, however. My head began to tingle and my vision to darken. I found myself walking again.

The race director, still running, passed me a second time. I resigned myself to defeat. Nothing mattered now but escaping my misery. But then I saw something in the distance ahead: a cluster of people, a banner—the finish line!

I launched myself into one last kamikaze push. The pain no longer mattered. At stake was my very dignity; I could bear any amount of suffering for the fifty or sixty seconds it would take to preserve what was left of it. Sprinting with the desperation of a cheetah-fleeing antelope, I put the race director behind me once and for all, eyes riveted to the finish line, where I spied a pair of familiar faces among the multitude. Recognizing me in return, Nataki put a hand to her slack mouth, and I knew I must look as bad as I felt. This was confirmed by the behavior of the person standing next to her, Greg, who grinned with undisguised glee, relishing the irony of my performing so pitifully in the sport I was paid to chronicle.

Less amused were the three ladies in Red Cross uniforms who swarmed me the moment I stopped, fussing over my bloody patches. Ignoring their ministrations, I checked my watch and was jolted by the discovery that Nataki's and my flight home was scheduled to take off in fifty-five minutes. The race had taken me almost an hour longer to complete than I had predicted. I swatted off the nurses, grabbed Nataki's hand, and lurched away, sipping from a bottle of water. All other comforts—a proper meal, a hot shower, clean clothes—would have to wait. Twenty minutes later, I screeched into the rental car return lot at Princess Juliana. No attendant visible, I parked where I saw fit, left the key in the ignition, and dragged our luggage—Nataki's and mine—across the steaming pavement, weaving and tottering like a drunken hotel porter.

The instant Nataki and I stepped through the plane's hatch, the door was sealed behind us. Smeared in blood, reeking of sweat, my race number still inked to my upper arms, I collected wondering looks from the other passengers as I limped down the aisle in search of our seats.

"You crazy, Booby," Nataki said as we zoomed down the runway.

I closed my eyes, let my head fall back, and sighed deeply. I could not deny that what I had just done was a little nutty. But that didn't mean I wouldn't do it again. To the contrary, although I had approached the St. Maarten International Triathlon as a one-off, something to do just for the hell of it, the experience itself had changed everything. At 38,000 feet, eating trail mix from a plastic baggie Nataki had produced, I thought about Greg's smirk and the race director's "Hang in there" and the chiseled race winner's obliviousness to my very existence. All these men believed I was a terrible athlete, utterly lacking in God-given ability, and not without justification, having seen no contrary evidence. I burned to prove them wrong. Why this was so was a question I did not consider. Much time would pass before I recognized that the consuming need I felt to avenge my latest athletic failure had deep roots, stretching all the way back to a soccer pitch in Hanover, New Hampshire, on a spring afternoon in 1988. The only thing I knew then was that I needed to race again—as soon as possible.

CHAPTER 8

LOVE IS SACRIFICE

(Runners Marathon of Reston)

ON OUR WAY to Reston, Virginia, for marathon number four of the eight, Nataki and I (and Queenie) made a one-night stopover in Overland Park, Kansas, just south of Kansas City. Exiting Interstate 435 at Metcalf Avenue, we came to a traffic light on the far side of which stood a multistory building with the words "INDOOR SKYDIVING" emblazoned on its exterior. My inner child lobbied hard for a spontaneous drop-in, but my inner adult swiftly vetoed the idea, citing the need to stay mission focused.

"Indoor skydiving!" Nataki read aloud. "We should do it!"

I turned to her in surprise. Nataki had never been much of a daredevil. Jet skiing on St. Maarten was about the limit of her thrill-seeking in our early years together. Later, with the onset of her illness, she became even more risk averse. Once able to sleep through takeoffs and landings, Nataki was now a reluctant flyer. And her newest medication, though effective, had reduced her stuntwoman potential still further by expanding her body to proportions unfriendly to bungee jumping and the like.

"Seriously?" I said. "Okay, sure."

My hope and expectation was that the whim would pass as soon as something else captured Nataki's attention. But in the hotel room that evening Nataki could talk about nothing else, interrupting my hair-pulling efforts to write a coherent blog post after a long day on the road to ask questions ("How much does it cost?") and voice concerns ("Do you think there's a weight limit?"). When I was done blogging I joined Nataki in bed with my MacBook, and together we found the facility's website and researched all the possible barriers, including price (the Spread Your Wings for Two package would set us back $139.95) and size (Nataki was under the maximum allowable weight of 300 pounds but above the 260-pound threshold at which "additional restrictions and instructor scheduling limitations may apply").

"So, what do you think?" I asked as I rose to turn out the lights, confident the fine print had chilled her enthusiasm.

"I think I want to do it," Nataki said.

"Sleep on it," I suggested.

Nine hours later, when Nataki woke up, I was again at the computer, working on a training plan for a runner I coached before heading out to jog with a local triathlete, Robbie, whom I'd met via Twitter the previous evening.

"I think I want to do it," she repeated.

I studied Nataki's face for a drawn-out moment, reading on it a complex hybrid emotion I'd never seen from her before—equal parts excitement, fear, and resolve. Only then did I fully grasp how important it was for her to fly. For whatever reason, Nataki wanted—perhaps needed—to challenge herself in this way.

"Let's go there and have a look after my run and then we can make a final decision," I said.

My concern was that Nataki's image of the experience lacked verisimilitude—that it digitally enhanced its fun aspect, as it were, and airbrushed the scary part. I pictured her losing her nerve at the last minute, when confronted with the full reality of what she'd signed up for. A bit of an adrenaline junkie myself in my New

Hampshire days, I'd seen this sort of thing play out many times, for example at the edge of a thirty-foot-high railroad trestle my high school classmates and I used to jump off (or not) into the Lamprey River.

I met Robbie at a trailhead on the west side of Overland Park. We traded the usual get-to-know-you questions as we loped along through cool air freshened by recent rain. I asked Robbie what he did for a living, and he told me he was about to start a new career as a substance-abuse counselor. I asked him where his interest in the field came from, and he told me he was a recovering alcoholic, sober for three and a half years. I then asked him why he'd started drinking, and he told me he'd been sexually abused as a boy.

None of this surprised me. Running has a unique way of getting strangers to open up to each other. People want to share their struggles, and to defy the shame that prevents such sharing, but they need to feel safe in doing so. Something about the act of matching strides with another person—the synchronization of movements, perhaps, the compromise on pace (you slow down for me, I speed up for you), the shared destination—impels runners to tell other runners, even those they've just met, things they wouldn't tell a cab driver, a hairdresser, or even a bartender.

I learned a lot more about Robbie in the ensuing miles. His was not the typical story. Many runners are former substance abusers who kicked their habit through running, finding in it a healthier outlet for hardwired addictive tendencies. Robbie was different. He drank five handles of vodka a week *while* training for and competing in Ironman triathlons. For him, being an endurance athlete was not an alternative to drinking; instead, it complemented his drinking, supplying episodic relief from the pain he carried inside, not by numbing it but by subjecting him to a substitute pain that he at least controlled.

After the run, Robbie took Nataki and me out to lunch at Mixx, a cafeteria-style healthy-food joint patronized by the low-body-fat set. I had told Robbie about Nataki's bipolar disorder (our sharing went both ways), and, as we ate, the two of them found many parallels in their respective diseases, particularly in the social stigma attached to each and in the long odds they had overcome to get to where they were now.

"It's not easy to admit you have mental illness when you hear how people talk about it," Nataki said. "I'm a black woman. I know about prejudice. You can't say 'colored' no more but it's okay to say 'crazy' all you want."

Hearing this, I recalled something that occurred a few months earlier, when a TV news commentator referred to a mentally ill man who had committed a mass shooting as a "monster." Nataki turned to me then and, with devastating sincerity, asked, "Am I a monster?"

Robbie told us that of the three or four dozen fellow addicts he'd encountered in rehab, he was, to the best of his knowledge, the only one who had stayed clean.

"Were you also the only endurance athlete?" I asked.

"You know, I never thought about that," he said. "But, now that you ask—yeah, I believe I was."

It was midafternoon when Nataki and I arrived at iFLY. At the reception desk, a college-age guy who seemed to really like his job told us we were in luck—another group of customers had just entered "the tunnel."

"No better way to see what it's all about!" he said.

We moved into a cavernous space at the center of which stood a clear-plastic cylinder some ten feet in diameter and about a hundred feet tall. Seating ourselves on a long, curved bench set back toward the wall, we looked on as a helmeted woman in a skydiving suit passed through a hatch, raised her arms overhead, teetered forward . . . and floated, the wind from a giant fan recessed into the floor holding her aloft. An instructor kept at least one hand on her at all times and (verbal communication being impossible because of the fan's roar) made signals with the other hand that conveyed instructions. (An ascending motion with an upturned palm, I deduced, indicated "Lift your chin!") Three friends of the flyer awaited their tries on a smaller bench located outside the tunnel's main chamber but within its outer shell, displaying such over-the-top enthusiasm for the show through their own mute gesticulations that I wondered briefly if they weren't friends at all but some kind of paid pep squad. I tried to see this tableau from Nataki's perspective, and I concluded that it probably terrified her.

"Are you up for it?" I asked.

"I'm ready!" Nataki said.

We returned to the reception area, forked over our money, and signed a waiver saying, in so many words, that if we died it was our fault. We then met Raleigh, a square-chinned stud who looked like an X-Games athlete and who talked like an X-Games TV commentator, totally stoked about everything. Raleigh showed us into a little classroom labeled "Flight School" and left us there to watch a five-minute video that offered four minutes of heart-pumping action footage set to a soundtrack of wailing guitars and one minute of education.

The moment the video ended, as though he'd been waiting outside the door, Raleigh came back, even more pumped than before. He reviewed the hand signals the video had taught us like they were bomb-defusing guidelines. We then suited up in ill-fitting skydiving suits and brain buckets and it was time to fly.

"I assume you want me to go before you," I told Nataki as we entered the tunnel's outer chamber.

Her face fell.

"Really?" I said. "Who *are* you? And what have you done with my wife?"

During her first turn in the tunnel (we would each get two), Nataki struggled to achieve a balanced floating position, twice careening toward the Plexiglass like a confused sparrow accidentally dive-bombing a bay window, and Raleigh struggled equally with her heft. The rushing air stretched her lips into a cartoonish rictus but did not disguise her primal fear.

In sixty seconds it was over. Nataki stumbled through the hatch waving a hand at her face like a southern belle complaining of the vapors. *I couldn't breathe!* she mouthed. All too soon, it was time for her second go. Raleigh reached a hand out to Nataki from the hatchway. She shook her head. Raleigh and I cajoled her with foot stomps and ushering hands. With a resigned sagging of the head, Nataki stepped forward.

She did not regret it. For the rest of the day, Nataki acted much like I do after running a marathon. Flushed with ecstatic relief, she relived the experience again and again, perfecting the story. She called her mom, Lorene, and her sister, Tayna, to recount it. She sent her father, Ray, a video of her flight that we'd bought from iFLY for an extortionary fee. She was proud of herself, and I was happy for her.

"What made you want to do that?" I asked during the short drive back to our hotel, where Queenie, cabin-fevered but ready to forgive, waited for us. My best guess was that watching me challenge myself as I'd been doing on our journey had inspired her to take on a challenge of her own.

Nope.

"Do you remember when I was looking at some of our old photos before we started our trip?" Nataki said. "I saw what a fun person I used to be before I got sick."

I saw a mental slideshow of the happy moments captured in the photo album in question. Nataki riding horseback. Nataki on an ocean cruise. Nataki taking Latin dance lessons.

"Yes, I remember," I said.

"I know I can't go back," she said, "but I want to be fun again."

At a loss for words, I drew Nataki to me and held her. Or maybe it was the other way around.

....

The Runners Marathon of Reston—as its very name suggests—is a people-focused event. Its organizers take great pains to foster a sense of community among participants, beginning with the registration process, which includes an invitation to submit a personal factoid for inclusion in the official *Runner and Spectator*

Information Guide. When I perused this document prior to leaving California, I was drawn to one factoid in particular, perhaps because it reminded me of my own introduction to running (and to the marathon) in 1983.

I have run 10 marathons with my dad! This will be our 11th together! (Michelle, 26, Brooklyn, NY)

"I'd like to meet these two," I said to Nataki, sharing the item with her as part of a general effort to involve her in something that, we both knew, was really my show.

"Sure, whatever," she said. "It's your show."

In any case, meet them we did, less than twenty-four hours before the race (and four days after our indoor skydiving experience), at Caffé Amouri, a neighborhood coffee shop located in the quaint northern Virginia town of Vienna, not far from Reston. Arriving there with Michelle and her father, Mike, was Michelle's boyfriend, Rob, who had ditched a promising career on Wall Street three years earlier to become a physical therapist so that he could, as he put it to me, "be more active and help runners." The five of us ordered drinks and took them outside to the patio, where we arranged ourselves around a glass-topped table.

"So, who slows down for whom?" I began.

"Oh, she definitely slows down for me," Mike said, laughing.

"But even when I run on my own," Michelle said, "I'm not setting any world records, so that's fine."

"Some runners wouldn't want to do that, though," I said, thinking of myself. "Why do you?"

"It's pretty fun when we cross the finish line together," Michelle said. "He normally tries to give me a hug, but he's pretty sweaty, so I try not to. But the high-five is great!"

Suddenly I was twelve years old again, my hair an inverted flaxen bowl, and I was running with my father on his favorite route, a six-mile out-and-back on pine-shaded mostly dirt roads in Madbury.

In the last mile, Dad picked up the pace, as was his custom. Overmatched, I watched him drift ahead of me, less frustrated by my inability to keep up than reassured by my father's strength. When I came around the final turn, he stood waiting at the end of our driveway. As I drew close, he spread his arms and I ran straight into a pungent, sopping embrace. A small part of me recoiled from the smelly basting. But a much bigger part treasured it.

"What do you get out of running marathons with your daughter?" I asked Mike.

"I played a lot of tennis with my dad when I was growing up," he said. "It's something I enjoyed, so I was happy when Michelle said that she wanted to run. It's a blast. We always go to an interesting place, have some nice meals at restaurants, and then we have a shared experience of doing something that's pretty hard to do. We finish it and we feel really good about each other. What's not to love?"

I bumped into Michelle, Mike, and Rob again the next morning in the student cafeteria at South Lakes High School, which had been commandeered to serve as a staging area for the marathon. After an exchange of greetings, Michelle gave me her phone and asked me to snap a photo of the trio. Noticing that Michelle wore a blue marathon bib, not a purple half-marathon bib as her father and boyfriend did, I was puzzled.

Two months earlier, on President's Day, Mike had collapsed while getting dressed for work. At the hospital he learned that a massive spike in blood pressure was responsible for the scare. Although Mike made a full recovery, by then he had missed a month of training, so he switched over from the marathon to the half. In a show of family solidarity, Michelle and Rob had switched also—or so I'd been told.

"I actually missed the deadline," Michelle confessed when I pointed out the discrepancy. "But I'm running the half, trust me. We all are."

"Would you have come here at all if your father was still sick and couldn't run?" I asked.

"If he wasn't running right now I wouldn't have bothered to come here," she said. "I would have done a long run by myself in Brooklyn instead."

This was more or less what I'd expected to hear, Mike having made it clear in our prior encounter that the thread of solidarity between father and daughter tugged both ways.

"I couldn't imagine ever stopping or bailing out with Michelle there," he said. "Having her with me keeps me going, and probably running a little harder than I would on my own."

At a quarter to seven, race director Anna Newcomb, who had facilitated my rendezvous with my new friends and whom I'd met in the flesh at the prerace dinner the night before, raised a hand-held sign ("Follow me to the start line!") and led a 547-person march outside to the start line, where, fifteen bone-chilling minutes later, the race began. I settled into a pace that split the difference between my need to save energy for the weeks ahead and my instinctual lust to run fast. At the end of the first loop, the half marathoners (who outnumbered marathoners three to one) peeled off toward the finish line, and I found myself alone, not a single other racer in sight, and I remained so, vaguely worried at times that I had gone off course, until the eighteenth mile, where I spotted a solitary figure striding far ahead of me on a long, straight stretch of road. Despite the distance, I could tell from the cut of her top and the angles of her gait that she was female.

What I couldn't tell, initially, was whether I was catching up to her or she was in sight only because we happened to be in an area of extended visibility. The next several minutes revealed that I was indeed gaining on her, albeit slowly, a sign that the runner was struggling but had not yet hit the wall. A veteran of numerous marathon meltdowns, I found myself rooting for her to keep it together, knowing I would catch her eventually regardless.

We had just passed the twenty-one-mile mark when I pulled abreast of the runner. "Let's go, Kacey," I said, having learned her name from the shouts of supporters she passed ahead of me.

My intent was to let Kacey know that I intended to help. Whether she actually wanted help was an open question. Personally, when I'm hitting the wall, I want to be left the fuck alone, so I was prepared to give Kacey her space at the slightest hint. There was also a gender calculus at play. For all I knew, she would be no less creeped out by my sidling up to her at the crisis stage of a marathon than she would be by my doing the same on a random Wednesday at the park. In any case, it was plain to see that Kacey could use a little help. Although her form still looked pretty good, her breathing was ragged and her brows were knitted. She was also, I noticed, very young.

"This is getting brutal," she said, words I interpreted to mean *I accept your offer of help—now please help me!*

"It's a marathon," I said, wondering if this was her first.

With one eye on Kacey and the other on the path ahead, I positioned myself a half step behind her to avoid pulling her out of rhythm and to allow her the cleanest line through the path's many tangents. We soon came upon a small group of race volunteers, one of many such groups scattered strategically across the racecourse to prevent wrong turns and to supply encouragement.

"Woohoo! First female!" they shouted.

"What am I, chopped liver?" I called back.

Kacey grunted in pained amusement.

I studied her closely with that one eye, looking for cues to guide my aid. One thing I picked up on was that she checked her watch frequently, a sign that her mind was still very much in the fight and that she had a goal she wouldn't let go of easily—either a personal best or a Boston Marathon qualifying time, I guessed. My job, then, was to push her as much as it was to encourage her.

We passed a sign marking twenty-three miles.

"Three to go," I said, rounding down. "You've got this."

"Thanks," Kacey said.

This exchange occurred on a long, snaking ascent through thick woods with no visible summit.

"I didn't realize this course was so hilly," Kacey said.

"It's a tough one," I granted.

Validate. Don't sugarcoat.

We kept climbing. Kacey's pace slackened, her shoulders cinched, and her breathing became even more ragged.

"Are we almost at the top?" she asked.

The worst mistake you can possibly make when you're trying to help another runner in such a situation is to tell a lie that will inevitably be exposed as such. Thankfully, we were in fact near the top, and I said so.

Just beyond the high point, the paved trail we'd been running on seemingly forever ended, and we merged onto a smooth, flat-to-downhill road that would take us almost all the way to the finish line. I squinted into the distance, willing the twenty-four-mile mark to appear. At last it came into view.

"This is my first marathon," Kacey said.

I told her she was killing it. And she was. But it was also killing her. Any momentum Kacey had gained after we came over the hill was lost as we pressed toward the final mile. Her stride tightened up noticeably, despite gravity's pull, and I began to worry. Feeling powerless to assist in any material way, I resorted to prayer. *Please, let her hang on,* I pleaded silently. *Let her achieve her goal.* Just then, Kacey stopped cold and grabbed both hamstrings, and I stopped too.

"Are you cramping?" I asked.

She nodded, her pain-filled eyes narrowed questioningly. I knew precisely what those eyes were asking: *Why are you doing this?*

Why *was* I doing this? Well, because it felt good—good in a way that was as new to me as the dreadful leadenness of Kacey's legs was to her. I had never been one to run for others in any of the myriad ways others do, despite being surrounded by such folks in my local running community. A neighbor of mine, Esther, an experienced ultrarunner, routinely climbs Mt. Whitney and Halfdome with children afflicted with spina bifida, often accompanied by her friend Steve. Steve, in turn, has guided a blind friend, also named Steve, through countless marathons. And blind Steve, in *his* turn, ran the 2017 Seattle Half Marathon exactly one year after the sudden death of his wife, Lynne, at the same event, to "take back that day for her," as he put it to me. The closest I'd ever come to experiencing this sort of athletic altruism was in 1983, on the streets of Boston, with my dad, when I was eleven. But as I read the question in Kacey's eyes, the whole running-for-others thing suddenly made sense to me, not just intellectually but viscerally.

Love is sacrifice. To love is to put another person's needs ahead of one's own—to donate a kidney to a dying sibling, to skip a few meals for God, to (as the song goes) "climb the highest mountain . . . only to be with you." The more we love, the more we are willing to sacrifice—or suffer—for the beloved. There's not much difference, if you think about it, between climbing a mountain to be with someone and running a marathon to cure cancer or to bring joy to a friend who used to run marathons before the accident.

A person may choose to run a marathon for personal or even selfish reasons initially, but once he's neck-deep in suffering at mile twenty-four, he starts to think of others, because that's just how the human heart works. A runner who's neck deep in suffering needs the most powerful motivator he can find to endure the suffering he must endure to finish the race, and nothing motivates like love. Even the most competitive runners—the professionals, the Olympians—who may seem to race only for money, fame, and the thrill of victory, if you talk to them about their motivators (as I have), will tell you they never run harder than when they are running for their family, their team, their tribe, their school, their god, or their country.

After a half-hearted stretch and a quick glance at her watch, Kacey resumed running. I fell in beside her, again tuning my tempo to hers, trying as best I could to literally *run for her*, imagining my legs propelling her body, continuing to pray that this young stranger would find within herself whatever it was she needed to achieve her goal.

"That's the last turn ahead," I said.

This *was* a lie, and one that would soon be exposed as such, but when that happened, I knew, Kacey would be within sight of the finish line and it wouldn't matter.

She stopped again. As though I were leashed to her, I stopped also.

"Just keep going," Kacey said, waving a hand at me.

"I'll see you on the other side," I said.

The race ended with a lap around the track at South Lakes High School—the very oval on which Alan Webb, the current American record holder in the mile, had run as a teenager, birthing his legend. By the time I completed the circuit, Kacey was visible on the backstretch, charging hard. She had rallied.

I loitered behind the finish line, sipping water with a medal draped around my neck, as Kacey powered home. The instant she stopped, she wobbled, causing excitement among the supernumerary volunteers who bunched around the women's champion of the 2017 Runners Marathon of Reston. Arms reached out to steady her and a folding chair was produced. Kacey plopped down and hung her head like a weary boxer between rounds. But not for long. As if hearing her name called, she looked up, eyes roaming, and soon found me hovering on the periphery, watching her. Kacey rose to her feet with less than perfect steadiness, against the protests of her helpers, and pushed toward me lock-kneed, fending off proffered water bottles.

"You were my guardian angel out there," she said when we were face to face. "I couldn't have done it without you. Seriously, I would have been walking at twenty-two miles."

These few words lifted me in a way that nothing I had achieved for myself as a runner ever did.

....

The next morning Nataki and I checked out of our hotel in Reston and made a quick drive that ended at an office building in Arlington. Inside, I punched the 8 button on the lobby's elevator console and a minute later we were buzzed into the offices of the Treatment Advocacy Center, an organization that works to re-move barriers to proper care for sufferers of serious mental illness and the official charity partner of the Life Is a Marathon Project.

We were greeted by Carol, the center's director of commu-nications, who wore thick-rimmed eyeglasses and appeared to be about my age. She gave us a brief tour of a workplace that screamed NONPROFIT, introduced us to a few colleagues, and then led us into a conference room where we seated ourselves at one end of a table that could have accommodated ten or twelve more. All at once Carol seemed ill at ease, her eyes flitting, hands fid-geting. A few weeks earlier, when I was planning our trip, she had asked me via e-mail whether she could use the opportunity of our visit to interview Nataki for the center's "personally speaking" blog, a request I'd gladly accepted after running it by Nataki, but Carol now seemed uncertain. She placed her iPhone down between us as though wanting to disassociate herself from the device. Open-ing the voice recorder app, she commenced to overexplain the purpose of the interview, wincing in anticipation of resistance as she told Nataki she would be taping their conversation.

"Whatever you're comfortable sharing," she kept saying, her pointer finger suspended over the record button.

I couldn't fault Carol for her apprehension. Paranoia is a com-mon symptom of bipolar disorder, and in Nataki's case there were many times when she believed her enemies were recording her with evil intent. Another symptom is anosognosia, or the inability to understand or perceive the reality of one's illness. It took Nataki five years to say out loud to anyone that she was bipolar. Carol knew as well as I did that trying to initiate a conversation with a bipolar individual about the disease can be like talking to an alco-holic about his drinking.

"First of all," she began, swallowing hard, "would you tell me about your experience with serious mental illness?"

"It's been hard," Nataki said, now seeming a little nervous her-self. "At first, everything was just kind of going out of control and I didn't know exactly what was wrong. But now that I have been treated for a while, it has been beneficial. But it's still a journey—each day is different."

The interview continued along these lines. I leaned back in my chair, my body releasing a tension I hadn't been aware of (the stuff's contagious), hearing Nataki's words against the backdrop of the past fourteen years, marveling at how far she had come. It's one thing to accept the reality of one's mental illness, quite another to go public with it.

"I want to help people," Nataki told me when we first discussed the possibility of sharing our story.

One by one, Carol drew lines through the questions she'd written out on a notepad that lay before her until there were no questions left, and then she showed us out, seeming more relaxed as the three of us stood together in the lobby, chatting informally. Nataki noticed a piece of silver in the shape of some arcane script dangling from a chain around Carol's neck.

"I like your necklace," she said. "Is it Arabic?"

"Hebrew, actually," Carol said. "It means 'determination.' That's my motto for this year." Carol looked at us as though seeking assurance, reminding me that courage is not the absence of fear but the willingness to face it.

We left, taking a quick peek inside the Fun Mobile to check on Queenie, whom we found chilling out in the backseat, patient as ever, before walking a couple of blocks to a kebab place Carol had recommended. With my usual post-marathon ravenousness appeased for the moment, I asked Siri to guide us to the nearest flower shop.

Nataki's paternal grandfather, Alfred, was buried at Arlington National Cemetery—a stone's throw from our present location. Nataki had never known him. Nor had Nataki's dad, for that matter. What they did know was that, after serving as an army corporal in World War II, in which he suffered some kind of head injury, Alfred returned to his native Arkansas just long enough to knock up Nataki's grandmother, who told Ray little about the man except that he drank heavily and got into a lot of fights (the only photograph Ray had ever seen of him showed Alfred with a bandaged nose). He'd died on December 10, 1958, two weeks shy of his forty-second birthday—almost exactly Nataki's current age. Nataki and I had learned this information and the location of Alfred's final resting place from the Veterans Administration.

The building Siri directed us to was occupied not by a florist but by a beauty salon. I gave her (Siri, that is) a piece of my mind and phoned the store, only to find out that the business had relocated to Fairfax three years earlier.

"I keep trying to get them to change it," the proprietor said unhelpfully.

Conscious of time (my goal was to reach Philadelphia before nightfall), I headed straight to the cemetery, hoping to spot another flower shop along the way. It was a terrible plan, and when we rolled onto the 642 acres that are the eternal home for some 400,000 departed souls, Nataki's eyes widening in wonder as she took in the immaculately tended grounds and larger-than-life classical architecture, we still had nothing to offer Alfred but ourselves.

"I'll bet they sell flowers in the welcome center," I said hopefully as an armed man in uniform pointed us toward the visitor parking lot.

The welcome center teemed with tourists from all four corners of the globe, and with folks like us who sought one specific headstone that no one else cared about. At the information desk, we were told what I had known in my heart already, that flowers were not sold on the premises. Turning away from the desk, we nearly bumped into a short man with a painter's brush mustache who carried a gorgeous white wreath in an open box.

"Where did you get that?" Nataki asked.

The man informed us that he had ordered the arrangement online. Understandably proud of his purchase, he gave us the full backstory, including a thumbnail biography of his own grandfather, whom the wreath was for. Nataki stopped listening as soon as she understood that she could not make a similar purchase immediately.

"What do you want to do?" I asked her.

"I want to give him flowers," Nataki said firmly.

I felt the tingle of déjà vu as I looked into Nataki's eyes, seeing in them the same determination I'd noted when she insisted on skydiving despite my efforts to pour cold water on the idea. I realized then that these flowers carried a similar kind of symbolism for her. Mental illness runs in Nataki's family, specifically on her father's side, and we've both wondered at times whether Grandpa Alfred's instability might not have been caused by something more organic than a war wound. Her resolve to honor him seemed to represent another step in Nataki's own healing process, a widening of the circle. If flying had been about reclaiming herself, the present pilgrimage was about reclaiming a deeper past. Nataki felt the need to *make an effort* for a forebear who perhaps suffered in a similar way, and indeed whose suffering she may have inherited. And I needed to make an effort for her. Philadelphia could wait.

"Let's go get some flowers," I said.

We returned to the car and gave Siri a second chance to guide us to the nearest florist. Forty-five minutes later, we were back at the cemetery with a lovely bouquet of Casablanca lilies. I pulled out my phone and opened the Arlington National Cemetery Explorer app, and we began our search for Section 39, Grave 836. It was a warm day, close to eighty degrees, and Nataki, who since hitting the road with me had not been walking as much as she did at home, where we covered two miles with Queenie every morning, showed signs of strain almost immediately. Sweat beaded on her forehead, and her lips parted in the pinched way they do when she's laboring for air.

We came to a hill—not a big hill but noticeable. Halfway up, Nataki stopped. I stopped with her.

"I just need a minute," she said.

In less than a minute we were walking again.

"That's Section 39 right there," I said, pointing ahead.

Nataki stopped a second time, and again I paused with her. When she was ready, we made one final push that brought us at last to her grandfather's grave marker. Nataki laid the bouquet at its foot and said a few words. I took some pictures. Unable to think of anything else to do, we turned around and began the long walk back to the welcome center, where Nataki plunked herself down on a wooden bench and hung her head while I visited the men's room. Seeming to sense my return, she looked up and scanned the crowd, seeking me. Only then did I recognize the striking parallels between my run with Kacey the day before and the walk I'd just completed with my wife.

We all have our marathons to run.

CHAPTER 9

HITTING THE WALL

THE LONGEST DAY of my life—one of the longest days, anyway—was October 4, 1998. This was the day I went straight from the finish line of the St. Maarten International Triathlon to the airport in Philipsburg and caught a flight home to California with Nataki, touching down at San Diego's Lindbergh Field in the last moments of the same calendar date on which I'd woken up hungover twenty-one hours earlier, having slept not a wink on the plane.

San Diego is a long way from San Francisco, of course, but I no longer lived in the Haight-Ashbury apartment Sean and I had acquired three years before by virtue of our good looks, nor did Nataki live in the house in West Oakland I had first seen on the night we met. We now shared a tiny one-bedroom rental near *Triathlete*'s new offices in Southern California, where I'd been obliged to relocate after a change in the magazine's ownership, and where Nataki—who had never before lived away from her mother—was persuaded to join me some months later. It was to this humble nest that we retreated in the wake of my ignominious return to endurance racing.

No sooner had I unpacked than I set about avenging my latest athletic disgrace. I bought a cheap secondhand bicycle and used the hell out of it, got a membership at a YMCA with an indoor pool that was kept way too warm in deference to the retirees who dominated its eight lanes, and continued to run three or four times a week. The preparation paid off. (Or was it the shaved legs?) Seven months after my Caribbean debacle, I completed a second triathlon, in Oceanside, California, covering the same distance more than thirty minutes faster.

Not quite satisfied, I stepped up my training and took aim at the US Triathlon Series Championship, also held in Oceanside, where in October 1999 I improved my time by another fifteen minutes. But I still wasn't content, so I kept at it, now a full-blown endorphin junkie, hooked on the high of going farther and faster. Like others of my type, I climbed the ladder of race distances, advancing from Olympic triathlons and 5K runs to half Ironman triathlons and 10K runs to half marathons and even a full Ironman, my training load increasing commensurately: eight hours per week, eleven hours, fourteen.

The more I worked out, the more I improved. I loved the straightforwardness of this equation, but what I loved even more was the ascent itself, the feeling of being better today than I was yesterday and knowing I would be better still tomorrow. It was like a second youth, a state of almost godlike expectation of acquiring ever greater aptitudes. Each time I pedaled up Torrey Pines Hill—a section of Highway 101 between La Jolla and Cardiff-by-the-Sea that rises 413 feet over 1.36 miles—I reached the top a little quicker. Each time I ran through Mission Bay Park, seven-minute miles felt a bit more effortless.

Looking back at this period, I am unable to pinpoint the precise moment when sports became my first priority and Nataki my second, but one thing is certain: it happened. Not that Nataki didn't have her own interests. A few weeks after we stuffed all her worldly possessions into her Mustang and made a one-way drive from the 510 area code to the 619, Nataki took a job as a stylist at a black hair salon in North County, working a flexible schedule that left her plenty of time to pursue her modeling and singing on the side. A Los Angeles–based talent agency scooped her up and began to cast her in rap music videos, whose directors seemed to share my appreciation for her Tina Turner legs. Between gigs she took music classes at MiraCosta College, where she met and befriended Alejandro, a gifted young guitarist with whom she wrote songs and eventually formed a band called Shades.

Nataki herself certainly did not lack for gifts, but she exercised them with something less than a fame-at-all-costs mind-set. In November 1998, for example, she turned down an opportunity to dance in Will Smith's "Miami" video because she had a pimple.

"But it's Will Smith!" I pleaded, desperate to change her mind. "What are makeup artists for, anyway?"

She shrugged. It wasn't that important.

Nor was Nataki likely to make any Faustian bargains in pursuit of a chart-topping record or status as the next celebrity black hairdresser. Shades performed publicly on just two occasions before the drummer quit and the whole thing fizzled. Around the same time, Nataki lost favor with her boss at the salon for the sin of taking another stylist's teenage son, Trey, under her wing. Trey was gay and HIV positive, which made him radioactive to some but an object of compassion to Nataki, who gave him rides to places he needed to go, helped him with his social services, and, perhaps most helpfully, got him laughing again, beginning with an impromptu dance-off between just the two of them.

"Where's your ambition?" the boss asked Nataki on the day she quit the salon to work at a women's shoe store.

Hers was just a different kind of ambition. What Nataki wanted from life, I discovered during our first year or two of living together, was a little bit of everything—a certain balance. She wanted to work some, play some, and do some good in the world, and yet, for her, our relationship remained the unchallenged center around which all else revolved. As I gave more and more of myself to my solitary training, Nataki continued to seek to involve me in her stuff. With her encouragement, I tagged along to a few of her photo shoots, and I even allowed myself to be talked into trying out for my own fitness modeling contract (no luck, unsurprisingly). Although I couldn't carry a tune or play an instrument, I was treated as a full-fledged member of Shades even so, writing about half the group's songs and delighting in the challenge of composing lyrics in Nataki's voice, which I did perhaps most successfully in the club banger, "Let Your Booty Out."

> *I don't care what the neighbors say*
> *I keep my booty locked up all day*
> *Don't tell me I don't have the right*
> *I'm gonna let my booty out tonight.*

Even most of my new friends in San Diego were really Nataki's friends—people like Alejandro whom *she* brought into our lives. Preoccupied as I was with swimming and cycling and running and lifting weights, I had scant energy to dedicate to doing my part to expand our social circle.

And I was just getting started. By December 1999 I was ready to tackle my first marathon. Wanting not just to go the distance but to kick ass, I chose the California International Marathon, a point-to-point race from Folsom to Sacramento that's popular among runners seeking Boston Marathon and Olympic Trials qualifying times on account of its net-downhill layout. The same hubris that had set me up for calamity on St. Maarten did me in again as I readied for this new challenge, causing me to commit a host of rookie errors. What I regret most about the whole sad affair is that I was warned. My friend Bernie, a veteran of more than a dozen marathons, urged me to set a conservative goal, treat the race as an opportunity to learn, and swing for the fences the next time. Instead I set a goal to beat Bernie's own marathon personal record (PR) of 2:46:38. To further increase the likelihood of disaster, I subsequently made zero effort to train on routes emulating CIM's rolling hills (topography's meat tenderizer), nor did I bother to test out the unfamiliar sports drink that would be served at official aid stations to see if it agreed with me (it didn't).

My self-sabotage continued on race day, when I ran the first mile out of twenty-six at the same pace I'd averaged in a *half* marathon a few weeks earlier. At nineteen miles I was walking, my quads feeling as though they'd been bludgeoned with crowbars for the preceding two hours. Disgusted, I tore off my number bib, crumpled it into a wad, and flung it into the gutter, resenting both the pity of the spectators who stood along Fair Oaks Boulevard and the pitilessness of the runners passing me in droves. Compounding my unhappiness was my physical discomfort, which my decision to surrender had not solved but only transformed, shifting the locus of pain from muscle to skin, for the air was a raw forty-seven degrees and I was half naked, my body generating a fraction of the heat it had churned out when I was still running. At my present rate of progress, I would need another two hours to reach the finish line, where Josh and Sean, who both now lived in San Francisco, awaited my triumphant arrival with my sweats.

A shopping plaza materialized on my righthand side. Seeming to have a mind of their own, my feet led me off the racecourse and across a parking lot to the entrance of a supermarket, where I found myself begging shoppers for spare change like some teenage runaway. My true plight, though unusual, required little explanation, and minutes later I was able to plunk thirty-five cents into a payphone and dial Sean's cell number. No answer.

The small ember of hope that had been kindled by my escape plan went dark. I returned to the road and resumed my defeated march toward downtown Sacramento.

Another hour brought me to a sign with the number 23 on it. Something about this figure made me think I could run again, and I eased into a tentative shuffle. This felt okay, so I tried jogging. No problem there, so I switched to a trot. By the time I reached the homestretch, I was in full gallop, shooting past runners who had shot past me earlier, having learned (or relearned) that the mind, not the body, is the limiter. My finish time was 3:38:40, a scant fifty-two minutes off my goal.

Thus began my twenty-years-long-and-counting apprenticeship in the marathon, an often frustrating, sometimes agonizing, never-regretted mission to master the twenty-six-mile, 385-yard footrace. I could not have known then what a long road (so to speak) lay ahead of me. I knew only that I needed to run a second marathon to exorcise the first.

Yet I took my time about it, putting in another summer of triathlon racing before I toed the start line of the Long Beach Marathon in November 2000. A year had taught me nothing. Once again I started out too aggressively, hit the wall way earlier than you're supposed to, tore off my number in disgust, and then finished the race anyway, taking no satisfaction whatsoever in lowering my time to 3:11:36.

The following June I gave the distance a third go, at the Rock 'n' Roll San Diego Marathon. Nataki and I now lived in Pacific Beach, just a few miles from the event's downtown start line, so I was able to sleep in my own bed the night before. Except I did not actually sleep but instead spent eight hours in a cold sweat, staring at the backs of my eyelids as Nataki reposed peacefully beside me. Thirteen years after the race I never ran because I was too chicken, my fear of the suffering of endurance racing was undiminished. What *had* changed was that I no longer made the same choices. When morning came, I was in the corrals with everyone else.

Despite the long night, I ran well—for a while. With less than two miles to go, I was still on pace to beat Bernie's time, finally. But the lack of sleep then caught up with me all at once and I ran the last mile a minute slower than the one before, crossing the finish line two seconds shy of the mark I sought.

Painful as this near miss was, it at least had the compensating virtue of qualifying me for the 2002 Boston Marathon, which I promptly signed up for, savoring the opportunity to return to where my running journey began. Training went well, and in February, a few weeks before Boston, I destroyed Bernie's half-marathon PR by four minutes. Ten days later, I suffered a pelvic stress fracture. Hopped up on codeine, I watched the marathon on television.

This was not the first injury I had experienced in the three years since my athletic rebirth. Not by a long shot. I had previously dealt with a severe case of iliotibial band syndrome (right leg), a yearlong battle with plantar fasciitis (right foot), a pair of calf strains (left leg), a prolonged struggle with piriformis syndrome (left side), several bouts of runner's knee, three separate occurrences of shin splints (left side), a mild case of swimmer's shoulder (left), a not-at-all-mild chest muscle tear (right), a sprained neck, on-and-off low back pain, hip flexor tendonitis (right side), a few hamstrings strains (both legs), a strained groin muscle (right), and Achilles tendonitis (left leg). It was as if I'd somehow traded my prior mental fragility for the physical equivalent—without having yet rid myself entirely of the former.

Some of these injuries were plainly the result of stupidity on my part—small trouble spots exacerbated into major breakdowns as I stubbornly insisted on training through pain's warnings. But I spent enough time around other athletes to know I was exceptionally delicate. My stress fracture, for example, was caused (according to the orthopedist I saw) by running too many counterclockwise laps around the track at UCSD.

"But *everybody* runs counterclockwise!" I vented. "Why don't you have a waiting room full of runners with the same injury?"

I deferred my Boston Marathon registration to the next year and started over. Training went well again, that is until the Sunday after Thanksgiving, when my right knee became tender during a sixteen-mile run around Mission Bay. Refusing to submit to yet another interruption of my progress, I continued to run over the next several days as the pain predictably worsened. When it became unbearable, I switched to bicycling to stay fit while the knee healed up. Symptom-free after six days, I did a test run, which hurt. I took ten more days off and eased back into running a second time, but the result was the same. A third and even longer period of rest proved equally fruitless.

As race day drew inexorably closer, I threw every treatment you can imagine at the ailing joint: ice, heat, oral anti-inflammatories, topical anti-inflammatories, analgesic creams, therapeutic taping, acupuncture, an orthopedic brace, physical therapy—nothing worked. Eventually, all hope of racing the 2003 Boston Marathon now gone, I tried the only thing I hadn't: surgery. In June, a highly regarded sports medicine specialist at the California Orthopedic Institute, a man with glowing teeth and an almost visible aura of confidence, scoped my knee, found a bunch of chewed-up cartilage, and filed it down all nice and smooth. In the recovery room he assured me that I would be running again within two weeks. And I was. And three weeks after that, the pain was back.

Nataki suggested that perhaps my body was sending me a message to slow down a bit. I took this counsel with a grain of salt, aware that she had her own reasons for wanting me to slow down. We were now husband and wife, having tied the knot on September 21, 2001, at the San Diego County Recorder's Office with my mom as the only witness. If Nataki's hope and expectation at the time of our low-key nuptials was that, in taking a solemn vow to put her before everyone and everything else in my life, I would actually do so, she was since disappointed. Simply put, we did not see eye to eye on the subject of my exercise habit. From her perspective as one who had never participated in any organized sports activity or regular fitness program, working out for two to three hours every day was as pointlessly excessive as devoting an equal amount of time to brushing one's teeth, and she came to resent those hours. Never one to hold back from expressing her feelings, Nataki got the last word in a thousand variations of the same argument.

"Hikin', bikin', jumpin'!" was her hollered refrain on these occasions. "That's all you care about!"

The fight I remember most vividly happened on a Friday, our customary date night. Having ridden my bike home from work, I burst into the apartment around half-past five, and by a quarter to six I was out the door again, now wearing running clothes, bent on squeezing in a few hard laps around the local high school track before we went out for dinner and a movie. The workout took longer than expected, and upon my return I informed Nataki that we'd have to grab takeout somewhere to avoid missing the movie we'd chosen. Nataki insisted on a proper dinner. I said okay, fine, but in that case we'd have to skip the movie. Nataki asked why we couldn't just see a later showing and I said I needed to get up early the next morning for a group bike ride. Nataki blew her stack.

"Hikin', bikin', jumpin'!" she hollered, right on cue. "That's all you care about! What about me? You keep me in a box!"

The box metaphor was new—and apt. I loved Nataki as much as ever—perhaps more than ever, because I knew her so much better. In any given week, my happiest moments were moments spent with her, whether I was helping her with an assignment she'd been given in one of her college classes to attend and write about a classical music concert, joining her in an African drum circle at Balboa Park, or dressing up in bespoke Pebbles and Bamm-Bamm costumes for Halloween. But something had changed in me on the island of St. Maarten. Accepting the challenge that had presented itself to me there, to finish business left unfinished in my late childhood, had set me on a course that I now felt powerless to deviate from. Whereas previously I had gladly squeezed exercise into the margins of time not filled by Nataki, I now wanted to compartmentalize the relationship—to remove my wife from her "box" when I was good and ready and not a minute sooner.

On another evening some weeks later Nataki and I sat together on a secondhand sofa we'd picked up in Orange County in happier days and watched a reality television show that required boyfriends and girlfriends who were in the doghouse to perform theatrical acts of penance. This particular episode featured an avid cyclist whose girlfriend made him slice his bike in half with a chainsaw to prove he was willing to make her number one in his life. People watching this show in other homes across America saw a selfish narcissist with bad priorities eating a well-deserved serving of humble pie. Nataki saw *me*—and said so.

I got it—to an extent. I knew I wasn't doing right by the woman I loved. At the same time, though, I felt a genuine need to continue the journey I had begun. Finding my physical and mental limits as an athlete seemed as necessary to my happiness as Nataki herself had become when she fed crab dip and crackers to my dying grandmother five years before. But how could two things that I truly needed be incompatible? I struggled to come up with a satisfactory answer to this question, and Nataki and I continued to grow apart. No more did she automatically invite me along to her beading classes and Reiki treatments and such, nor did I always bother to mention when I had a race coming up, instead sometimes just rising early and slipping out.

Understandably, Nataki began to look elsewhere for what she wasn't getting from me, and in time she found it—in Jesus. Her transformation from nominal Baptist to holy roller began on an ordinary Sunday at Truth Apostolic Community Church, a black Pentecostal house of worship located in Spring Valley, a low-rent part of San Diego, where we had a standing invitation from Nataki's friend Latrice, a lifelong member. We arrived about an hour after the service had started and more than three hours before it would end, a sullen youth outfitted in a worn blazer and a hand-me-down tie ushering us to open seats in the fourth or fifth pew of a sanctuary that was spacious but shabby, in need of repairs and renovations that were unlikely to come anytime soon given the pinched finances of its tithers.

By this time in my life, being the only white person in a crowd of two hundred was no big deal. But I had not yet found myself in an environment quite like this one. The spectacle I witnessed over the remainder of the morning and well into the afternoon made the black church scene of *The Blues Brothers*, with James Brown howling from the pulpit and fan-waving sisters high-stepping in the center aisle, seem like a Quaker meeting in comparison. Pastor Anthony Charles Williams III's winding sermon unfolded like an improvisational blues, his gravelly tenor responding with exquisite sensitivity to the keyed-up emotions of the congregation, soaring and plunging in volume and pitch until just the right note was struck to bring on the holy ghost, at which point the man of God fell silent and nodded approvingly as a contagion of wild dancing and glossolalia spread across the room, egged on by the frenzied playing of a five-piece band with serious chops.

Williams's eyes drifted repeatedly in my direction as the performance wore on. The ninth or tenth time this happened, his gaze lingered.

"Sister Latrice," Williams said, "I see you've brought some guests. Would you like to introduce them?"

Latrice rose and introduced us.

"Matt and Nataki," Williams repeated, trying out the names. "Welcome to Truth. May I ask you to come to the altar?"

I led Nataki to the front of the room with a thudding heart and clammy palms. Williams shook our hands and asked us a couple of softball questions (where did we live, were we married) before turning his full attention on me, the smile dropping from his face.

"Do you believe the Lord Jesus Christ died for your sins?" he asked.

The building went silent. I might have picked up the rustle of a Kleenex in a control room located behind soundproof glass on the mezzanine level at the back of the sanctuary. Everyone waited to hear what I would say. *I* waited to hear what I would say.

"No," I said eventually.

Gasps from the pews.

"I admire your honesty," Williams said quickly. "Let me ask you this, then: Do you believe in prayer?"

"Sure," I said.

Ignoring the noncommittal tone of this response, the pastor asked me to close my eyes and spread my arms. He then put a hand on my face and prayed that God would open my heart to His Word and I would accept Christ into my life, now and forevermore. Next thing I knew I was on the floor, Williams having given my head a subtle surprise shove that laid me out as though I had been "slain by the Holy Spirit."

I left the church that day assuming the experience was a one-off. Nataki had other ideas. Within a month she was attending Sunday morning service (which seldom let out until midafternoon) weekly. Then she started going back for evening service—another three hours, on average. Then she added Wednesday night Bible study to her routine and began attending special events at Truth and other churches on Tuesdays, Saturdays, whenever.

At home, Nataki spent more and more time reading the Bible, praying, fasting, and watching Christian television, until she was scarcely doing anything else. She turned virtually every conversation, private and public, in the direction of God, urging her friends to stop sinning in whatever ways she thought they were and handing out Pentecostal leaflets to strangers.

For a while this new path brought Nataki great happiness. In the lexicon of her evangelical community she was a "babe in Christ" who was "on fire for God." Indeed, her passion for serving the Lord reminded me more than a little of my own passion for endurance. But then something changed. An air of desperation entered Nataki's 24/7 focus on doing right and being good. She seemed to live in unrelenting fear of God's judgment, consumed by feelings of guilt and condemnation for past sins, most especially the sin of prior dalliances with other traditions: getting her chakras balanced, having her palm read, patronizing New Age bookstores.

As the months passed, Nataki gradually lost the ability to enjoy just about everything in life that had once brought her pleasure and satisfaction. She stopped listening to secular music, reading secular books, and watching secular television and films. She stopped buying clothes and jewelry and gave away or threw out most of what she had. She became a reluctant sex partner, referring to the mating act as doing her "wifely duties," and eventually our lovemaking ceased altogether.

In the early days of my obsession with working out, Nataki, in an effort to be supportive, had gone for a run with me, quitting after a quarter mile with pain in her bunioned, archless feet. Not everyone is born to run. In the same spirit, I now made an effort

to join Nataki on the spiritual path she had chosen. I read the
Bible with her daily, accumulating a personal collection of favorite
scriptures ("We count them happy who endure"—James 5:11). I
prayed with her, becoming comfortable enough with the ritual after a while that I sometimes found myself speaking to God spontaneously on my own (mostly about injuries). I fasted with her now
and again, discovering an interesting parallel between the "mortification of the flesh" that was achieved through this practice and
the mind-over-muscle experience I sought as an athlete. I attended
Truth's shorter Sunday evening services and signed up for the new
converts class, a sort of enhanced Bible study where fresh recruits
to the faith (and the occasional godless infiltrator) were taught the
Pentecostal denomination's doctrine and history. I even went and
got myself baptized, though not until later and not at Truth.

Meanwhile, Nataki's unraveling continued. She stopped bath-
ing and fasted herself down to skin and bones. Her sleep became
severely disrupted, dwindling to no more than four nonconsecutive
hours a night. She spent the better part of each day locked in our
bedroom, kneeling in front of her Bible, wailing piteously in un-
known tongues. One day she asked me in dead earnest if I was Jesus.

It was all leading somewhere, but exactly where I dared not
imagine. In the spring of 2004, Nataki's deteriorating mental state
took an alarming turn toward paranoia. She went from thinking I
might be Jesus to accusing me of being the devil. I somehow convinced her that she ought to see a psychiatrist, but as luck would
have it, this happened on the Saturday of a long (Memorial Day)
weekend, and nobody answered her calls. Within another twenty-
four hours Nataki was almost completely helpless, requiring con-
stant monitoring. One minute she was cackling for no reason, the
next minute sobbing, and a minute after that blaming me for the
punishment God was inflicting on her. She seemed to believe that
the apocalyptic "rapture" foretold in the book of Revelation had
begun and she had been left behind with me and all the other hell-
bound heathens. My only goal was to get us through the day, and
then the next—to just hang on until we could get some help.

I prepared turkey burgers for dinner that evening. Nataki took one bite of hers and spat it back onto her plate.

"It tastes funny," she said.

A chill ran through my body. I knew with inexplicable certainty that she believed I had poisoned her food. To forestall an accusation, I assured Nataki that nobody had tampered with her burger and offered to swap plates. In response to this she burst into tears. I watched in horror as Nataki's bawling transformed into a kind of seizure, her torso convulsing jerkily, her chin jutting forward with each spasm, her lips issuing a mournful vibrating sound, some hellish perversion of the noise a child makes when trying to imitate a motorboat.

I reached a comforting hand toward my wife's shoulder, but before it got there she leapt up from her seat, balled her hands, and shouted, "I'm TIRED!" I shrank back like a scolded puppy. Nataki then stormed into the kitchen and withdrew a large blade from the knife block. I sat frozen, disbelieving.

Not once in the seven years I'd been with Nataki had I heard her express hatred or even disdain for another human being. She gave money to every charity that sent her an appeal in the mail because every cause seemed worthy to her. Watching the evening news was torture for Nataki, the pain of the man whose house had burned down and of the woman whose child had been killed in a drive-by shooting affecting her as deeply as if she knew and loved these people. She once said to me, with heartrending innocence, "I wish nothing bad would ever happen to anyone."

Knife in hand, Nataki stomped back to where I sat and raised her arm overhead. I looked into her eyes and saw someone I didn't know. I fought a reflexive urge to lift my own arms in self-defense, hoping to restore her trust in me with a reckless display of my trust in her. It didn't work. As the knife came swooping down toward my Adam's apple, instinct took over. My right hand shot out and knocked away the blade before it could open my jugular vein. Blood spewed from the web of meat between my thumb and index finger and I sprang from my chair and sprinted toward the front door, barefoot, snatching my keys from a wall-mounted metal rack as I passed.

Nataki was right on my heels, still wielding the knife, raving. We tore through the courtyard outside our building like prey and predator. A young couple appeared ahead of me, directly in my line of flight, their mouths falling open as they leapt aside. I made two right turns, sprinted across a parking lot, and scrambled inside the aged and unreliable Ford Taurus (nicknamed Moldy Pumpkin) I'd recently inherited from Sean. It took three tries to jab the key into the ignition switch, just like the movies. When the engine roared to life, I looked up and saw Nataki streaking toward the car, looking very much intent on finishing the job.

I threw the transmission into reverse and kicked the accelerator, shooting backward until I had clearance, then cranked the steering wheel to the left and screeched away. Having left my cell phone behind in the apartment, I drove to the nearest supermarket, where I deposited coins into a payphone for the first time since I hit the wall at the 1999 California International Marathon.

"Please, don't take her to jail," I begged the 9-1-1 dispatcher. "She's not a criminal. I think she's sick!"

The responding officers came to the same conclusion, invoking Code 5150 to take Nataki into involuntary custody for evaluation and treatment. I returned to the apartment complex just in time to see her being chivied into the back of a police car, wrists cuffed behind her—precisely the treatment I had hoped to protect her from. Rage bubbled up in me and I imagined myself shooting the cop in the temple with his own .38.

"What should I do?" I asked a second officer, who had taken a statement from me while his partner separated my wife from her freedom.

"Forget about her, man," he said.

The cruiser rolled away, Nataki's unkempt Afro framed in the rear window. It was this image, strangely, and not anything that came before it, that made me realize my life had changed forever. I forced myself to watch until the vehicle disappeared from sight.

The following night I drove to the private psychiatric hospital where Nataki had been taken after a check of her insurance status. I signed in at a prison-like reception window and took an elevator to the locked ward, where I was buzzed in. An orderly led me down a wanly lighted hall bordered on either side by thick-windowed rooms occupied by jabbering, rocking men and women in whom it was impossible to discern the slightest hope of future lucidity. I found Nataki sitting in a drug-induced stupor on an institutional twin bed, the faintest flicker of recognition showing in her heavy-lidded eyes as I entered.

I had brought with me Nataki's most comfortable cotton dress (she wore only dresses now, for pietistic reasons), a couple of her favorite snack treats (potato chips, beef jerky), and Mr. Pajamas, the pajama-clad pink stuffed bunny Nataki had given me at the end of our first date. I sat down on the bed next to her and asked how she was doing.

"Oh, well, you know," she said vacantly.

It appeared I would have to do most of the talking—not the norm in our relationship. I asked the obvious questions. Was she being treated okay? What kind of medication had she been given? Had she met with a doctor yet? I might as well have posed these questions to Mr. Pajamas. Nataki was almost catatonic, seeming to have little idea where she was or why, let alone the names of the drugs that were responsible for her current muddle. So I stopped grilling her and just said whatever came into my head. I pointed out how the phrase "Protect the animals" appeared in a pattern all over Mr. Pajamas's outfit. Nataki looked at me in amazement, as if she'd never noticed this, and smiled hugely. Taking a measure of encouragement from her reaction, I gestured toward an empty second bed in the room.

"Have you met your roommate yet?" I asked.

Nataki's smile vanished and her face went hard.

"Did you get all the information you needed?" she demanded. "Did you record everything on your microphone? I know you're all in on it!"

Voice rising, Nataki bounded from one unlikely fear to the next, accusing me of using her for her body parts, conspiring against her with Latrice, and telling her secrets to my family.

"I'd better go," I said quietly, already rising.

Nataki shadowed my long retreat down the hallway, hissing further indictments. As I approached the orderly who was guarding the exit, our eyes met and he shook his head in small sympathy. I turned my attention back to Nataki, wanting one last look at her before I completed my escape, and at that moment her bearing transformed again, as suddenly and drastically as before, but in the opposite direction. The hard look left her eyes, replaced by one of childlike terror.

"Please, don't go!" she pleaded, grabbing my shirtsleeve.

My heart exploded inside my chest. I reeled out the door, driven to my own brief madness by the unbearable cruelty of what had just happened. Outside on the landing I flung my body against a wall and howled liked a wounded animal. Only now did the awful truth hit me, that I had fallen out of love with Nataki during her long descent into sickness, having felt that she was turning into someone else, not understanding that, in a completely different sense, *she was turning into someone else.* But I had just caught a flashing glimpse of the real Nataki, the woman I had fallen in love with in the first place, seen her fighting for her very soul inside whatever awful malady had swallowed her up, and my love for her had come flooding back in the most excruciating way possible. She needed me—needed me and deserved the most heroic effort I could muster to save her from the curse that had been wrought upon her so unfairly.

I dried my face on the same shirtsleeve Nataki had lately pulled at and punched the elevator call button. As I slid downward I vowed silently that I would never give up on Nataki, never allow her to fight alone, never stop trying to be the blessing in her life that balanced out the curse, no matter how much I suffered for it or for how long.

Forget her? No fucking way.

CHAPTER 10

TO MEASURE UP

(Boston Marathon)

IT'S EASY TO spot the first-timers at the Boston Marathon Health and Fitness Expo. They're the giddy ones jabbering nonstop at their friends and family members as they flounce across the crowded floor of the Hynes Convention Center, punctuating their manic speech with overloud laughter at things both funny and unfunny like teenage girls meeting their favorite pop star. Or else they're the awestruck ones drifting about dazedly in wide-eyed, reverent silence like pilgrims at a holy site.

I could tell Rome (short for Romadel) was a first-timer the moment I laid eyes on him. He represented the second, awestruck type. Our meeting occurred two days before the big race at a booth where I was signing books and where Rome, passing by after collecting his race bag and recognizing me, stopped to introduce himself. Business was slow, so we were able to chat for a while, and I got to hear a good bit of Rome's story.

Some runners qualify for Boston on their first attempt. Others need a few tries. It took Rome *twenty years* to punch his ticket to

133

the Mecca of running. His first marathon was the 1996 Los Angeles Marathon, which he ran as a bandit on zero training after hearing a coworker brag about her runner boyfriend, an innocent expression of amorous pride that had the unintended effect of compelling Rome to prove that running 26.2 miles was no big deal.

On race day, Rome made it all of 1.5 miles before he hit the skids and staggered into a donut shop to refuel. It's a wonder he got even that far: at five foot two, Rome weighed 180 pounds and he smoked the occasional cigarette to boot. After demolishing a Boston cream kismet, he returned to the racecourse and pressed on. Hours later, most of the other racers having finished the race and gone home, an angel appeared to Rome in the form of Flo from *Good Times* and walked him to the finish line. Just before he got there, however, he stopped.

"What's wrong?" Flo asked.

"I can't cross," Rome said. "I'm a bandit."

"Wait here," he was told.

Flo—who in fact was neither a real angel nor Flo from *Good Times* but just another runner—crossed the finish line on her own, unpinned her number bib, and returned with it to Rome, who then completed his first marathon. It was three o'clock in the afternoon. The race had started at seven in the morning.

The type of person who will run a marathon on zero training is also the type of person who, after suffering through the event for eight hours, will come back for more. By 2004, Rome had completed ten marathons and four Ironmans. But though he'd gotten a lot faster, he hadn't yet met the Boston Marathon qualifying standard for his age group, and that bothered him—a lot. For reasons he did not yet fully understand, Rome still needed to prove to himself whatever it was he'd *really* been trying to prove when he jumped into his first marathon without preparation, and making it to Boston seemed like the way to do it.

A lieutenant commander in the US Navy, Rome was sent to war the following year. To deal with the stress of his deployment, he started smoking again. Then he quit training. Before long he was back up to his pre-running weight.

In 2014, now forty-seven years old, Rome launched a comeback, but this time he took a different approach. Having done some soul searching during his time overseas, Rome realized the reason he'd failed to achieve his goal in the past was fear—specifically fear of failure, which led him to create excuses for falling short, ensuring he *did* fall short. Rome's first marathon, though impressive in its way, had created a self-limiting paradigm for everything that followed. While he may not have ever again attempted to run 26.2 miles on zero training, he still insisted on winging his workouts, never sticking to any plan. And if he no longer fueled his running with Boston cream kismets, his overall diet remained a C+, *maybe* a B−. Determined not to repeat these mistakes in his second go-around, Rome hired a coach and a nutritionist, and he did everything they asked him to, right down to the very last detail, as he readied for the 2016 Rocket City Marathon.

Twenty miles into that race, Rome was on pace to qualify for Boston at long last when his calves cramped up—a terrific excuse to fail yet again.

"Before, I would have quit," he told me. "But this time I didn't."

Rome gutted out the final miles and just squeaked under the time he needed to hit to stand where he now stood.

"What does running the Boston Marathon mean to you?" I asked him, repeating a question I'd posed to Josh before we ran the Modesto Marathon together four weeks back.

Rome parted his lips to answer but no words came out. Instead his eyes filled and his lower lip trembled. Mouthing the word *sorry*, he raised an index finger to signal "Give me a minute" and dropped his chin to his chest.

"I've always had a complex about being a shorter guy," he said eventually. "Making it to Boston validated that I could be as good as anybody else—that I was a real runner despite being five foot two."

Growing up in the first percentile for height in suburban Seattle had been difficult for Rome in the customary ways: he was overlooked by the prettier girls, challenged by the tougher guys, and teased by friends and enemies alike. Although he loved physical competition, he felt his stature prevented him from being taken seriously as an athlete at sports-crazy John F. Kennedy High School. By the time he took up running as an adult, Rome had internalized these judgments, causing him to doubt his own ability to achieve goals like Boston qualification. When he did qualify, he performed a little research and learned that he was the first male graduate of JFK High ever to do so.

"Making it to Boston validated for me that I could be as good as anybody else," Rome told me. "I know it sounds silly, but I've been kind of emotional ever since I picked up my race number."

I told Rome this didn't sound silly to me at all.

....

The next morning I took the T from Somerville to downtown Boston. My starting point was a house on Pembroke Street where Nataki and Queenie and I were staying, a house belonging to none other than Dori, our old family friend, who had put me up before both of my prior Boston Marathons and whom Nataki had not seen since Dori came to California for a party we threw on our fifth wedding anniversary. My destination was a retail space on Newbury Street that had been cleared out to serve as the meeting place for a group run organized by Black Roses NYC, a New York City running club. Stage lights and a green screen had been set up against one wall for photos and videos. Hip-hop music pulsed from a DJ station at the back. A racial rainbow of young harriers was arrayed about the room, shedding outer layers, chatting in small groups, stretching.

I found myself wishing Nataki were with me to witness this refreshing diversity, but she had stayed behind to have her hair braided at an African salon she'd discovered in Dori's neighborhood. Gone were the days when Nataki spent two, sometimes three hours getting ready for a night on the town, but gone too, thankfully, were the days when she wore the same musty frock for a week straight and sometimes forgot to brush her teeth until I commented on her breath. Her current approach to style and grooming split the difference between these past extremes, fake eyelashes one day, leopard-print satin pajamas at noon the next—whatever felt right.

For Nataki's fortieth birthday I paid a photographer friend to blow up and box frame a selection of images from one of her old photo shoots, which I then hung in a cool geometric pattern on a wall in one of our guest bedrooms, my way of acknowledging her grief over the loss of the physical beauty captured in those pictures. Yet Nataki had never been one to take excessive pride in her looks. Even at the height of her radiance, whenever someone spoke to Nataki critically of another woman's appearance, she would leap to that person's defense, pointing out that with a little more attention to her hair and a dress that better flattered her figure (or whatever), she would look quite nice indeed, and Nataki applied this same attitude to herself after her figure filled out and she was no longer asked to show ID when she bought beer for me. "Work with what you got," she often said.

A week or two before we left for our trip, a package arrived on our doorstep, and twenty minutes later Nataki appeared in the doorway to my office modeling an elegant cream-colored pantsuit with flared legs in size 22, pirouetting with her arms spread wide as she asked me what I thought, her girlish smile proof she'd already made up her own mind about the garment. It occurred to me then—not for the first time—that if life is going to hit you with the double-whammy of a major mood disorder and the sledgehammer drugs used to treat it, it sure helps to have been born an old soul.

After a quick tour of the room, I spotted the leader of the Black Roses, Knox Robinson, a handsome forty-two-year-old with a neatly trimmed Afro and matching beard and the bird-boned body of a high-level distance runner, and greeted him with a hearty bro hug.

"Glad you made it," Knox said, already half-distracted by the next person wanting his attention.

"Wouldn't have missed it," I said.

I had known Knox for all of five days, having first met him when Nataki and I passed through the Big Apple on our way north from Virginia. A past editor in chief of the music magazine *Fader* and a former NCAA Division I track and field athlete, Knox occupied a singular position in the running community at the intersection of hip-hop culture and the running cognoscenti. In interviews, he quoted the likes of Amiri Baraka and Hunter S. Thompson without ever coming off as pretentious. Confident he had a unique perspective to offer on the magic of the marathon, I'd made sure to include an encounter with Black Roses NYC in my travels.

It was midafternoon on the Tuesday before Boston when the Fun Mobile rolled into Brooklyn. After settling my road-weary wife and pet into a hotel that compromised between the locally incompatible virtues of affordability and tolerability, I called Knox to confirm an arrangement I'd made with him previously to drop in on the club's weekly track workout on Manhattan's Lower East Side. He gave me some sketchy-sounding directions to a place that turned out to be a 330-yard cinder oval with a hummock at one end. It was located right under the Williamsburg Bridge, thrumming then with rush-hour traffic, so that all conversation below had to be shouted, as in a crowded bar. It wasn't an actual running track, but it served well enough as a venue for speed work and also, I soon discovered, as a symbol of the Black Roses' scrappy approach to running.

About two dozen runners showed up for the workout. They were a perfect cross section of the city, an even mix of blacks, whites, Asians, and Latinos, and the gender balance was pretty good too, though I was by far the oldest person present. The next-oldest, Knox himself, convened the evening's session with some announcements.

"So, the author of *The Endurance Diet* is with us tonight," he said by way of introducing me. "He's here to fat-shame those of you who have been slacking on your food choices."

I shook my head in denial as the runners sized me up. Knox quickly moved on, delivering individual shout-outs to club members who were racing Boston in six days. I confess I was more than a little surprised by the number, as these folks, by and large, did not have the look of the prototypical Boston Marathon qualifier. There were tattoos everywhere, alternative hairstyles, clothes not designed for running being used for running. I liked it.

"Let's see, have I missed anyone?" Knox said.

A tall white guy at the back of the group raised his right arm.

"Oh, right, Mackay!" Knox said.

Everyone clapped for him.

"Mackay's visa's running out in a few weeks," Knox continued, "so he's checking a few things off his bucket list before we Trump him the fuck back to Syria!"

I learned later in the evening that Mackay was Australian by birth, lived in England, and had never been to Syria.

Knox concluded his announcements with an overview of the workout. We were to run six hard laps around the track (such as it was) with ninety-second standing recoveries between laps. These would be followed by a ten-minute tempo segment and finally a set of four 30-second strides. It wasn't the toughest workout ever drawn up, but it made me nervous, saddled as I was with a balky left Achilles that raised hell whenever I subjected it to speed work too abruptly—and I hadn't run faster than marathon pace in months.

We warmed up with seven or eight easy laps. I fell into rhythm with a guy named José, who had started running as a way to lose weight. Two years later, getting rid of flab was his last concern. "I just want to get faster," he told me more than once as we ran in circles together.

Out of consideration for my Achilles, I ran the first interval in third gear, taking Knox's instruction to "ease into" the session a touch further than he'd intended. Ahead of me the younger guys tore through the circuit like greyhounds. A leggy African American woman in booty shorts and a bra top surged past me just before the line, her competitive vibes palpable.

After the second lap, Knox ordered us to "start getting after it." My Achilles was already grumbling, but otherwise I felt good, my lower extremities showing more bounce than I would have expected from them given the one-sidedness of my recent training. I completed the interval ahead of Ms. Booty Shorts. Barely.

While we recovered from the third lap, openmouthed, hands on hips, Knox offered fresh commands.

"I don't want any sandbagging on this next one," he warned. "You're only cheating yourself if you do. The workout won't serve its purpose, and you'll have no one but yourself to blame."

"Man, what a hardass!" I stage-whispered at Jeb, a club member who had recently run the Tokyo Marathon. Jeb laughed politely, but his eyes said it was no joke.

During a short break between the interval and tempo portions of the workout, José took me aside and pointed at various other members of the group.

"He's run 2:42," José said, referring to the marathon time of the runner who had won all the intervals. "That dude next to him has run 2:45. We have another guy who's run 2:45, but he's not here tonight. Sam there has run 3:04. And, of course, Knox has run 2:36."

My eyes lingered on Sam. I would not have pegged him as a three-hour marathoner. He looked to me more like a sprinter or a running back or even a boxer. After the workout, I spoke to Sam and learned that he had been a sprinter in high school, a football player in college, and a middleweight boxer after college. Now, like his teammates, he just wanted to get faster.

We moved outside the park for the next part of the workout. Huddled together on the sidewalk, Knox and his charges argued back and forth for several minutes about whether to go north or south. I still had no idea which way I was supposed to run when Knox gave the command to start and everyone else went north, so I followed.

I got a chance to talk to Knox one on one after it was all over, as we walked together toward his car and my subway stop.

"So, what did you think?" he asked.

"Don't take this the wrong way," I said, "but the whole time I was out there I kept thinking about those sports movies like *Mighty Ducks* where an unconventional coach brings together a motley band of misfit athletes and turns them into champions. There's a *Bad News Bears* quality to your group—serious but not too serious. Where does that come from?"

"No offense taken," Knox said. "When I created Black Roses five years ago, it was to address what I perceived as a dearth of information in the urban running community about how to approach performance. People thought it was cool to stay out all night and then run a marathon the next morning, or to jump in a race with no preparation just to say they did it. As everyone knows, when you run a marathon, and you have a tough one, you start to reflect and ask questions, like, 'What could I have done better?' 'What are the elements of success?' 'How do you put together a good race?' Marathons are addictive because they're logistical challenges. You try to figure out how to make it right. 'If I had only fueled correctly.' 'If I had only paced properly.' 'If I had only had a little more preparation.'"

I nodded along as Knox spoke, thinking back on my own long struggle to solve the logistical challenges of the marathon distance.

"I had kept my running to myself up to that point," Knox continued. "People thought I was just a cool guy in our group who hung out with rappers at Fashion Week in Paris. But other runners knew I could run, and they would come to me with questions, looking for help. Eventually, I decided I wanted to have a more codified way of delivering whatever insights I had gleaned. My goal was to share these elite-level tools for unlocking performance."

I recalled these words four days later when I met Rome at the Boston Marathon expo. If Rome's personal mission was to prove he could be a "real runner," as he put it, despite being short, then Knox, it seemed, was on a mission to convince young urbanites that they, too, could be real runners regardless of where they came from, how they spoke, or what they wore.

At my second encounter with Black Roses NYC, in Boston, I saw a mix of new and familiar faces. Among the latter was Nadia, a South African spitfire with the physique of a gymnast, diminutive and powerful. When Knox had named her as one of the club's first-time Boston qualifiers back in New York, Nadia had pogoed like a circus dog, shouting "Boing!" at the apex of each astonishingly high leap.

"Did you save any energy for tomorrow?" I asked her now.

"No!" she blurted defiantly, running in place with fast feet.

A piercing whistle silenced the room. Its source, Knox, took advantage of the hush to invite the gathering to follow him outside, where, on the front stoop of the building, he delivered a short speech that included another off-the-cuff jab at the current leader of the free world. A few group photos were taken, and the run began, the Black Roses swarming the streets with little regard for cars, pedestrians, or traffic lights.

In Boston, on the day before the marathon, running groups are as ubiquitous as mosquitos in Arkansas, but our crew stood out, attracting stares from fellow runners and civilians alike as we rumbled through the Back Bay. There was an aura of danger surrounding the charging horde, a vaguely piratical energy. Indeed, the Black Roses NYC flag, draped around the bare back of a sinewy young club member, could easily have been mistaken for the Jolly Roger from a distance. It was Easter Sunday, and as we passed by a long queue of stooped, silver-haired worshippers awaiting entry to a Catholic church, the flag-wearer bellowed, "Happy Easter, everybody!" in a tone that seemed somehow both reverent and irreverent.

The run ended at (where else?) the Black Rose, an Irish pub near Quincy Market. In New York, I had asked Knox about the origin of his club's name.

"'Black Roses' is the title of a 1990s dancehall classic by Barrington Levy," he said. "It's about the rarest flower, a flower that you never find, that you never see. A lot of times, I'm with this group and I think of that line from *Fear and Loathing in Las Vegas:* 'There he goes. One of God's own prototypes. A high-powered mutant of some kind never even considered for mass production. Too weird to live, and too rare to die.' Because these guys I've got running for me are crazy! They bring the idea of black roses to life."

At a booth inside the Black Rose, I asked Knox one last question, one that had been on my mind since our first meeting.

"When I talked to you in New York," I began, dropping my eyes to my phone to verify that it was recording, "you told me that you created Black Roses NYC because, in so many words, you wanted people in the urban running community to take running seriously—to take it all the way. Can I infer from this that you feel runners who *don't* test their limits are missing out on something?"

Knox considered the question. "Yeah, I do feel kind of bad for the folks who don't take the whole trip," he said carefully. "Running has unfathomable riches to share. Someone who endeavors to put together the full modern runner's tool kit and really understand the marathon, beyond just completing it and getting a finisher's medal, ends up learning more, I think, about himself or herself and what it means to be human. That's what those tools are for."

....

Five hours later, the doorbell rang at Dori's house, a tastefully maintained Victorian in which old and new are blended just right (quirky original colonial door locks balanced out by a modern kitchen) where Dori and Nataki were now preparing dinner while I blogged in the living room.

"It's Mike!" I caroled, leaping from my seat and skipping toward the foyer like a kid whose favorite cousin has just arrived for a sleepover.

I flung open the door and there he was: my high school best friend and former daily running partner, a man I'd last seen seven years before, when I ran my first Boston Marathon, and had last run with sixteen years before, in Central Park, on the eve of his wedding. Mike had given up competitive running at the same time as me, quitting the Oyster River High School track team in a show of solidarity after Coach Bronson booted me for gross insubordination. From there we went in very different directions with our running, Mike moving on to other athletic interests as I returned to the sport in a big way in my late twenties. A short stint of competitive lumberjacking at the University of New Hampshire was followed by a couple of seasons of rowing at the University of Rochester. Then came a mountain biking phase in San Francisco and an ongoing love affair with downhill skiing, which he shared with his wife, Alison, and their four children in (as fate would have it) Hanover, New Hampshire. Mike's own running comeback began after my second tilt at Boston in 2016, which had somehow inspired my friend to try to qualify. And now here he was, weighing fifteen pounds less than he had the last time I'd set eyes on him.

"You look like a real runner!" I said, ushering him in.

A slight yet noticeable flinch preceded Mike's verbal response ("I'm trying!") to this greeting, as though I had called him fat instead of the opposite. Puzzling over his reaction, I led Mike into the kitchen to greet Nataki and to meet Dori. I offered him a beer and he declined. With a *suit yourself* shrug I popped the top off a single bottle and waved Mike into the living room, where we sat in adjacent vintage armchairs to go over the race plan.

"Let's start with your goal," I said. "What are you thinking?"

"I want to break three hours," Mike said.

It came to me now why Mike had startled at the doorway. *I'm not a real runner anyway.* One month earlier, Mike had written these words to me in an e-mail listing his reasons for having decided to treat the Boston Marathon as a fun run instead of a race—"a victory lap," as he called it. But since then Mike's forty-six-year-old legs had shown flashes, more and more frequent, of the zip that had once powered him to a 4:24 mile. In his qualifying event, Mike ran 3:00:00—perhaps the most excruciating time a marathoner can possibly run. First Rome, now Mike—what was this *real runner* business all about?

"Just to be clear," I asked Mike now, "is your goal to break three hours or to run as fast as you can?"

"I just want to break three," Mike said.

"So, as far as you're concerned, 2:59:59 is as good as any faster time?"

"That's exactly right."

This meant Mike would be running 6:50 miles, a pace I felt I could keep up for about twenty miles without jeopardizing my greater mission (assuming my sore Achilles behaved). I told Mike I would pace him to the base of Heartbreak Hill and then back off, leaving him to soar away to individual glory.

"Soup's on!" Nataki called from the kitchen.

We filled our plates from the stove with fresh artisanal pastas and sauces Dori had procured from the same neighborhood shop that supplied the last supper (so to speak) before my disastrous first Boston Marathon in 2009 and carried them to the dining room, where the conversation remained marathon focused. I asked Mike—as I'd asked Rome before him and Josh before *him*—what running the Boston Marathon meant to him.

"I'm a really goal-oriented person," he said, leaning back. "I set goals and then I work very hard to achieve them. And then I set different goals and I work very hard to achieve those. Running the Boston Marathon is yet another goal."

The contrast between this rather flat response and Rome's tearful earlier answer to the same question could not have been starker. How casually Mike lumped Boston in with his past goals! For as long as I'd known him, Mike had kept his emotions well contained, never letting anyone see him sweat. I wondered: Was this because he was afraid to show the doubts and fears that existed within him as they do in all of us or because he truly didn't sweat? I had no idea, despite our almost thirty years of friendship. Perhaps there was a clue in the concern he and Rome shared about whether they were or were not real runners. Or maybe the poker-faced gentleman forking fettuccini into his mouth on the other side of the table was the only runner on earth for whom a marathon, even the Boston Marathon, was 26.2 miles, nothing more.

....

Whether by coincidence or by fate, Mike and Rome met face to face the next morning, in Hopkinton, one hour before race time. Mike and I were jogging back and forth along a short stretch of road tracing the boundary of the Athletes Village when a familiar-looking figure approached us, an economically proportioned Filipino man with salt-and-pepper hair.

"Rome!" I called.

We paused our respective warm-ups and introductions were made. While the two first-time Boston Marathon runners shook hands, I looked Rome over, admiring his snazzy black uniform with pink trim. At the upper right corner of the singlet was a cross made up of letters and numbers.

4
E N E
3

Later Rome told me that the alphanumeric configuration referred to his Auntie Emy, who had died of breast cancer in 2014. "I lifted her as a pallbearer," he told me. "She lifts me on race days."

"How are you feeling?" I asked him now.

"Honestly, I'm a little nervous," he said.

Rome didn't look nervous to me—he looked pants-shitting petrified. I cautioned my new friend to run conservatively (it was a seventy-degree day), and we went our separate ways.

Forty-five minutes later, Mike and I stood pressed together in the corrals, surrounded by the cream of Earth's amateur running population. The national anthem was sung. Fighter jets ripped overhead, their roar briefly drowning out the thrum of a hovering TV helicopter. Ten or twelve of the world's greatest professional distance runners were recognized over the public address system.

A sudden commotion occurred to our left. A female runner had fallen to the pavement, where she lay insensate, the apparent victim of an anxiety attack. I had done my best the previous evening to prepare Mike for this madness, but in my heart I knew it was like expecting a soldier to be fully prepared for his first taste of combat.

"Forget what I said last night," Mike told me as we watched a police officer scramble over a barricade that separated him from the collapsed woman's limp form. "This is not just another goal for me. I'm about to bust out of my skin!"

The starter's pistol cracked, and a cheer went up all around us—and then everyone just stood there. Mike and I were in Corral 7, stuck behind 6,000 other runners like idling cars in a long backup at a traffic light that's just turned green. By the time we crossed the timing mat and were officially on the clock, the male pros were already almost a mile up the road, and even then the field remained so closely bunched that our rate of progress scarcely matched that of our earlier warm-up as we muddled through what should have been the fastest section of the course: a four-mile, 310-foot free fall toward Ashland. Mike's body language communicated an impatience bordering on distress.

When at last the glacial floe of bodies loosened up enough to allow Mike to accelerate toward his goal pace without barreling through people, he did just that, darting left and right and executing abrupt forward bursts to slip through slim gaps between human obstacles. I played the same game, and in no time Mike and I had developed a sophisticated system of teamwork in which whoever found the next gap led the way for the other, using gestures of the head and hands to signal imminent moves and to prevent collisions.

Suddenly the past twenty-nine years were obliterated. Everything was as it had been half a lifetime ago: Mike's exasperatingly erratic pacing, his penchant for half-stepping me (running six inches ahead when we were ostensibly running together), the fraternally nuanced nonverbal communication between us—*this* was what it had been like to race with Mike in 1986, and nothing had changed. I was seized then by an aching cognizance of the preciousness of the moment, a feeling akin to what an aging crooner might feel on reuniting with his former accompanist for "One Night Only" after decades apart and unexpectedly finding, relishing, that old magic.

We completed the first mile and I checked my watch. "Even with all of that, we still ran six fifty-five," I told Mike. "We're fine."

Mike made no reply, but his actions spoke volumes. The more dispersed the cattle drive became, the faster he ran, leading us through the next four miles at an average pace of 6:36 per mile.

"Are you running this fast on purpose?" I asked him.

"Yes," he said flatly.

I realized then that Mike was not running to break three hours. He was running as fast as his middle-age heart would drive his slightly bowed legs, risking catastrophe in unfavorable conditions in a bid to leave absolutely everything he had to give on the racecourse. He was, in short, taking Knox Robinson's whole trip.

As we worked our way through mile six, a male voice, heavily accented, hailed me from behind. I swiveled my head and identified the speaker as a pint-sized South American–looking dude.

"Are you Matt Fitzgerald?" he repeated. I said I was.

"I have your *Racing Weight*," said the fan, offering me a hand to shake, a very awkward procedure given our relative positions. "And now we are suffering here together!"

I turned toward Mike with an expectant smile, certain he was remembering any of a number of embarrassing episodes from my past, like the night during our sophomore year when we camped out in my neighborhood and I left a huge puddle of beery vomit right outside the tent door, forcing us both to leap over it in the morning, and that he would be unable to resist saying something to take me down a peg. But no. His eyes stayed locked on the road ahead.

A few miles farther on, we passed by a spectator who held a large sign in front of him, a professional-looking rendering of the 2017 Super Bowl scoreboard. It showed the Atlanta Falcons leading the New England Patriots by a score of 28 to 3 with 2:12 left in the third quarter. The implicit punch line, of course, was that the Patriots had gone on to win the game in overtime, proving forevermore that in sports, no matter how bad it looks at any given moment, it ain't over till it's over. I laughed out loud, imagining the effect this message might have had on me in some of my worst marathon moments. Mike remained expressionless, oblivious to everything but a distant finish line visible only in his mind.

At the next aid station, congestion caused Mike to miss the cup he wanted. Seeing this, I grabbed an extra and handed it to him. He dumped it over his head.

"That was Gatorade," I said, trying but failing to suppress an apologetic giggle.

Mike's face stayed as still as a photograph. Tossing the empty cup aside, he pressed on.

We passed the halfway mark of the race in 1:27:47, well ahead of Mike's stated goal pace. Soon we entered the famous Wellesley College Scream Tunnel, no longer quite the gooseflesh-raising sonic assault it had been before the post-bombing security crackdown forced the coeds behind barricades, but Mike's tempo lifted slightly even so. Ears ringing under the onslaught of a thousand treble voices, I thought of Kathrine Switzer, who had defied a traditional ban on female participants to become the first woman finisher of the Boston Marathon in 1967, and who was running the race again today, fifty years later. "If you are losing faith in human nature," Switzer once said, "go out and watch a marathon." How many of these fresh-faced spectators, I thought, were right now changing their minds about our imperfect species as they witnessed women and men from ninety-nine countries striving in common purpose, driving themselves to the brink of breakdown in an effort to create meaning out of meaninglessness, to become more than they were?

After Wellesley came Newton and its dreaded hills. On the first of these, Mike bogged down a little more than he had on prior climbs, his stride losing some of its characteristic jauntiness, his eyes taking on an unfocused look, lips bent in a frozen scowl. My watch beeped, marking the completion of mile seventeen. Seven minutes flat—our slowest yet.

"Looking good, Mike," I said.

We came to the base of Heartbreak Hill, the last and toughest ascent of the race. My injured left Achilles tendon blazed with pain. The Glass City Marathon was six days away. I had promised Nataki I wouldn't do anything stupid. But at the precise moment my foot touched the spot where I had planned to back off, Mike, whose water cups I had continued to fetch for him over the last several miles, groaned involuntarily.

I stayed with him.

At the top of the hill, my watch chimed again: 7:08. I began to pray, even more urgently than I'd prayed for Kacey eight days before, words bubbling up spontaneously from my deepest inner depths: *Please, God, let us have this. Please, God . . .*

The fire in my ailing leg intensified. Mike's fatigue visibly increased. But we kept moving, and the passing of each subsequent mile marker—twenty-two, twenty-three, twenty-four—seemed to me an incremental unfolding of an answer to my divine petition. I made myself as useful as I could by grabbing more drinks, guiding Mike as linearly as possible through the road's tangents, even moving ahead of him at one point to block the headwind that had kicked up. Mike, meanwhile, checked his watch obsessively, and from this I knew that he was still battling, trying not merely to survive but to conquer. My heart swelled with brotherly pride, and something grape-sized lodged in my throat.

"Let's go, Mike," I said as we approached the next, and next-to-last, mile marker.

Mike sped up, having apparently misinterpreted my encouragement as a directive, and it was then I realized that Mike was not pushing himself to the absolute limit for his own sake entirely but also for mine—that my presence and support made him want to give his very best effort. But he could not sustain the surge and soon fell back into the funereal 6:45-per-mile rhythm we had kept up since coming over the top of Heartbreak.

We turned right onto Hereford Street and then left onto Boylston—the long, iconic homestretch of the world's greatest footrace. Seeing the finish line banner ahead, Mike surged again, fighting for every last second until there were no seconds left to fight for. We had overtaken nearly 5,000 runners to this point, and we continued to reel in flagging competitors as we approached the line. The grape in my throat burst and I began to cry, absurdly, a grown man weeping and running as thousands watched.

One thing I had never said to Mike in all the years of our friendship was, "I love you, man." His Spock-like emotional containment doesn't invite such effusions, and, for that matter, no one has ever accused me of being the touchy-feely type. Even hugging is awkward between us. But what better way for two old running buddies to say, "I love you, man," than to stride shoulder-to-shoulder to the finish of the Boston Marathon in shared struggle, an agony freely chosen by each as a gift to the other?

We crossed the line at 2:57:45. Mike and I became separated almost immediately as I limped behind and he speed-walked ahead like a Manhattan pedestrian, fearful (he confessed afterward) that if he stopped moving his legs would cramp, and that if he turned to face me his own feelings would overflow. Just when I was beginning to think my friend had forgotten about me, he wheeled around. I made fists of my hands and let out a primal scream. Mike smiled queasily and raised his palms overhead, initiating a weary high-ten.

"That's all I could do," he said. "I couldn't have run any faster."

To a non-runner, these words might have smacked of disappointment, but to me they conveyed the deepest fulfillment—the satisfaction of having taken the whole trip.

....

Mike woke up two days later in an unfamiliar bed at Homewood Suites in Washington, DC, where he had driven with his family all-too-immediately after the race for an enriching spring holiday. Separating his sore body from the sheets with some difficulty, he dressed proudly in the neon-yellow long-sleeve official Boston Marathon participant shirt that had come in his race bag and took the elevator down to breakfast with Alison and the kids.

In the dining room, Mike began to have second thoughts about his clothing selection. Feeling the eyes of the other eaters on his back, he worried that he might be giving the wrong impression, falsely passing himself off as a real runner. At home in Hanover, Mike was surrounded by serious athletes—skiers and cyclists and others whom, he felt, he didn't measure up to in midlife, decades after his glory days as a high school runner. But these second thoughts gave way to third thoughts as it occurred to Mike that his high-achieving athlete friends and acquaintances probably viewed him the same way he viewed them—at least now, if not before. After all, he'd just placed among the top 4 percent of finishers and the top 3 percent of men his age in the world's most prestigious running event, smashing the hallowed three-hour barrier in tough conditions that had brought down many a more experienced marathoner.

Back at the room, while the kids got ready for a day of sightseeing, Mike sat down with his computer to answer some questions I'd asked him about how his Boston Marathon experience had affected or perhaps even changed him. Mike described his choice of shirt and the self-consciousness it had caused him at breakfast and the introspection that followed.

"So maybe it's time I gave myself permission to think of myself as a real runner," he concluded. "Maybe that's what's changed."

When I received Mike's reply, I was seated at an imitation cherrywood desk in a hotel room in Danbury, Connecticut, where Nataki and I were stopping over on the way to Toledo, Ohio, and marathon number six in my search for the magic of the marathon. While I worked, Nataki relaxed on the bed with her back braced against the headboard, conversing by phone with Tayna, something she does every day without fail as part of her self-care regimen. As I read my friend's words, there appeared suddenly in my mind's eye the forgotten image of a strawberry birthmark that was conspicuously visible on Mike's left cheek when I first knew him—a blemish that he'd traveled to (wait for it) Boston at age sixteen to have blasted off with a medical laser. Mike took some good-natured jibing from his teammates, including me, about the procedure, and he took it sportingly, but I remembered now catching a hint of strain in his smile, sensing an eagerness for the subject to be dropped.

Of course! Underneath his impenetrable sangfroid, Mike truly was as human as the rest of us and cared what other people thought. It all made sense. Mike's initial hesitance to take aim at the three-hour marathon barrier in Boston was rooted in a natural fear of putting himself out there, of stepping forward for public measurement and possibly coming up short. That he would do so in the company of a man whom Mike once measured himself against as a runner—me—could only have intensified his trepidation.

All at once, I understood what this real runner stuff was really about. We humans are social animals, and as such we measure ourselves against each other in all kinds of instinctual ways. As a consequence, our happiness depends on our self-esteem, which in turn depends, to some degree, on how others perceive us. It is often said that we shouldn't worry about what other people think, that our sense of personal worth should come from within. But self-esteem cannot be manufactured out of thin air. An undersized

boy whose ego has been damaged by bullying and teasing and being overlooked must find something of real value inside himself
before he can walk tall. A city girl whom society has repeatedly
given the message that people who look like her cannot excel in a
particular sport needs a fair opportunity to prove otherwise before
she can fully believe otherwise. This is what running did for Rome
and has done for certain members of Black Roses NYC, and it's
what running does generally.

From the outside, running may seem like just another way to fail
to measure up—an unnecessary one, at that. Height and ethnicity
are beyond our control, but a marathon is a choice. A non-runner
can be forgiven for assuming that only the winner gets an ego
boost from a race—that the novice runner who can't finish a 5K
without walking feels inadequate next to the marathon finisher,
who in turn feels inadequate next to the Boston qualifier, who in
turn feels inadequate next to the Olympian. In fact, running is a
reliable self-esteem builder across the entire spectrum of abilities.

You'll see this if you watch the first printed results being posted
in the finish area of a local road race. Runners scrum around the
pages like honeybees, eager to find out how they measured up.
"I was fourth in my age group!" shouts a man with a running cap
covering his balding head. "I was less than a minute behind Rick!"
says a college-age woman in reference to her boyfriend. Everyone
has a different result, a unique takeaway. Yet *everyone* is pleased.
(Well, almost everyone.)

All runners yearn to be "real" runners. The definition of this
term, however, is relative, not absolute. The runner who cannot
yet complete a 5K without walking may define a real runner as
one who can, and strive to do so. The runner who can already run
a full 5K but has never run farther may define a real runner as one
who has completed a marathon, and strive to do so. And so on. At
every level, runners define "real runner" in such a way that it is just
within their reach to become one, but only if they take the whole
trip, giving everything they've got to realize whatever amount of
potential they have.

And therein lies the magic. For our self-esteem is not determined *entirely* by how we measure up against our peers. It is influenced as well by how we see ourselves independent of others' judgments. All runners who try as hard as they can to become the best runner they can be discover something in themselves—what Mike described to me in his response to my written questions as "a real satisfaction that I've got the fire in the belly to dig deep and not fade away when the going gets tough"—that heightens their self-image. *All* runners who try as hard as they possibly can to measure up, do.

CHAPTER 11

NO END IN SIGHT

ON JUNE 4, 2004, Nataki was discharged from the psychiatric hospital that the San Diego police had delivered her to in handcuffs twelve days before. She came home to me with a diagnosis of bipolar disorder and a prescription for antipsychotic medication. A month later, we relocated to the Silicon Valley city of Fremont to be closer to Nataki's family, a move made possible by my having left *Triathlete* to work as an independent endurance sports writer.

Scarcely had the last picture been hung in our new apartment when Nataki secretly stopped taking her medicine, convinced perhaps by its very effectiveness that she didn't need it and loathing its side effects, which included drowsiness, muddled thinking, and joint pain. The psychiatrist she'd seen back in San Diego warned me this might happen, explaining that most people with Nataki's illness had to "bottom out a few times," as he put it, before they accepted the reality of their condition and complied with its imperfect treatment. So I was less surprised than I was disappointed when Nataki began to unravel, insomnia leading to mood swings, mood swings to paranoia.

One night I was awakened by a gentle unweighting of Nataki's side of the bed as she slipped from the sheets with her Bible. It was well past midnight, hours before dawn.

"You stopped taking your meds, didn't you?" I said through the darkness.

"Please don't be mad at me!" Nataki pleaded.

"I'm not mad at you," I sighed. "I mean, I wish you would keep taking them. But I can't say I wouldn't do the same thing in your place."

A few days earlier I'd accidentally ingested one of Nataki's pills. For the next forty-eight hours I'd felt as if my brain had been replaced with a big wad of soggy wool. Walking a mile in her shoes had greatly increased my appreciation for her no-win situation.

Within another week, Nataki's mind was as disordered as it had been on the night she came after me with a kitchen knife. Not fancying an encore, I begged her to let me find help. She relented, and the next day I called half a dozen psychiatrists and hospitals and had the same frustrating conversation with receptionists at each of them.

ME: I'd like to make an appointment for my wife.

RECEPTIONIST: Is she a current patient or new?

ME: She's a new patient.

RECEPTIONIST: Our next opening is in five weeks, is that okay?

ME: It's urgent. I'd like to get her in right away.

RECEPTIONIST: I'm afraid that's not possible. But you can always call 9-1-1 in the meantime if there's an emergency.

ME: I'll try somewhere else.

My last call was to a clinic in Palo Alto, whose receptionist informed me that their next opening was five weeks out and that I should dial 9-1-1 if an emergency happened in the meantime. I lost my temper.

"That's excellent advice, ma'am, thank you!" I raved. "Let's all just wait for a tragedy to happen and *then* do something!"

It wasn't my finest moment, but I don't regret it—Nataki got a next-day appointment with a young resident who prescribed a different drug that, according to clinical trials, had less onerous side effects. My relief was oceanic.

In the spring of 2005 we bought a house, our first, a not-yet-built track home in Oakdale, California, a Central Valley cow town located ninety-seven miles east of San Francisco. We moved in just before Thanksgiving, and by Christmas I'd begun to suspect that Nataki had gone noncompliant a second time. An abrupt reversal of her medicine-induced weight gain tipped me off. I then watched helplessly as a series of increasingly worrisome indicators (a hyper-religious new voicemail greeting on her cell phone, complaints about vampire spirits sucking out her energy and ventriloquist spirits taking over her tongue) followed.

I was blending a smoothie in the kitchen one morning after swimming laps at a health club in Modesto when Nataki stormed into the room and accused me of marrying her for the purpose of stealing her anointing, an all-too-familiar charge.

"Tell me the truth, Kitty," I said. "Did you stop taking your pills again?"

"No!" she protested, all wounded innocence. "I'm still taking them, I promise!"

I chose to believe her, but within a week Nataki was railing against the puppet master spirit that was trying to control her body. I asked her whether it was possible that this spirit was in fact a symptom of her disease.

"You're all against me!" she shouted.

"I'm not against you, Nataki," I said with forced calm. "I think whoever or whatever really is against you is trying to convince you I'm against you."

"I'm tired!" she cried.

My skin prickled at the sound of these remembered words, last spoken as Nataki made a sudden dash for the knife block. Sure enough, she now went for it again. Why had we even kept the damn thing?

"Nataki, stop!" I commanded. "Don't let the enemy control your mind!"

My use of Nataki's own church vocabulary was unpremeditated but effectual. She let go of the seven-inch santoku she had seized and faced me. Pressing my advantage, I gently proposed that we call her doctor. This was less well received. Nataki's jaw tightened, and in the next instant she was all over me, clawed fingers tearing at my cheeks and hair.

"Nobody's going to save you this time!" she shrieked. "You're all alone!"

I broke away and raced toward the front door. My thumb had just found the latch when I heard a crack and at the same time felt a searing lash across my back. I wheeled around to discover that the studded leather belt Nataki had been wearing moments earlier was now in her right hand, gripped by the buckle. I suffered two more painful swipes—one to each wrist, sacrificed to save my face—before I was able to scramble out the door.

Shoeless, I ran down the middle of the street without a thought as to where I was going. The injury to my right knee that had kept me from running the Boston Marathon three years earlier continued to limit my training, and I felt my lack of fitness profoundly as I fled. After fifty or sixty yards I hazarded a look back. Nataki was close behind, her face a mask of deadly intent. I ran another fifty yards or so and looked again. Still there. Fueled now as much by embarrassment as by terror (I could picture the headline: "Local Marathoner Outrun, Killed by Sedentary Wife"), I gave everything I had to the next fifty. When I glanced back a third time, Nataki was walking. Even then, I dared not slacken my pace but continued to run hard until I had circled the block, returning to the house from the opposite side.

I slipped through the front door and bolted it behind me, grabbed my phone and a set of keys, dashed to the back of the house, fastened the sliding glass door that gave access to the back-yard, bounded upstairs, and shut myself inside the master bed-room, where I called for help.

"Nine-one-one. What's your emergency?"

The voice was female, jaded, possibly sleepy. I described my emergency in as few words as possible, breathless. Seemingly un-moved, the dispatcher told me she would send help just as soon as she got some necessary information. A heavy thudding sound came from below.

"Okay, fine," I said.

My assumption was that I would be asked to provide a few details pertinent to my rescue, but the questions just kept coming:

Was my wife under a doctor's care?
Had I noticed any recent changes in her behavior?
Was she taking her medication?
Did she have a history of violence?
Were there any weapons in the home?

"My favorite color is blue!" I cut in. "Are you going to send help or what?"

There was a brief silence on the other end, followed by one of those pointedly forbearing customer service scoldings ("Sir, I'm only . . . ") intended to make you feel like an ass. Having reasserted her authority, the dispatcher resumed her quizzing. Meanwhile, Nataki stopped pounding on the front door and moved to the back of house, where she came into view through a large south-facing window. I watched in disbelief as my wife ran straight at the slid-ing glass door and launched her body into it, bouncing off like something made of rubber. Thinking better of a second attempt, she changed tactics, hurling a series of flower pots against the door, to no effect. Having run out of smaller projectiles, she lifted a four-foot plaster bird bath with Herculean ease and flung it against the glass. Amazingly, the plaster shattered but the door held.

I described all of this to the dispatcher, who, at last comprehending the seriousness of the situation, asked if I could possibly escape the house and get into a vehicle. I decided to give it a shot.

Confirming with a final peek out the window that Nataki was still in the backyard, I rumbled down the stairs and fled out the front door. The Honda Element I'd bought a few days after Nataki's release from the hospital sat in our driveway. I pressed a button on the key fob to deactivate the alarm and winced when the vehicle announced its obedience with the blaring double-honk that had inspired its nickname: Meep Meep. As I backed out of the driveway, Nataki burst through the side gate and leapt on top of the car's roof like a Hollywood stuntwoman.

Not knowing what else to do, I continued to reverse, Nataki meanwhile bouncing on the roof with her rear end, kicking the windshield with her heels and screaming threats and curses. The dispatcher, hearing me narrate these developments, advised me to stop moving, lest Nataki be thrown off and snap her neck. I pressed the brake and sat idling on the street, watching indentations form inches above my head, feeling blood soak through the back of my shirt, waiting for the Oakdale police to arrive and consummate our degradation.

Minutes passed like hours. An especially violent blow to the glass in front of me put an end to my patience. Defying the dispatcher's injunction, I shifted into drive and crept forward. I'd made it almost all the way to the main road before a slow-moving police cruiser appeared, lights off, siren mute, stopping to discharge a fleshy patrolman who commenced a waddling, gunslinger's walk in our direction. In less time than it takes to fry an egg, he diagnosed our situation as a garden-variety domestic dispute and told us to go home and work it out.

"You both seem calm enough now," he concluded.

Nataki was still sitting on the roof.

"You're going to have blood on your hands," I called out as the cop swaggered back to his vehicle. He spun around.

"What was that?" he said, showing his teeth.

"Never mind," I said.

Nataki suffered her next psychotic break a few days later. Again I dialed 9-1-1. Another man in blue showed up and told us to work it out. This time, though, I was able to convince Nataki to accompany me to the local psychiatric hospital for an evaluation. A nurse there immediately saw what the cops had missed and took her into protective custody.

When the same nurse asked her to hand over her medication, Nataki fumbled inside her purse and produced a bottle of pain pills with another woman's name on the label. After a baffled moment, it hit me: some slacker at the pharmacy had given Nataki the wrong prescription, a nearly fatal fuckup. And I realized something else: that the hurt I'd heard in Nataki's voice when she defended herself against my accusation that she had stopped taking her medicine was authentic. It wasn't her fault.

Loathe to see Nataki hospitalized unnecessarily, I convinced the nurse to rescind the involuntary hold and let her return home with me. But it was too late. Nataki's downward spiral had already gained more momentum than could be stalled by the usual dose of her proper medication, and so it continued.

I knew the crash was coming when Nataki came home from a trip to the sporting goods store with an aluminum baseball bat and a pellet gun. My blood ran cold as she displayed her new purchases with artificial breeziness and a rehearsed story about needing a healthy outlet for her frustrations. Certain that one or both of these instruments would be used on my person if I did not act decisively to prevent it, I urged Nataki to return them immediately, making up my own excuse about not being able to afford silly impulse buys with the new mortgage and all. Braced for an explosion, I felt every muscle in my body relax when Nataki backed down with no resistance beyond a bit of you're-no-fun chiding.

As soon as she had left the house I called Lorene, Nataki's mom, to let her know what was up.

"What do you want me to do?" she asked.

"Well, there's not a lot you can do," I said. "When she gets home I'm going to talk to her about seeing the doctor. If she calls you, just tell her you think it's a good idea."

On returning, Nataki shot down my proposal with the haughty disdain of an empress asked to wash dishes. Having more or less expected this reaction, I pressed on, asking Nataki whether she would at least consider talking to her mom about it. Darkly delighted by this suggestion, she snatched up her phone as though she were about to settle a bet. I withdrew to the kitchen to fix myself an unneeded snack, out of sight but within earshot. Continuing to speak in the tone of insulted royalty, Nataki explained to her mother that I thought she was "flipping out" and should be "locked up." When she fell silent I knew Lorene was carrying out my request, and I practically held my breath.

Nataki appeared suddenly from the hallway, cocked an arm back, and flung her cell phone against a wall, shattering it.

"So, you're working together!" she shouted.

"Nataki, calm down, please!" I said, dropping my toast and jam.

She rushed at me, arms windmilling. I tried to ward her off with a side kick to the stomach but it came up short. Nataki responded with a kick of her own, landing a square hit on the outside of my recovering right knee. A cry of pain escaped me as the joint buckled, drawing a triumphant laugh from Nataki.

Knowing my life might depend on it, I forced myself to stay upright, putting all my weight on my left foot, and slammed my wife's chest with both palms. Still unbalanced from her successful strike, she staggered backward into a sectional that marked the boundary between the kitchen and the family room and tumbled over it.

While Nataki struggled to figure out which way was up, I hopped toward the front door, my right leg folded like a broken wing. Aware that our neighbors Katie and Wes never locked their own front door, I bounded in their direction, saying a silent prayer of thanks as the latch gave under the pressure of my thumb.

"Is anybody home?" I called out.

No answer. I locked the door behind me, pulled my cell phone out of my pocket, and dialed 9-1-1. Again.

I was standing in Wes's office, surveilling the street through open French shutters, when a police cruiser pulled up to the curb. Two doors opened and two cops emerged, one sauntering unhurriedly toward the front door of the house I occupied while the other took his time approaching the home I'd flown. I hopped outside and met the first cop on the front porch. He had the bulging forearms of a serious weightlifter.

"Did you call 9-1-1?" he asked, flipping a wad of gum from one side of his mouth to the other.

"Yes," I answered, distracted by a mirror image of our tableau to my left: the second cop questioning Nataki.

"Wait here," said my cop after I'd given him my side of the story.

He strutted back to the sidewalk and conferred with his partner. Minutes later, the officers gestured both of us forward. Standing side by side like siblings forced to apologize after a spat, Nataki and I traded sidelong looks of resentment.

"Sounds like you two can work this out," said the first cop.

"What!" I exclaimed. "You're kidding me! Can't you see this woman needs help? You've got to take her to the hospital!"

"I haven't seen enough to warrant that," he said. "She could go voluntarily, but I can't force her."

"What about him?" Nataki argued. "He's the crazy one!"

"He could go in voluntarily too," the second cop replied, taking her seriously.

"Actually, that sounds like a good idea," I said, changing my tone. "What do you say, Kitty?"

I looked Nataki straight in the eye, hoping to disguise my true intent, which was to get her once again in front of someone more competent to judge her mental state.

"I'm not going unless you go," she said.

A crushing weight of pity fell on me. Somewhere behind those hard eyes was a scared young woman who knew she needed help.

"I'm going," I said.

"Okay, then, if you two need anything else from us, just give me a call," said the first cop, handing me a business card as though he were a contractor who'd just given a pair of besotted newlyweds an estimate on a bathroom renovation.

Nataki and I rode in silence to the hospital. We knew the way blindfolded. A receptionist passed me two clipboards with attached pens and paperwork through a slit in bulletproof glass, and I handed one to Nataki. We sat in nonadjacent chairs to fill out our forms.

Ignoring requests for my name, address, and insurance information, I scrawled the following message across the page: "My wife has bipolar disorder with a history of violence. She attacked me unprovoked this afternoon. The police were called, but they refused to declare her 5150. She agreed to come here on the condition that I be evaluated as well. She needs help."

Nataki did not come home with me.

The following evening, I returned to the hospital for visiting hours, where I found Nataki sitting in the common room with a motley assortment of her fellow patients, all paying scant attention to a droning television tuned to a game show. Expecting the dopey and docile Nataki I had seen in the early days of her first hospitalization (and her second), I was confronted instead by the same truculent spouse who had practiced karate on my right knee the day before.

"What are they doing with your medication?" I asked, slipping this question between less pointed ones to avoid getting her guard up.

"They have me on ten," she said.

"Ten milligrams? That's it?"

"I'm not taking fifteen. It jacks me up."

I closed my eyes in dismay. A psychiatrist I was not, but I knew from hard experience that nothing short of the maximum allowable dose of Nataki's current medication—thirty milligrams—would suffice to stabilize her. On my way out of the building I stopped by the nurse's station.

"Which doctor is treating Nataki Fitzgerald?" I asked a balding gentleman whose surviving hair was tied into a long, graying ponytail.

"That would be Dr. Reyes," he said. "Teresa Reyes."

"Is she here? May I speak with her?"

"She's not here," he said guardedly, catching the agitation in my voice. "If you'd like I can have her call you tomorrow."

"Please do."

In the morning I tried to write but managed only to sit inert at my desk, staring emptily at my computer keyboard, incapable of forming an idea coherent enough to type out. At length I abandoned the effort and slunk upstairs, where I flopped onto the bed and lay for hours, curled into a fetal position with my eyes open, trying to decide whether to call Sean or Josh or my parents for emotional succor or drive to that guns and ammo store in Modesto whose billboard I passed all the time and purchase a firearm suitable for self-slaughter. But I knew from past experience that a call to my family would only spread the unhappiness, and though oblivion's attraction was strong, there still remained a mustard seed of hope inside me. So I did nothing. Around two o'clock in the afternoon the home phone rang, the screen identifying the call as coming from the hospital.

"Hello?" I croaked, realizing this was the first word I had spoken all day.

"Is this Mr. Fitzgerald?" asked a female voice.

I said it was.

"Hi, this is Dr. Reyes," the woman said. "I'm here with your wife, Nataki. We've been talking about releasing her from the hospital, and before we do that I want to hear your thoughts about how she's doing."

I was speechless.

"Are you there?" asked the doctor.

"Terrible!" I sputtered. "She hasn't improved at all. She's not even close to being ready to come home."

"Well, by our standards there's really no justification to extend her seventy-two-hour hold," Dr. Reyes rejoined. "Nataki is eating and grooming normally and she does not seem to be a threat to herself."

"She was eating and taking baths before she even got there!" I said. "And she's *never* been a threat to herself. She's a threat to *me!*"

"If there's ever an emergency, you can always call 9-1-1," she said, adopting a tone of high-handed tolerance.

"Oh, not that again!" I fumed. "Do you have any clue how much suffering comes before each one of those calls?"

The question was rhetorical, and Dr. Reyes did not answer it.

"Listen," I said, forcing myself to calm down. "You're wasting an opportunity here. I know that being in a psychiatric hospital sucks, and I want Nataki out of there as soon as she's ready. That's why you should be doing whatever it takes to stabilize her. But you've barely changed her treatment at all."

"We did increase her dosage from five to ten milligrams," said Dr. Reyes, "and I recommended fifteen, but there was an issue with compliance, and my job is to serve the patient."

"So you literally let the lunatics run the asylum?" I spat.

"There will be a release hearing tomorrow," Dr. Reyes said evenly. "Your opinion will be presented, along with the hospital's recommendation."

Having received no phone call from Nataki or the hospital by midafternoon the next day, I drove there for normal visiting hours. At the reception desk I was informed that Nataki had indeed been released. Aware that her purse sat on a barstool at home, I felt my stomach drop. Dr. Reyes had allowed an unstable and disoriented woman to walk out the door without money or identification because she swallowed her food and used soap.

On a hunch, I drove back toward the house by an alternate route—the route I would have taken if I were attempting the eight-mile walk. About halfway home I spotted a forsaken-looking female figure shambling along the edge of the road, a busy two-lane country highway that lacked sidewalks and shoulders, rumbling pickups passing within inches of her defenseless body every ten or twelve seconds. Sorrow and rage seized my heart at opposite ends and stretched it like a medieval torture victim. I turned on the hazard lights, stopped the car, and reached over to open the passenger door.

"Get in," I said.

As I had foreseen, Nataki's struggles picked up right where they'd left off at the time of her squandered confinement. A few days after she came home, she threw on a ball gown and a tiara and promenaded up and down the block with Queenie, who was just a puppy then, waving at houses like a county fair princess on a parade float. A couple of nights later, frustrated by insomnia, Nataki got out of bed in the middle of the night, tiptoed downstairs, and blasted gospel music on our seven-hundred-watt home theater system (which included ceiling speakers located right underneath our bed), waking me as violently as if she had whacked me over the head with a pillow, which she in fact did the very next night. The following week, Nataki drove Glamour Puss—the brand-new Mercedes-Benz CLK350 convertible I had gifted her for Christmas, after months of saving and years of scheming to procure her dream car—seventy miles per hour in a forty-five zone, on the wrong side of the same country highway I'd rescued her on after her premature hospital release, while I sat in the passenger seat, gritting my teeth and trying my best to appear unfazed.

Then came the day I found Nataki in the kitchen tearing up some of her Christian books and trying to set fire to them.

"Kitty, you need to stop that," I said, chasing her around the island like an ineffectual parent attempting to corral a refractory three-year-old. "Give me the lighter."

She quickened her pace and continued applying flame to paper. Rather than persist in the absurd chase, I halted.

"I think you might need to go back to the hospital," I said, hastening the inevitable.

Nataki's face curdled. She dropped the ruined volume and the lighter onto the countertop and strode swiftly to the knife block.

This time she selected a six-inch vegetable chopper, which she raised overhead while moving toward me, her eyes opaque.

"Please, Nataki, don't," I said, more resigned than afraid, raising my palms protectively.

"I'm sick of your mind games," she said. "If you want to leave me, just leave me! You don't have to lock me up and pump me full of drugs."

"Put the knife down," I said firmly.

Nataki pursed her lips and drove the knife downward in the direction of my left eyeball. I delivered a forearm shiver to her wrist, halting the knife's progress with the point of the blade less than a foot away from turning me into a cyclops. Undeterred, Nataki seized my throat with her left hand and clenched. Instinctively, I did the same to her. As we stood there suffocating each other, Nataki cocked her right arm and again plunged the knife at my face. This time I caught her wrist with my left hand.

"I think you *want* me to kill you!" Nataki hissed.

She squeezed my throat with renewed force and pressed her knife arm against my hand with shocking strength. My elbow buckled and the blade sliced through the hair at my temple. Momentarily stunned by the close shave, I was unprepared for the sudden shove to the neck that followed. I stumbled backward into our sectional and began to topple, just as Nataki had done during our last brawl. Tightening my hold on her own neck as I fell, I pulled her down with me. We landed upside down in a tangle, our heads against the carpet, feet in the air.

When my vision refocused, I saw the knife lying on the carpet an inch from my chin. Then it moved. Nataki still had it. Acting on raw, animal reflex, I plowed a fist into Nataki's cheek.

"Argh!" she cried.

"Drop the knife!" I screamed.

"I will, if you get off of me!"

"Drop it!" I repeated.

She did not. I hit her again, harder, dazing her, and scrambled to my feet. Stocking-footed, I sprinted to the front door and out, made two quick rights, and blundered my way inside Wes and Katie's never-locked house.

This time it wasn't empty. I found Wes seated on a sofa in the TV room in back, surrounded by four children between the ages of four and six—two of them his own, two from other houses on the block.

"Call 9-1-1!" I shouted. "Nataki just attacked me with a knife!"

"Holy shit!" Wes said.

The children's faces took on excited expressions and they ran to the front of the house for a glimpse of the perpetrator.

"I see a black lady running!" shouted the eldest girl, gleefully, as though she had just seen a miniature sleigh drawn by eight tiny reindeer swooping over the rooftop of the house across the street. "And she has *two* knives!"

Anything seemed possible at this point—but *two* knives?

I peered out the same window the kids were gathered before but saw no one. Wes tapped my elbow and handed me his cell phone, having gotten a dispatcher on the line. I described the situation and hung up to await the cavalry. Only then did I notice that my left hand was throbbing from its encounters with Nataki's cheek.

I hustled the kids away from the window and kept a lookout for my rescuers. After what seemed an eternity, a pair of police cruisers rounded the corner up the street with screeching tires, gunned their engines down the homestretch, and skidded to a stop in front of the two adjacent houses, lights flashing. Four cops spilled out like paratroopers plunging into battle. Three of them drew guns and ran to the front door of Nataki's and my house. Wild with panic, I burst out onto Wes and Katie's porch and screamed.

"For God's sake, don't shoot her!"

Just then Nataki emerged calmly and the guns were holstered. At the same time the fourth officer, a burly Latino guy, strode toward me. Wes had come outside to stand at my side. Behind us, the kids watched jubilantly from the doorway.

"Does anyone here live in the house next door?" the Latino cop asked.

"I do," I said, raising a hand.

"Why don't you have a seat in the car while we sort out what happened?" he said. It was a demand, not a question.

Wes shot me an alarmed look. I shrugged and followed the policeman to his car, where he opened a rear door for me like a valet and shut it firmly behind me.

I twisted around in the backseat and watched as all four cops crowded around Nataki in the driveway, listening to her version of events. Turning forward again, I discovered that several clusters of neighbors had gathered on their front porches to gawk.

After fifteen or twenty minutes, the officer who had detained me walked back to Wes's house and sat down with him. An ambulance arrived, and Nataki was gently escorted inside the emergency vehicle by a pair of cops. A paramedic applied a bag of ice to her head.

The door nearest to me opened and I found myself looking at what appeared to be a fifteen-year-old boy wearing a borrowed uniform as a Halloween costume.

"Okay, I'm going to take your statement," he said. "But first I'm going to explain your rights. You have the right to remain silent. Uh . . ."

"You have the right to an attorney," I coached.

The young deputy picked it up from there and finished the script flawlessly. Knowing already that I would spend the night in jail, I offered my recollection of the scuffle with apathetic terseness. The rookie seemed interested only in knowing how many times I had struck Nataki and whether I had done so with an open hand or a closed fist. Satisfied, he shut the door and conferred with the other badge-wearers before returning to me.

"You're under arrest for misdemeanor domestic assault," he said. "We're going to take you to the station and write up a report. Then you'll be transferred to Stanislaus County Jail for processing."

An unconscious smile of contempt twisted my lips. The Latino officer, peeping in through another window, caught it and spoke.

"I know it probably doesn't seem fair to you, but there's a certain way we have to do stuff," he said. "The most important thing is to separate you two until you've had a chance to cool off. Your wife is going to Oakland to stay with her mother for a few days."

Rookie asked me to turn away from him and clasp my hands together behind my back. I did so, wincing at the bite of the manacles against my bony wrists. My captor then installed himself in the driver's seat and we made the short trip to the station in downtown Oakdale, where I was placed alone in a high-ceilinged, all-white room with a small square of glass in the door that was almost indistinguishable from a racquetball court. Shivering in my shorts and T-shirt, I paced around the perimeter in my socks to stay warm as I awaited whatever came next.

During my 839th lap (or thereabout), Rookie returned, cuffed me again, and led me back to his car. As soon as we had cleared the town outskirts and passed into farmland, he hit the gas and sent the car hurtling toward Modesto at speeds that would have earned a mere citizen a reckless driving citation, taking his right hand off the wheel to pop open a can of Mountain Dew, from which he drank in huge, adolescent gulps. All four windows were cracked, allowing chilly night air to rush in, raising gooseflesh on my exposed forearms. The radio came on. Appearing to recognize a song he liked, Rookie turned it up loud. It was one of those angst-rock anthems with slashing guitars backing a reedy-voiced singer. The lyrics caught my attention:

How could this happen to me? I've made my
mistakes Got nowhere to run The night goes on
as I'm fading away I'm sick of this life I just
want to scream How could this happen to me?

We arrived at what looked like the rear entrance to a hastily constructed military compound. Rookie frog-marched me inside and through a labyrinth of narrow, low-ceilinged hallways and small offices filled with dim fluorescent light and stale air. At last I was deposited in a chair facing a rickety metal desk behind which sat a bald-headed black man who, reading from a screening form, asked me a long list of questions about my health and medical history. We hit a snag when I gave an affirmative answer to the question of whether I had ever considered suicide.

"Recently?" he asked.

I nodded, earning myself a visit to a nurse for follow-up questioning. She asked me why I wanted to end it all.

"My wife is bipolar," I said. "It's a nightmare. She can't control herself. I'm not safe with her. But if I left her, I couldn't live with myself, knowing she was out there alone, suffering . . . "

"You feel trapped," she said.

Tears sprang to my eyes, and I dropped my head in embarrassment.

From the nurse's desk I was taken to a holding cell to await booking. Its only other occupant was a venerable doll-sized man in grimy clothes who spoke no English. I went straight to the pay phone and called a bail bondswoman chosen randomly from a list on the wall. Then I called our neighbors Eugene and Edith, a Ghanaian couple with whom Nataki and I had become close over the preceding year. It was Edith—who happened to have passed the California Bar Exam three weeks earlier—who answered. She took down the number of the bondswoman I had spoken to already and agreed to spot me $500.

"Matt, I'm so sorry," she said.

When I hung up the receiver, I turned around to find the holding cell carpeted with snoring men collectively reeking of tequila. It had turned into a busy night—an unfortunate development, as it would hold up my booking.

Having no alternative, I joined the others on the foul cement floor and rested my forehead on my knees. Hours passed. Around three o'clock in the morning, the door creaked open, and we were joined by a middle-aged cat daddy with a crafty smile and a felt hat perched rakishly on a corner of his head. Awake the entire

night, I'd overheard a booking clerk interviewing him earlier outside the cell.

"Sexual preference: male, female, or both?" she asked.

I had been asked the same question.

"I'll take male," he said slyly, as though ordering a decadent
confection off a dessert menu. I laughed despite myself.

Dawn was breaking when I walked out the jail's Twelfth Street
exit, where I found a shiny new BMW, presumably paid for by
criminals like me, waiting at the curb. I climbed into the back and
was driven three blocks to a small office in which a drowsy Edith
greeted me in the unsmiling way people do at funerals.

"Thanks, Edith," I said wearily as we settled into her car.

She put a finger to her lips. Following her eyes, I saw her two
young daughters dozing in the back seat. Their slack, innocent
faces made me suddenly conscious of my own exhaustion. I felt as
though I could sleep for a week, or maybe forever.

"I can't even imagine what you're going through," Edith said
softly as she drove.

Considering these words, I was struck by the unexpected re-
alization that the desperate hopelessness I felt right then was not
entirely unfamiliar in my own experience. Indeed, I had felt something very much like it in marathons and other races, specifically
in those moments when I knew I was not going to make it to the
finish line, having suffered too much to face the suffering ahead—
those moments that came just before the moment I gave up. I kept
these reflections to myself, however, wary of trivializing my current
situation by comparing it to a mere sporting event. How could
Edith possibly understand that, to me, these self-sought athletic
crises seemed truly life or death, that finishing was as important
as living, quitting as unthinkable as dying, even as I chose to quit?

Edith let me out in front of the house and waited until I'd
succeeded in climbing through an unlocked ground-floor window
(I was keyless yet again, as well as shoeless) before driving off. I
tiptoed upstairs and checked the bed to confirm that Nataki had
gone to Lorene's house in Oakland. No sign of Queenie, either.

My next stop was a linen cabinet located at the top of the staircase, from which I extracted a couple of old blankets. I carried them back to the ground floor, grabbed my keys off their hook, and entered the garage. I placed one blanket at the base of the door leading to the backyard and the other underneath the door I'd just come through. Satisfied that I'd created an airtight seal, I got inside the Meep Meep, started the engine, and opened all the windows.

Almost immediately the air turned thick with the noxious stench of exhaust fumes. Not knowing what to expect, I turned my attention inward, waiting for internal symptoms to manifest. And waited. And waited.

Just when I was beginning to wonder if I was somehow immune to the toxic effects of carbon monoxide, I became aware of a heightened visual acuity, my eyes zooming in on the tiniest details of my surroundings, the orange-peel texture of the steering wheel pulling me in like a hypnotist's voice. My brain began to throb. Time lost all meaning. I didn't know if a minute or an hour had passed since I'd twisted the key in the ignition switch. The throbbing became a tingling, the painful kind you feel when your arm falls asleep. My sight went muddy around the edges. I sensed my entire consciousness—sight, thought, everything—contracting toward a point.

An image appeared in my mind's eye. I saw an emaciated Nataki dressed in rags, her hair a ratty bird's nest, shuffling along a garbage-strewn urban street, hollering garbled invective at revolted pedestrians giving her a wide berth. I understood that this was the future—an almost inevitable future in our society for a woman with serious mental illness whose husband lacks the courage or endurance to save her from such a fate.

I felt a beckoning—a silent, urgent summons, weirdly similar to a long-ago summons I had never forgiven myself for refusing. This time, however, it was not a high school track official calling but life itself, drawing me back to face a test I dreaded, a test I doubted my ability to bear, but a test I had chosen, however indirectly, and one that a better man would face despite his dread.

My right hand shot out, as if by its own initiative, and cut the engine. My left hand fumbled for and found the door release. I tumbled out of the car and onto the cool concrete, got to my feet, and staggered blindly toward safety, breath held. Shouldering through the door, I lost consciousness and sprawled onto the tiled kitchen floor, where I lay with my lungs heaving, as they were so used to doing.

CHAPTER 12

ME TIME

(Glass City Marathon)

THREE DAYS BEFORE the Glass City Marathon, at half past one on a raw afternoon that felt more like the twelfth of March than the twentieth of April, I steered the Fun Mobile into the University of Scranton's Ridge Row parking lot, where I had arranged to meet a Facebook friend for an easy run to loosen up my legs ahead of race number six in Nataki's and my eight-week expedition.

At least I hoped it was the Ridge Row parking lot. Only time would tell, for the location lacked identifying signage and I had arrived thirty minutes early, so all I could do was hang around and see whether John showed up.

I cut the engine and studied our surroundings more closely. They were the very image of rust-belt decline. The parking lot itself was surfaced in sooty gravel and abutted a corroded set of railroad tracks. Across the tracks, behind a sagging chain-link fence, stood a pair of toilets, portable in name only, and behind these a set of tennis courts that looked more likely to host narcotics transactions than doubles matches. The road we'd come in on was not a road at all but a narrow, potholed alley, on the far side of which stood a derelict warehouse. A low ceiling of smoky clouds completed the setting's gray theme. Cold drizzle misted our windshield. Queenie whined in the backseat.

"This is a strange place to meet for a run," I said to Nataki.

Like most of my Facebook friends, John was not a person I had ever actually met. All I knew about him was that he liked to run and he lived in Scranton. Our impending meet-up had been orchestrated a few weeks earlier, when John, having seen my announcement of the Life Is a Marathon Project on Facebook, messaged me with an invitation to run with him if my travels should happen to include an east-west crossing of Pennsylvania on Interstate 84. Before accepting the overture, I scrolled through our few prior interactions, all of them initiated by John, each of them peculiar in some way. Take, for example, this exchange from December of the previous year:

> JOHN: merry Christmas brother
> ME: Same to you, my man
> JOHN: ty. love you too

The phrase *odd little duck*, a designation my mother applied to the likably eccentric when I was growing up, came to mind. I was curious to know what running did for a guy like John, and now here I was.

While Nataki and I waited for two o'clock to roll around, I reviewed the directions John had given me. They included the line, "It is near the opposite side of the railroad tracks." Only now did I recognize how vague this guidance was, each side of a railway being by definition opposite the other.

After twenty minutes or so, a little white Toyota pulled into the lot across the tracks from where we sat and parked near the toilets. The occupant was, like John, a middle-age male, and he appeared from my vantage to be executing a change of footwear before emerging fully from his compact sedan—a very runner-like thing to do.

"That's him!" I blurted.

I scrambled out of the car and strode toward the gentleman. I waved. He waved back—a little uncertainly, it seemed.

"Are you John?" I asked when his face was no longer obscured by metal, glass, and distance.

"No," he said. "I'm here to play tennis."

I returned to the Fun Mobile. Two o'clock came and went. Quite certain now that I was in the wrong place, I started the engine and drove farther along the crumbling alley, soon coming upon a second parking area. Remembering that I had described my vehicle to John, I circled the lot several times, hopeful that if he was present he would flag me down. Nobody did.

Phoning him was not an option. John hadn't given me a number, and I had a hunch it was because he had no number to give. So I sent him a Facebook message apprising him of my location. Several minutes passed before I received his reply.

JOHN: I was just there. where are you now?
ME: Ridge Row lot.
JOHN: pull out of lot over tracks, head behind buildings.
   i have green compression socks on. be there in 10
   minutes

Lot over tracks? Buildings? From what I'd seen, there were *two* parking lots that could be described as sitting "over" the railroad tracks. And there were buildings all around us—I had no clue which ones he meant.

"I'm starting to think this guy's an idiot," I said.

"Maybe he's just having a bad day," Nataki suggested.

My wife does not believe in idiots. In early grade school she was briefly placed in a special education class, where a plurality had Down syndrome, as the result of her performance in standardized testing. She was later diagnosed with a learning disability. Today she can quote more scripture (in King James English) than a lot of preachers, and if there's a more morally perspicacious person on this earth, I haven't met her.

"You're probably right," I said.

I started the car again and drove around randomly in search of a physical reality that corresponded to John's description. Nothing did. Or rather, *everything* did to some degree. I became exasperated. Several important items on my day's to-do list remained unchecked, not the least of which was going for a run.

ME: Directions are unclear. I'm doing a lot of guessing here.

Receiving no immediate response to this unsubtle expression of peeve, I drove back to my original parking spot, near which a transit coach with an Irish theme sat idling, and messaged John again.

ME: I'm near the Leprechaun bus. Find me.

Time passed.

ME: Leaving in five.

More time passed. I now began to suspect that John didn't even have a phone—that he was messaging me from a computer in some nearby building between attempts to find me, and that he was completely unable to communicate electronically during these sorties.

Exhaling theatrically, I pressed the ignition button once more, threw the transmission into reverse, and kicked the accelerator. A wake of gravel spewed out in front of the car as we shot backward. According to the car's navigation system, our hotel in Wilkes-Barre was twenty-five minutes away. I figured I could cut it to nineteen.

Speeding out of town on a poorly maintained street barely wide enough for two vehicles to pass, I was forced to slow down by an oncoming car driven by an anxious-looking middle-age man whom, I realized with a jolt, I had seen earlier, going the other way, when we were parked.

"That's him!" I said, certain this time.

I made an illegal U-turn and sped after the car, flashing my lights. After half a mile of pursuit—long past the point where the driver must have noticed me—the car pulled over and I rolled up next to it. Nataki dropped her window.

"Excuse me," she said at my prompting. "Are you John?"

The man responded with an almost imperceptible shake of the head, evidently assuming we had it in for this John character.

Just then, a new message arrived from the real John. Then another. And another.

> where are you?
> are you still near the bus?
> hello?
> you still want to run?
> you here?

Unable to answer while driving, I returned to our original parking spot yet again and addressed the last of John's questions.

ME: Have been.
JOHN: by bus?
ME: It's leaving.
JOHN: The bus?
ME: Yes.
JOHN: i guess no run then?
ME: I'm not on the bus!
JOHN: ok I will be there in 10 minutes. Hang tough.
ME: Dude, how hard can this be?
JOHN: it is not. be there shortly.

Precisely ten minutes later, I saw a figure with neon-green shanks hurrying toward the Fun Mobile from the direction of the second parking lot. I got out and began to shed my sweat suit.

"Kind of a strange meeting place," I said pointedly as John and I shook hands.

John himself appeared neither upset, as I was, nor stressed out, as I also was, nor embarrassed, as I felt he should have been, but only a bit nervous, his eyes darting back and forth between my unsmiling face and Nataki's shadowy silhouette inside the car.

"That's okay," he said. "Don't worry about it."

Wait. *What?* I wasn't apologizing—I was fishing for an apology!

I had just opened my mouth to give John a piece of my mind when it struck me that I'd had a little trouble understanding what he said. His speech, I noticed on a two-second delay, was very slightly imprecise, not unlike that of a deaf person who wasn't born deaf. My anger vanished instantly, vaporized by shame. John was neither an idiot nor having a bad day; he was just different, an odd little duck indeed, who deserved a little more forbearance than I'd been inclined to afford him.

"What do you want to do?" John asked, his words again a bit woolly around the edges.

It was now almost three o'clock. Our plan had been to run for an hour and then go out for a meal, John's treat. But the post-run items on my to-do list (checking in to our hotel, walking and feeding Queenie, writing a blog post) were heavy on my mind. I told John I'd run with him for half an hour and take a rain check on dinner.

"We'll go this way, then," John said, pointing back in the direction he'd come from.

We set off together and bumbled our way into conversation, John doing most of the talking while I concentrated on his every syllable. Within a mile I knew that John had spent his entire life in Scranton, as had most of his surviving family members. Now fifty-three, he started running in the seventh grade and never stopped, except briefly in the early 2000s when he battled and beat basal cell carcinoma.

"Are you married?" I asked.

"Not yet," John replied in the same hopeful tone a recent college graduate might have used.

As we shuffled through the university campus and into downtown Scranton, John played tour guide, pointing out landmarks ("That's the bookstore; I can help you get your books in there if you want"), stopping frequently at intersections (John did not like to jaywalk). Every third or fourth person we met greeted him warmly.

"Do you know all these people?" I asked.

"I know everyone in this town," John said proudly. "And everyone knows me."

Our dialogue turned inevitably to the subject of running. John informed me that he had run seven marathons and thirteen half marathons. I noticed that numbers anchored nearly every story he told me about himself. Three months and six days was how long it had taken John to get his first job, at a local restaurant, after he graduated from high school. Two thousand seven hundred and fifty miles was how far he had ridden his bicycle in 2016.

"What do you like about running?" I asked as we turned right onto Vine Street and back toward our starting point.

"Running is good for the mind," he said. "It helps me overcome fears."

I did not have to wait long to learn what sorts of fears John strove to overcome. In 1999, he told me, after twenty-one years in the restaurant business, he'd decided to pursue higher education—at Scranton, naturally. Eleven years later, at the age of forty-seven, he received a bachelor's degree in communications. It hadn't been easy. He had to give a presentation once in front of 153 classmates. The prospect of speaking before so many people, all of them less than half his age, terrified John, but with a compassionate teacher's help he faced his fear of judgment and earned an A.

In what seemed the blink of an eye, we were approaching the Ridge Row parking lot, or whatever the fuck it was, and the end of our time together. Conscious of this, John spoke a kind of summation.

"I can tell you one thing," he said. "God has you on the right path."

"I'm glad you think so," I said. "How about you? Has God put you on the right path?"

"Mmm," John said evasively, as though I'd asked him to rate an inedible goulash I'd cooked for him. "Kind of."

"What would you change?" I asked.

John mulled it over.

"Nothing, I guess," he said. "I just have to keep going."

We came to the Fun Mobile and stopped.

"Well, that should be just about thirty minutes," John said.

I looked at my watch. We'd run for twenty-three minutes. I checked John's wrists: No watch.

I opened both left-side doors so John could say farewell to Nataki and Queenie.

"Come back when you can spend more time," he said. I detected a hint of disappointment in his voice, and was tempted to reverse my decision on dinner, but I didn't.

"I like that guy," Nataki said as we drove off.

"Me too," I said.

You learn a lot about what compatibility really means when you're married to someone as different from you as Nataki is from me. Shared race isn't compatibility. Nor is shared culture, shared hobbies, shared religion, or even shared personality traits. But in my experience, liking the same people definitely *is* a part of true compatibility.

At the hotel that evening I received another Facebook message from John:

> thanks again for the run. Appreciate it. it was nice meeting the mrs and queenie

I thanked John in return and then, on a whim, I visited his Facebook page, where I scrolled through his posts in an effort to further satisfy my curiosity about the man. I was struck by the number of posts that were self-defining in some way. Many were little billboards borrowed from a certain website that seemed to exist for the specific purpose of helping people express their identity online. It presented users with all kinds of personal questions ("Which one word describes your life?" . . . "What's the brutally honest truth about you?") that invited introspection. If a question was selected, the site then analyzed the user's Facebook page to generate a personalized answer in the form of a mini poster, which could be posted directly onto Facebook. John had done this many, many times. Among his most recent posts was one that answered the question, "Which five letters describe you?" They were "L" for loyal, "O" for open-hearted, "V" for valiant, "E" for enthusiastic, and "R" for romantic, and they spelled "LOVER."

The problem for people who stand out from the crowd is that the crowd tries to define them. John had probably dealt with a lot of this when he was younger and had learned to seize control of defining who he was, not just through Facebook but also, surely, through running. The activity of running puts people alone with themselves in a way almost nothing else does. It clears away the distractions of everyday life and, according to neuroscience, induces a mental state—characterized by heightened activity in the brain's so-called default network—that is conducive to free thinking, reflection, and self-discovery. And when runners test their limits in marathons and similar events, their consciousness is further simplified, the mind's stage emptied of all characters save the will to continue and the urge to quit. In negotiating this internal conflict, each individual runner discovers *why* he wants to quit and what motivates or enables him to keep going, excavating parts of his being that lie hidden in most other contexts. You might say running is the ultimate "me time."

The ancient Greek temple at Delphi commanded, "Know thyself." Everyone agrees this is sound advice, not only because learning about oneself is inherently satisfying but also because knowledge is power, and thus the better you know yourself, the more control you have over your life. But how does one come to know oneself? Run a marathon or two.

....

We arrived in Toledo Friday afternoon. The next morning, after breakfast, I drove to the University of Toledo's Savage Hall, the school's main indoor sports arena, to pick up my Glass City Marathon race packet. Having fulfilled this mission, I returned to the lobby of the building, where I met Lisa, another complete stranger I'd connected with online. She greeted me with a Sharpie and a well-worn copy of one of my books. Not immune to flattery, I felt well disposed toward Lisa as I tried to come up with a clever inscription. Failing in this effort, I went with *best wishes.*

Lisa had offered to give me a running tour of parts of the marathon route in exchange for a cup of coffee. We took a photo together, and then she led me outside and onto a smooth, tree-shaded bike path that matched my vision of the perfect marathon course. It didn't hurt that the weather, too, was ideal for running: sunny and cool without a breath of wind. Tomorrow couldn't come soon enough.

Lisa explained where we were in relation to the start and finish lines and listed several highlights of the Glass City Marathon experience, which included a mannequin dressed up in a Santa costume that a guy who lived along the route trotted out every year, a charming duck pond I would encounter around mile nineteen, and Glass City Glory, a beer brewed especially for the event, served in the finish area, that was christened by Lisa herself through a naming contest.

"How long have you been running?" I asked her.

"I started running in 2009," she said. "Growing up, I didn't do any sports or exercise, and I hated running. I had to run a timed mile in school and it was hell. When I got married, I started going to the gym with my husband, Alan, not for myself, really, but because he did. But when Alan started getting more into running, I gave it another try and found that I enjoyed it."

"What do you enjoy about it?" I asked.

"It's a very rare day that I come back from a run feeling worse than when I started. I tend to lose my focus and interest in doing other workouts. I come up with a lot of other things I should be doing when trying to follow a workout video, but I can run for hours, which a lot of non-runners think would be boring."

"I feel kind of sorry for people who think running is boring," I said. "To me it means they can't stand being alone with themselves. Hurts your knees? Fine, I get that. But boring? That's tragic."

"Running clears my mind, and a lot of times it also helps me solve problems," Lisa said. "When I run before work in the morning, it gives me a feeling of calmness and a confidence that I can solve all the challenges the day will bring."

Through running Lisa not only experienced healthy time alone but also discovered a whole new dimension of herself, a physicality that had been latent inside her to that point. As her body became stronger, she was amazed time and time again by what it could do: run for two hours straight, three hours, four.

When she was forty-three, Lisa signed up for a marathon. The prospect of completing the required training, let alone the event itself, overwhelmed her. But her second marathon caused her no such anxiety. Meanwhile, parts of Lisa's everyday life that had overwhelmed her previously—stressful days at the office, drama at home—bothered her less. Little by little, Lisa at Her Best was becoming Lisa All the Time.

Three miles into our short shakeout, we paused our watches and popped inside a Starbucks, where I ordered a vanilla latte and Lisa asked for something called a double chocolate bold. Forty-nine years old then and the mother of three, Lisa appeared not to have an ounce of flab on her body despite indulging in the occasional four-hundred-calorie beverage. We found an open table and sat.

"What have you learned about yourself through running?" I asked.

Lisa's mind went back to her toughest moment as a runner, which occurred in the 2012 Columbus Marathon, her first attempt to qualify for Boston (something she later succeeded in doing). At twenty-four miles, losing steam, she realized her goal was out of reach, and her suffering therefore pointless, and she became angry—at herself. *What the fuck is wrong with you?* an inner voice demanded. *Why the fuck can't you do this?* To a mind reader, these thoughts might have seemed symptomatic of low self-esteem, but in fact they were a manifestation of the very opposite: high personal standards—an expectation of greatness stemming from a newfound self-belief that Lisa did not even know she lacked until she became a runner.

At the twenty-five-mile mark, Alan, having finished the same race and come back to help his wife, fell in beside her and began to offer encouragement, but Lisa silenced him with a raised palm.

"I don't want to talk," she said.

Lisa knew instinctively that no voice other than her own (salty as it was) could talk her to the finish line in less than four hours—her new goal. She loved Alan as much as she loved anyone on earth, but even his supportive words couldn't help her—in fact, they could only hurt. It was up to Lisa at Her Best, the Lisa that running itself had birthed and nurtured, to make the most of a bad situation. On crossing the finish line (her time: 3:59:34), she crumpled into Alan's arms, sobbing.

"I've learned that I'm stronger than I thought," she said to me.

....

On the evening before the race, Nataki's aunt Margie and uncle Nate drove up from their home in Youngstown to dine with us. Having been informed that they were big fish eaters, I got us a table at the Rose & Thistle, a well-reviewed seafood place a few miles from the hotel where Nataki and I were staying. Midway through the meal, the conversation split along gender lines, Nate quizzing me about my running, which fascinated him ("Fifty miles? That's, like, from Youngstown to Akron!") and the women talking about who-knows-what until a sudden shift in the vibe on the yin side of the booth drew Nate's and my attention to our wives.

"Don't you believe God can heal?" Margie was asking Nataki.

"I do," Nataki answered. "But what do you do when God *doesn't* heal? A couple of years ago I had a lump on my breast. I prayed and God healed it. Before that, I had a node on my vocal cord. I prayed and God healed it. But I had fibroids for seven years, and even though I prayed and prayed, I had to have surgery. It's the same with my mind. I don't know why, but God never healed it."

"And are you okay with that?" Margie asked doubtfully.

"You know what?" Nataki said. "I am okay now. I am."

"It just sounds like you're giving up," Margie persisted.

"I thought so too for a long time," Nataki said. "But even in the Bible God didn't always heal everybody. Remember Paul? Paul asked him three times to remove a thorn from his side. But God left it in, because it had a purpose. *I'm* like that. Going through everything I've gone through has brought me into my purpose. I had anger issues I needed to work on. This disease *made me* work on them. It's brought me closer to my family, closer to my husband. I've always wanted to help people. I do that better now. You can't help nobody if you ain't been through nothing yourself."

I never said that *only* by running marathons can we become our best selves.

....

By this point in our journey, my race-day routine was rote, something I was able to do (and did) three-quarters asleep, and the morning of the Glass City Marathon was no exception. Rising at four thirty, I dressed in the previous day's clothes and took Queenie outside to relieve herself while the coffee maker heated water for my instant oatmeal. After a trip to the bathroom, I stripped down and put on my racing attire, number bib already pinned to the singlet. I then organized my nutrition: energy gels, cherry juice, caffeine pills, and water.

Next came technology. I burrowed a hand inside the zippered compartment of my backpack where I kept all my gadgetry, fishing out an ancient iPod and earbuds. But after studying the small silver square and the coiled wire for a few seconds I put them back where I'd found them. Not today.

A second search of the same pocket produced a true essential: my GPS watch. I began to strap it on my wrist, but again some irresistible impulse said no. The watch too went back in its pocket.

At the race site, still operating under the same spell, I avoided contact with my fellow runners, hiding out in the Fun Mobile until it was time to warm up and then warming up on a relatively unpeopled side street before entering the corrals at the last possible moment. Perhaps it was my natural introversion reasserting itself after five weeks spent going out of my way to make meaningful contact with my fellow marathoners. Or perhaps it was the influence of my recent interactions with John and Lisa, two runners who had reminded me of the value of running's interior journey. Whatever the season, I just wanted to be left alone with my private thoughts, free of distractions both electronic and human, in this particular marathon.

"Hey, are you Matt?"

Of the 1,069 people participating in today's race, I knew exactly one (and again only through Facebook), and I had unwittingly positioned myself right next to him. Having never met Brian face to face, I would not have recognized the Georgia-based ultrarunner and triathlete, but he recognized me. He held a sign identifying him as the leader of the 3:20 pace group and wore a thermal hat that I eyed covetously through the cold vapor of my exhaled breath as we shook hands. We had a short conversation that petered out when Brian, noting my terse answers to his questions and my total failure to ask him anything in return, got the message that I did not wish to talk, something he probably attributed to competitive focus, though in fact competition was far from my thoughts on this morning.

The race began. Despite my warm-up, I felt stiff and creaky during the initial eastward rumble down Bancroft Street, each heel-ground collision as unpleasant as kicking a frozen football shoeless. Hemmed in by other runners, I could not help but over-hear the conversations taking place around me ("Oh God, I have to pee already" . . . "I *told* you to try and go one more time") as my eyes roamed among the well-bundled spectators standing curbside, squinting into the herd in search of friends and family. I wished they would all go away.

Two miles in, I passed by a pair of women holding signs that delivered a joke in two parts, setup and punch line, like the old Burma Shave billboards:

ALTERNATIVE FACT   ⟶   THIS IS THE LAST MILE.

I could have screamed. My goal was to escape reality, and here it was chasing me!

Despite this unwelcome encroachment of politics on running's safe space, my body soon began to loosen up, and as the rhythmic scissoring of my legs and the counterbalancing swing of my arms became more fluid, my pace gently quickened. I must have passed a hundred runners in the fourth mile, which took us through moneyed neighborhoods to the west of campus. Small clusters of well-nourished white people, many wrapped in bathrobes, stood at the feet of long driveways clutching steaming mugs. Seeing them made me conscious of the time of day, and I wondered what Nataki was doing at that moment.

It was precisely then that my mind divorced itself from the external. One moment my attention was wholly absorbed in my physical context, the next moment I was on autopilot, focused 100 percent internally, no more conscious of the shift that had just occurred than one is conscious of falling asleep.

The thought of Nataki drew my mind back to the previous night. Things had taken an odd turn when our foursome returned

to the hotel from the restaurant and Nataki, in reply to a leading question from Nate, invited him and Margie up to our room.
Mindful of my early wake-up, I silently cursed this unexpected
prolongation of the evening, but our guests had driven two and
a half hours to see us, so I could hardly object. Inside the room,
though, I went straight about my normal race-eve regimen of
stretching and pinning my number bib to my singlet and taking a
sleeping pill as though Nataki and I were alone, leaving her to do
the entertaining.

At nine o'clock, having nothing left to do but go to bed, I went
to bed. Alas, I am not the kind of person who can fall asleep while
others converse within spitting distance of the bed I'm lying in,
even with pharmaceutical assistance. Thus, instead of drifting off
into dreamland, I followed the conversation involuntarily in a state
of mounting resentment. Nataki *knew* I had to get up early and
run a marathon the next morning. She *knew* I was already sleep
deprived and fighting a cold I'd picked up in Connecticut. Nate
and Marge were *her* family, not mine. If she had any consideration
for me, she would kick them out—politely, of course. Instead, *she*
was the one doing most of the talking.

I considered my options. The most obvious course of action
was to take charge and kick them out myself. I let this scenario
play out in my head and saw that it would expose me as an asshole, so I rejected it.

Alternatively, I could take the passive-aggressive route, booking
a separate room in the same hotel and removing myself to it. This
option appealed to me for the wounding effect it would have on
Nataki's conscience, but even with my reason half paralyzed by
pique I recognized the irrationality of following through on the
idea.

The only other solution I could think of was to rise from bed
and pretend to rejoin the discussion with the true intention of
feeding Nataki a private signal. But I knew this scheme wouldn't
work either, having tried it often in the past without success,

Nataki either missing my signal or choosing to ignore it without fail. When my wife wanted to talk, she would talk.

As absorbed as I was in the *fact* of Nataki's relentless yakking, I paid little attention to the actual content of her speech until I ran out of ideas to save myself from my plight and decided to wait for tomorrow to let Nataki know how much she had put me out. Only then did I realize that what she was talking about was us.

I'd heard the story—a favorite of hers, which she tended to share when she was feeling good about our relationship—many times. In the spring of 2002, Nataki and I moved into an upscale apartment community in the Mission Valley area of San Diego—the very home in which, two years later, she would suffer her first psychotic break. Agreeing that our improved living situation deserved better furnishings, we woke up early on our first Saturday at the new address and drove north to the furniture district in San Marcos to search for a couch set. By late afternoon I'd had enough; my blood sugar was dropping, I'd exceeded my four-hour tolerance for shopping of any kind, and I wanted to go home. Nataki begged me to let her try just one more store, and in it she discovered a massive French rococo–style sofa, a monstrosity of chenille and tassels with matching armchair, that she fell in love with. I told her it was the ugliest thing I'd seen all day and I wouldn't be caught dead with it in my home. Nataki's feelings were hurt and the day ended badly.

That same night, the living room pieces Nataki loved and I loathed appeared to me in a dream, and I saw them with new eyes. In the morning, I remembered the dream, and, for whatever reason, I still loved the furniture I had previously loathed, so I told Nataki about my nocturnal change in taste, and we bought the set. I'd seldom seen her so happy.

Nataki treasures this episode as evidence of God's operation in our relationship, proof that he wants us to succeed and will intervene when necessary to ensure that we do. I see in the same incident a chastening reminder of the power I possess to make Nataki happy and of how often I fail to exercise it.

As Nataki finished telling the story, I realized I had an opportunity to make her happy—or at least to avoid making her unhappy—right then. All I had to do was quit worrying about my precious sleep and allow her to enjoy this time with her aunt and uncle. I could count on one hand the things we had done on our trip to this point (a two-day visit with her dad in Oklahoma City, dinner at a Michelin-starred restaurant with Dori in Somerville . . .) because *she* wanted to do them. Far more often she had found herself alone in hotel rooms while I was off doing marathons and signing books and interviewing runners, a neglect she had accepted without complaint. On this night Nataki needed to talk to her family more than I needed to rest, and only a true asshole would have denied her such a simple joy merely because it inconvenienced him slightly.

Two things happened in the wake of this attitude adjustment. First, my obsessive concern about sleep simply vanished. Then Nate, who had been mostly silent since entering our room, cleared his throat and said, "Well, I think we ought to be heading home now."

A crashing sound to my right interrupted my reverie. I looked toward the ruckus and saw a deer dashing through the woods. A minute later, I passed a sign marking the nine-mile point of the marathon. *Nine miles?* I had no recollection of seeing the signs for five, six, seven, and eight miles.

The deer disappeared into the trees and my attention turned inward again. I went back to the moment in the hotel room the previous night when my perspective had shifted, when a better part of me had shone a light on my instinctive selfishness and made the right choice. Moments like this were happening more and more often lately. Drip by drip, the state of calm self-trust that I had first experienced in running was seeping into my everyday life. Slowly but surely, The Person I Want to Be was becoming . . . me.

A large pack of runners appeared in the distance ahead. One of them held a pace-group sign, and I wondered whether he was Brian. When I got closer, however, I discovered that I had caught not the 3:20 pace group but the 3:10. Had I sped up that much?

I overtook the group just beyond the eighteen-mile mark. In less than an hour I'd be done. The sun was shining, the road friendly, my energy boundless. Never before had I wanted a marathon to last longer than it would, but I did now.

Alone again, I relapsed into trance, recalling the many conversations I've had with Nataki over the years on the topic of self-love. I have always insisted to her, truthfully, that I do not love myself. Nataki has consistently countered that no man who does not love himself would take such great care of himself. I have repeatedly rejoined that there's a difference between loving yourself and loving your life, and that, whereas I do love *being* me, I don't love *me*.

"How can you love anyone else if you don't love yourself?" Nataki says, invariably, at this point in the discussion.

"Why do people always say that?" I say. "It makes no logical sense!"

In my experience, nothing could be easier than loving others without loving oneself. What I have a much harder time understanding is how *anyone* loves himself or herself. We know too much! We think evil thoughts of others. We secretly smear boogers on chair bottoms. What's to love?

Nataki takes it as axiomatic as well that a person cannot be happy in the absence of self-love, but I don't think this is true either. I don't even *want* to love myself; it seems in poor taste. But there's a difference between not loving yourself, which isn't necessarily a problem, and not respecting yourself, which most certainly is a problem, for the simple reason that self-respect, unlike self-love, is conditional. You have to earn it by living up to your personal standards.

On May 21, 1988, on a soccer pitch in Hanover, New Hampshire, I failed to live up to my personal standards in a big way, and I lost respect for myself. Only when I returned to running years later was I forced to confront my cowardice head-on and begin to work seriously at becoming a man I could respect. But at the same time that it gave me courage, running, in the context of my relationship with Nataki, exposed and perhaps even exacerbated a second flaw in my character: an almost solipsistic self-absorption. It was for the sake of my running, after all, that I was tempted to ruin Nataki's family time the night before. But had not running also given me the self-awareness and personal agency that had enabled me to avoid behaving like an asshole? Was running the problem or the solution? Yes.

In any case, as I crossed the finish line of the Glass City Marathon—noting but indifferent to the clock (3:03:22)—it struck me that, for the first time in my adult life, I sort of liked myself.

CHAPTER 13

MONKEYS ON MY BACK

IN JANUARY 2008, after eight years of self-employment, I accepted an offer to go to work for Competitor Group, a newly formed endurance sports media and events conglomerate based in San Diego. I confess that I did so not because I wanted the job but because life at home with Nataki had been so intense for so long that I regarded the prospect of spending eight hours a day trapped alone inside a cubicle as a kind of freedom. Having tried and failed to kill myself (and having no intention of trying again), I leapt at this less-absolute means of escape, renting out the house in Oakdale and moving with Nataki back to America's Finest City.

They say you can't outrun your problems, and we certainly didn't. One morning not long after we took up residence in a swanky new midrise in Little Italy, Nataki told me she'd felt something come out of her head during the night.

"I think God healed me," she said.

Here we go, I thought. Sure enough, convinced that this time would be different, Nataki went off her medication. Five weeks later, I received a call at work from the manager of our building, who informed me that Nataki had deliberately pulled a fire alarm for no reason and been taken to a psychiatric hospital by first responders.

Nataki was compliant with doctor's orders thereafter, but to little effect. Her disease seemed to have its own rhythm, an emotional ebb and flow that was as unalterable as the tide and that the drugs could not stop but could only contain—and only to a point.

To escape the notoriety we had acquired in the swanky midrise, Nataki and I moved to a condominium located nearer Competitor's Mira Mesa headquarters on the heels of her release from her fourth hospitalization. There Nataki began to complain of mysterious bite marks on her forearms, marks I could not see. I knew then that another crisis was coming, and it came soon, on a spring-like afternoon in the middle of March. I was seated in the oversize upholstered chair that had come with our prized chenille sofa, reading Jhumpa Lahiri's latest, when a shadow fell on me, and I looked up to find Nataki looming over me, looking displeased. As she commenced to charge me with practicing witchcraft on her, I became acutely conscious of how the chair's cozy wraparound design sort of entraps its occupant. I suggested to Nataki that she take one of her antianxiety pills. She leapt on top of me and throttled me with both hands. I freed myself with no small difficulty and bolted for the door, shoeless as always.

I was down the stairs and halfway across the parking lot before I noticed that Queenie was scampering at my feet, smiling happily, thinking daddy was playing. Still running, I pulled my cell phone out of my pocket and thumbed a too-familiar three-digit number. I was crouching behind a hedge near the front gate when Nataki came roaring by behind the wheel of Glamour Puss. I ducked even lower as she screeched out onto the main road without so much as pausing to look for crossing traffic.

The cops arrived. I gave them a description of Nataki's car, and they put out an all-points bulletin. Not until the authorities left did I recognize the quandary I was in: sock-footed, keyless, *sans* wallet, and almost certainly locked out of my home. I led Queenie back to the apartment and tried the door. Nataki had indeed locked it, whether out of responsibility or spite I couldn't guess. Night had fallen, and the temperature was dropping. The property's management office had closed for the day, and there was nobody I could call for help. Since moving back to San Diego I had been singularly antisocial, keeping my coworkers and training buddies at arm's length, reticent to expose others to the nightmare we were living.

There was a lounge in the resident community center that stayed open until ten o'clock. I went there and lay down on a sofa with Queenie and buried us under oversize pillows for warmth. At ten sharp, a baby-faced security officer in a rumpled uniform entered. Seeing me, he froze, his eyes crossing in an effort to classify the situation I presented. With as few words as possible, I explained my fix and asked him to let me stay where I was until the morning. He said he could not and then, very kindly, he kicked me out into the dark.

I had one last idea. Using words in lieu of a leash, I walked Queenie back toward the apartment and waded through a thick layer of groundcover that carpeted the space between the back of our building and the one next to it. Our apartment was on the second floor. It had a small balcony with an iron balustrade that we accessed through a sliding glass door, which was usually kept unlocked. When I reached the apartment beneath ours, I climbed on top of a three-foot plaster wall enclosing its porch. Reaching up, I was just able to grip the base of a rail in each hand.

Now what? If not for the balustrade, my strategy would have been to pull myself aloft by the arms and then swing a leg up to gain purchase on the floor of the balcony with my shin. Lacking this option, I would have to somehow get over the railing with no help from my lower extremities.

I took a deep breath and looked down. Queenie sat directly below, almost completely swallowed up in vegetation, watching me with worried eyes, aware now that this was no game. I squeezed the rails and hauled my body upward, the edge of the balcony digging into my forearms as my elbows flexed. When my head reached the level of my hands, I let go of the rail with my left hand and slammed the back of my upper arm down on the balcony floor between rails, transferring some of the load to other muscles.

The final step would decide everything. If it succeeded, I would at least get a chance to find out if the sliding door was open. If it failed, I would fall ten feet onto my back and squash my dog.

Putting all my weight on my left triceps, I let go of the rail with my right hand and shot the arm overhead. The very tips of my fingers found the top rail, gripping it fiercely. When I had a decent hold, I dangled briefly from my right hand before launching its mate up to join it. Quivering with fatigue, I then performed a second chin-up, got an elbow over the top rail, and dragged the rest of my body over, inch by inch. I dropped like a jellyfish onto the hard floor of the balcony, were I lay supine, heart thumping, until I was sufficiently recovered to get up and see about the door. It was unlocked.

Meanwhile Nataki was driving through the night (so much for the APB) to Tayna's place up north in Antioch, where the two sisters had attended high school and Tayna had since returned to work as a bus driver. I reached Nataki there by phone in the morning. She asked me to box up some of her clothes and other necessaries and ship them to her.

"When are you coming back?" I asked.

"Why do you care?" she said. "You'll be happier without me. You can hike and bike and jump all day. I won't get in your way no more."

I protested, but the truth of the matter was that a piece of me—a rather large piece—rejoiced at the prospect of time apart from Nataki. The past six years of shared struggle felt as if they had aged me sixty years. And the thought of exercising all day appealed to me very much. I had been mostly injury-free in the past year and was racing well as a result. But I was about to turn thirty-eight, and I felt a sense of urgency. If there was ever a time to commit fully to the pursuit of the race I believed was in me but hadn't yet come out of me, it was now.

That phone call—the first of dozens in what would become a nine-month separation—ended with my hanging up on Nataki. I now had the power to silence her recriminations, and I didn't mind using it. The next day's call didn't go much better. But, over the next several weeks, Nataki began to sound more and more like herself, a trend that was helped along by the attentions of a new psychiatrist—a rare African American woman in the field—who had an office not far from Tayna's place. Yet even as our communications improved, we remained in no hurry to reconnect. We both needed a break.

Where I had hoped to find relief, however, I found only emptiness. The thing I always forgot in my fantasies of escape was that Nataki and I were still a beautiful match on our good days, and we had experienced many good days in the half-dozen years since she'd gotten sick, enjoying the soul-feeding perks of any healthy long-term romance: an easy intimacy, a quirky private language, and a vast repertoire of inside jokes. A hand placed gently on the other's cheek in bed at night meant "Roll over, you're snoring"—no need to speak the actual words. A small scratching motion made with hooked fingers, accompanied by an openmouthed, almost-silent feline hiss, expressed mild annoyance, a playful gesture that usually succeeded in dispelling the very emotion it communicated. Nataki named my one and only dance move, a goofy two-step I adapted to everything from slow jams to head bangers, The Person. I teased her about her many malapropisms (*gracamole*, *Pissbird*, *flamingo dancers*). Nataki's sudden absence from my life served as a painful reminder that she was more than worth all the travail. Alone, I sank into a pathetic bachelorhood, dining on unhealthy prepared meals purchased from the neighborhood supermarket, drinking a six-pack of strong beer every night, and sometimes making it through an entire weekend without uttering a single word to another human being face-to-face.

Less than a month after Nataki left, I flew east to take a second whack at my first Boston Marathon. Having finally surpassed my friend Bernie's marathon time the previous fall, I now had my sights set on my friend T.J.'s best mark of 2:38:18. In February, I set a new personal record in the half marathon, notching a time that, according to the various online calculators, indicated this new goal was well within my reach.

Marathons are run on the road, however, not on calculators. They do not reward potential but demand execution—and, let's face it, a little luck. In Boston my luck ran out the moment the starting pistol cracked, when the runner behind me clipped my left heel with his toe, taking the shoe clean off. Judging it unwise to run 26.2 miles with one shoe, I stopped and bent over to fix the "flat tire," making a target of my butt for the thousands of runners bearing down on me. Knocked around like a piñata at a keg party, I was forced in the end to step off the road to reshoe.

Things went south from there. Thigh pain is inescapable in the Boston Marathon, as in any marathon that features a lot of downhill running, but I felt the first twinge at twelve miles—way too early. By sixteen miles, where my family (Mom and Dad, Josh and his wife, Jennifer, and good old Dori) stood huddling in a bone-chilling wind, I was already slowing, bitterly resigned to another disaster. Spotting me, my brother bolted from the sidelines for a quick check-in. Although he was running little himself at the time, Josh had enough running experience to know by the grim set of my features and the stiffness of my gait that I was coming apart.

"How's it going?" he asked anyway.

"Terrible," I said.

"Why? What happened?"

"Why?" I snapped. "Because I suck at running marathons!"

I considered quitting then and there, but, impelled by a combination of pride and self-spite, I chose instead to embrace the full catastrophe. Through the hills of Newton and into Boston proper my will engaged in a hopeless stare-down with my suffering, the pain in my legs intensifying steadily until, at twenty-three miles, I resorted to the familiar soft-quit of walking. Head down, I wished myself invisible to the thousands of hollering Bostonians on either side of me as I hobbled along Commonwealth Avenue wrapped against a cold drizzle in a flimsy space blanket I'd grabbed at an aid station.

After thirty minutes of this purgatory, I came to Cleveland Circle, the very spot where, twenty-six years before, I had become a runner, breaking from the curb with my brothers to pilot our father to the finish line. Having learned from past meltdowns that I can *always* jog the last mile, I looked for an appropriate place to toss away my heat sheet, making accidental eye contact with a posse of beer-swilling college guys attired in Red Sox merchandise—backward-worn cap on one, fleece hoodie on another, game jersey on a third. They appeared to be having the time of their lives, belching and laughing and picking out individual runners to support with half-mocking encouragement. Now it was my turn in the spotlight.

"Come on, Number 1233!" they bellowed. "Run! You can do it!"

With a rueful shake of the head, knowing how this was going to look, I cast aside the metallic cape and began to trot. The college guys went berserk, roaring and high-fiving as rapturously as they might have done if the Sox won the World Series with a two-out walk-off grand-slam homer. I laughed in spite of myself and went on to finish the marathon in a time I could have beaten wearing hiking boots on any other day.

....

I returned to California with a sore left heel and a monkey on my back. The sore heel made it inadvisable for me to rush to remove the monkey, but I did so anyway, starting the Orange County Marathon just thirteen days after Boston. I say "started" because I didn't finish. Within ten miles, my foot issue had become a full-blown case of plantar fasciitis. Lucky for me, the racecourse passed by my hotel at the halfway point, where the yummy brunch smell that emanated from the building when I got there sealed my decision to bail out.

This latest athletic fiasco not only compounded my monkey problem but also set back my early preparations for Ironman

Arizona, which was six months away and was itself an attempt to rid myself of a monkey I had acquired in my first Ironman, where I missed out on a World Championship qualifying slot by twenty-three seconds after suffering through a tragicomic series of setbacks beginning with a calf muscle cramp that stopped me dead in the water *two minutes* into the ten-hour race. The whole point of the second act of my life as an endurance athlete was to avenge the first, but it seemed that each attempt I made to redeem past failures gave me something new to deliver myself from, like one of those kitchen disasters where you keep adding extra ingredients to save a bad dish and only make it worse.

Having done no swimming or cycling in the lead-up to Boston, I threw myself into these activities and took a break from running to let my injured heel recuperate. After two weeks, however, the foot was still painful to walk on. Desperate to resume running before I lost any more fitness, I tried jogging on a treadmill set at an incline. This measure yielded the desired effect of taking pressure off my heel—and the undesired effect of transferring that pressure to my Achilles tendon, which developed a small but debilitating tear that throbbed even as I lay in bed at night.

Ordered by a sports medicine specialist to extend my break from running at least four more weeks, I doubled down on cycling, riding six days a week, one hundred miles every Saturday. The result was that I got really good at riding a bike. By midsummer my regular training partners simply couldn't keep up with me, nor could the many strangers who challenged me out on the roads, young men (always) who flew into a panic when I overtook them and scrambled to return the favor. I tortured these young men for sport, slowly cranking up the heat of my tempo until they boiled alive like the frogs in that old fable.

In the second week of August, I got a rare chance to ride with an athlete who was my match and more on a bicycle: Eneko Llanos, a thirty-three-year-old pro triathlete from Spain who had taken second place in the previous year's Ironman World Championship.

It was to be a five-and-a-half-hour rolling interview for a profile of Eneko that I was penning for *Triathlete*, which Competitor Group now owned.

We met early on a Technicolor Sunday morning at Nytro, a triathlon store located in the beachside city of Encinitas. From there we cruised northward along the Pacific Coast Highway, sunshine dancing on the gray-blue chop of the Pacific Ocean to our left. At Oceanside, we cut east on a bike path that at length dumped us onto Mission Avenue, near the salon where Nataki once worked. We then pressed farther inland until we hit Old Highway 395 and turned north, making it all the way to Escondido before at last reversing course.

Eneko had requested a flat route, but it is almost impossible to ride for five and a half hours in San Diego County without encountering a few serious hills. And so it was that, at sixty-seven miles, we hit a real quad-buster, a ramp-like slope ascending for 2.5 miles at a gradient of 6 to 7 percent. A few minutes into the climb, my companion fell silent. With sidelong glances I noted additional signs of exertional discomfort: hunched posture, clenched fingers, a fixedly downcast head position. After several more minutes, Eneko spoke.

"Is that where we turn?" he asked, gesturing toward a flat intersecting road branching off to the right.

"Yes," I said.

"Good," he said.

My chest swelled with pride. I would have killed for a witness. *Did you hear that? I just made the reigning Ironman runner-up suffer on a hill climb!* With a single word, Eneko had released in me a feeling of achievement that surpassed anything I had experienced in an actual race. But wait—wasn't this rather pathetic? Taking a mental step back, I saw my pride for what it was: empty vanity. Eneko's nod to my cycling chops was fool's gold, attractive but lacking real value. Ego strokes from elite athletes were not the rewards I sought and never had been. Beating my friends' race times, achieving coveted qualifying standards—these were no more than signposts toward the true goal. Only now that I had attained such a reward did I see how little they meant if they came easily, leaving me the same person I was before.

As Eneko and I made that right turn, it struck me that what I really wanted was *to conquer hard*. I wanted a race experience that was as tough and as painful as any of my many failures but that, for once, did not end in failure. Only this would redeem my first and greatest failure—the one I had carried inside as an unhealed psychic wound since I was seventeen years old. In a dim way, I had perceived the deeper nature of the completion I sought from the very moment I decided, on that long flight home from St. Maarten with Nataki, to become an athlete again. But like an insect mistaking light for warmth, I had allowed myself to be distracted from the core mission by the bright, shiny objects of recognition and ranking, overlooking the basic fact that it was myself I needed to impress, that *doing* better in sport was not an end but a means to the end of *being* better as a man. I had no clue what my race of redemption would look like, but I knew for damn sure it hadn't happened yet and was confident I would know it for what it was when it did happen—if it ever did.

....

The perspective shift that occurred during my bike ride with Eneko Llanos was still setting in when my boss asked me to attend and report on the Interbike bicycle industry expo in Las Vegas in the third week of September. As chance would have it, this event coincided with Nataki's and my eighth wedding anniversary. Feeling the time had come for us to test our readiness for a return to marital normalcy, I proposed to Nataki that we meet up in Sin City to mark the occasion, and she agreed.

I found Nataki waiting for her suitcase at baggage carousel 2 at McCarron International Airport, having just arrived on a ninety-minute flight from Oakland. Whichever brain cell of mine stored the memory of my very first encounter with her outside

T.G.I. Friday's was set faintly aglow as we greeted each other after our longest separation since that moment.

"You're so skinny!" Nataki said.

"So are you!" I said, gratefully, my embarrassment annihilated by Nataki's typical lack thereof.

Ironman training had removed the last two or three pounds of expendable weight from my body. Jenny Craig (Tayna's idea), meanwhile, had stripped away the usual ten pounds of "medicine weight" Nataki had gained after her most recent mental health timeout, restoring her old modeling figure, or nearabout.

"I just got a text message from Teisha," Nataki said, looking at her phone. "She said her brother found tickets for $245."

Teisha, the woman responsible for that first encounter outside T.G.I. Friday's, now lived in Vegas, as did her younger brother, Tony. When Nataki told Teisha we were coming to town and mentioned that we were interested in seeing Floyd Mayweather's highly anticipated return to the boxing ring against Juan Manuel Márquez, Teisha tipped her that Tony, a man of connections, might be able to cadge a pair of seats at the MGM Grand for less than the four figures they were going for online.

"Is that $245 apiece?" I asked.

"I think so," Nataki said.

"Tell her we'll take them," I said.

Celebrating eight years of wedded bliss by watching two men chase each other around a cage was Nataki's idea, not mine. Boxing was the only sport that ever made any sense to her, and she'd been attracted to the spectacle of major title bouts since Mike Tyson's reign as heavyweight champ in the late 1980s. Such avidity for the "sweet science" of pugilism had always struck me as a funny inconsistency in a personality that was otherwise pacifistic in the extreme. (Nataki once expressed reluctance to purchase a Bullet brand blender on account of its name.) But every personality has its inconsistencies.

After collecting Nataki's suitcase, we picked up our rental car and drove to the nearest Wells Fargo, where I deposited $490 into

Tony's checking account before heading on to the Wynn, a place of happy memories for us. As we unpacked, I extracted Mr. Pajamas from my carry-on bag and propped him up against a bed pillow. It took a minute for Nataki to notice him, and when she did she stared so long I began to worry I'd made a mistake, but then she stepped forward into my arms, pressing her cheek to my shoulder. Eventually my hands began to wander.

"I'm on my you-know-what," Nataki said.

"Naturally," I said, deflated.

The scene at the MGM Grand was everything we'd hoped for and more, a caricature of our preconceived image. The crowd's predominant female type was bubble breasted, expensively coifed, minidressed, and stiletto heeled. Every third man we saw resembled some celebrity, and indeed many really were the person they looked like: Kid Rock, Tyrese, P. Diddy, Mike Tyson in the flesh. The fight seemed almost an afterthought, Mayweather winning easily in his usual unexciting, defensive style, disappointing the largely pro-Marquez crowd.

The following day, Nataki and I drove twenty miles north to visit Teisha in the apartment she shared with her nine-year-old daughter, Aryanna, and her five-month-old son, Torres. To my delight, Arilou (as everyone calls her) behaved as though it had been three days, not three years, since she'd last seen us. Entrusting a soft little hand to me, she guided me to the community fitness room so I could squeeze in a run (I was now running a bit) while her mom and my wife caught up, gabbling happily about life in the third grade and being a big sister.

Later we went out for Mexican food at a bustling family restaurant in the neighborhood. As we attacked a nacho appetizer, Nataki began to recount one of our favorite Arilou stories from a few years back, when we used to see each other more often. Teisha and her daughter were visiting our home in Oakdale, and it was lunchtime. Assuming Arilou was like other five-year-olds, Nataki started to make a sandwich for her, asking a series of questions about what she wanted on it.

"I'll never forget it," Teisha laughed, taking over. "Nataki, you came rushing out of the kitchen like you'd been booted, and you said to me, all serious, 'Arilou says she can make her own sandwich.'"

Arilou squealed with delight and buried her face in a throw pillow in feigned embarrassment.

"Do you remember that?" I asked.

"No!" she said.

"But it sounds like you, doesn't it?"

At that moment I wanted a daughter just like Arilou, and I said as much to Nataki as we drove back toward the Strip at dusk.

"Teisha is blessed," she said simply.

In the morning, the calendar having flipped to the 21st of September overnight, Nataki and I breakfasted in our hotel room.

"Happy anniversary," I said, raising a glass of orange juice.

Within an hour we were on our way to the airport, where Nataki would catch a flight back to Oakland while I transferred to a cheaper, employer-approved hotel and prepared for Interbike. On the way we discussed our immediate future, agreeing that a little more time apart wouldn't hurt. I'd get my Ironman out of the way, she'd continue working with her new doctor, and we'd effect a permanent reunion around the holidays, perhaps.

Then my phone rang. I saw my brother Josh's number and knew instantly what the call was about.

"What's the good word?" I said.

"Jennifer's at the hospital," he said. "It looks like this is it."

Josh and Jennifer's first child, Caleb, would be born before the sun set. I was overjoyed by the news, not only because my brother's happiness was my happiness but also because Jennifer had suffered through a difficult pregnancy. Lurking underneath my joy, however, was a seed of envy.

"Are you glad we never had children?" I asked Nataki after relaying the news.

My use of the word "never" was premature, in one sense, as Nataki was still only thirty-four years old. But not in the sense that mattered.

"Yes," Nataki said quickly. "Aren't you?"

"Well," I said, focusing my thoughts, "on the one hand I grant that it would have been dreadful for a child to have been caught up in all of this. But on the other hand, I think you would have been a wonderful mother. And everyone says we would have made beautiful children together. I always picture a girl."

Nataki's initial reason for not wanting kids, as expressed on our first date, was self-focused. Having seen what Tayna's body went through in pregnancy and childbirth, she wanted nothing to do with it. A lot had happened since then.

"But what if she came out like me?" Nataki asked, her voice thickening.

How many times can a man's heart break for a woman?

....

On October 10, six weeks before Ironman Arizona, I raced a half Ironman in the hills north of Santa Clarita. Aptly named Magic Mountain Man, the race featured a punishing bike course that packed 5,500 feet of climbing into fifty-six miles. It was my first triathlon in six years, and I could hardly contain my excitement. Though still hobbled somewhat by my left Achilles tendon, I felt my running legs beginning to come back, and I thirsted for the opportunity to do against real competition what I had been doing to the cyclists of San Diego County all summer.

The day before the race, I pulled my wetsuit out of storage, left Queenie with a dog sitter, and drove three hours north to the race site, arriving in plenty of time to tour the bike route. I laughed out loud as the Meep Meep strained its way up a seven-mile, 1,700-foot ascent that commenced (sadistically, it seemed, as though the race director rather than plate tectonics had put it there) straight out of the swim-bike transition area. After checking in to the host hotel and attending an athlete meeting, I grabbed dinner at a nearby Red Lobster, limiting my booze intake to two pints of Samuel Adams. I had my game face on.

Early the next morning, I ate a banana and a PowerBar and choked down a bottle of Boost before heading over to Castaic Lake, where predawn darkness and a fifty-one-degree chill created an atmosphere of foreboding. At the start line I positioned myself rather optimistically in the first row of racers. Moments before the starting horn sounded, I felt a tap on my shoulder. Spinning around, I saw an olive-skinned beauty smiling at me. I smiled in return, vaguely expecting some form of flattery.

"Do you want me to zip you up the rest of the way?" she asked.

It seemed the zipper of my wetsuit had gotten caught in the fabric of the triathlon racing suit I wore underneath. My smile dropped and my face warmed, as if Kim Kardashian had caught me with my fly open. My kindly helper fixed the snag and I shuddered away a second premonition of doom.

The start of the race was the usual liquid melee. I swallowed water, got kicked in the head, suffered a mild panic attack, and forgot all the technique cues I'd been practicing in the pool as the field of three hundred-plus funneled toward the first turn buoy. But things spread out eventually, and on the way back to shore I found myself quite alone. What's more, when I lifted my head for sighting I detected no splashing ahead, and it occurred to me then that I might actually be leading the race. I reached the shallows, stood up, and scampered toward the bike racks, and still not a single other racer was visible before me. It was true! I was in first place! Either that or—

"And now we're getting into the heart of the field," said the race announcer over a PA system.

Eleven other athletes were already on their bikes, minutes up the road. I had washed ashore at the front of a pack of guppies.

Prior to the race, I clipped my bike shoes into the pedals like the pros do. I had not actually rehearsed a barefoot bike mount in training, however, and I paid dearly for my lack of preparation at the transition exit, where amused spectators watched me struggle like a 1930s pratfall comic against the laws of bicycle physics (*Law #5: A pedal with an empty shoe attached will always come to rest shoe side down*), losing even more time to the stronger swimmers.

I felt a perverse sense of relief as I started the seven-mile climb. Like that weird kid in Mrs. Johnson's third-grade class who celebrated the cancellation of recess, enjoying what everyone else hated, I bounded merrily up the mountain, passing seven gasping competitors within the first few miles, each of them turning to me with a just-shoot-me expression as I whistled by. Near the top of the climb I reeled in an eighth cyclist, this one neither gasping nor wearing a just-shoot-me expression, his two-digit race number (12) indicating he was a pro. Seeing me appear on his left side, he accelerated violently, as though his very manhood depended on not letting me by. Wary of getting caught up in a pissing match with fifty miles of cycling left to do, I dropped back, waited for the inevitable sag in Number 12's tempo, then stood on the pedals and made a decisive pass.

My reward for summiting the mountain was a white-knuckled plunge down the other side at forty-five miles per hour. Number 12 managed fifty and was back ahead of me at the bottom. The course then turned onto a desolate stretch of highway leading to a turnaround point seven miles away. Two massive hills stood between me and that point, and I was delighted to have to climb them twice in each direction. Number 12 was not so delighted. I shook him off once and for all on the first of these climbs and shifted my focus to the road ahead, wondering how many other opponents remained in front of me.

This question was answered near the turnaround, where a pair of police motorcycles cruised by me, lights flashing. Tucked in behind them was the race leader, riding flat-backed on a gleaming white Look 576. Two more athletes—both also wearing two-digit pro numbers—came past before I reached the turnaround. I was in fourth place.

On the second lap, the frontrunner and I met each other again, somewhat farther from the turnaround, confirming that he was riding faster than me, but I'd gained ground on the other two. Finding plenty of strength left in my legs, I rode the final climb one gear higher than I had the previous time, hoping to claw my way into second place before I reached the run, where the goal was more modest: survival.

The bike leg concluded with a bobsled ride down the seven-mile hill I had climbed two hours before. As I coasted into the transition area, I withdrew my feet from the shoes and executed a respectable pro-style flying dismount. A volunteer directed me to the spot where my running gear awaited. Those first few strides on pre-fatigued legs are always shocking, but on this occasion I felt not only the usual wading-through-slop sensation but also a keen consciousness that my longest run in the past six months was 10 miles, or 3.1 miles less than I was now attempting after the hardest bike ride I had ever done.

"Pray for me!" I called out as I plodded past a knot of spectators standing just outside the transition area's fenced perimeter.

Although I hadn't checked out the run course, I knew from the prerace meeting that it was a simple out-and-back, mostly straight with a couple of turns, along an exposed bike path on the Santa Clara River. I chose a conservative pace, both out of consideration for my injury and my recent paucity of run training and because I felt large and bumbling, like the 206-pound me who sometimes jogged home from bars late at night in those early days in San Francisco. Over the next several miles, my discomforts multiplied, symptoms of dehydration, hyperthermia, and glycogen depletion joining my original complaints.

With less than three miles to go, old Number 12 caught and passed me, relegating me to fifth place. I hooked my eyes on his back and imagined him towing me to the finish line. We came to a bridge and began to tramp toward the far side, but halfway across my challenger suddenly stopped and wheeled around.

"I think we missed a turn," he said.

"We're okay," I said, stopping also. "Look, there's an arrow." I pointed at a chalk arrow on the sidewalk ahead.

"No, *this is an out-and-back*," Number 12 insisted, already beginning to retrace his steps.

I put my trust in the arrow and pressed forward, studying my surroundings, looking for specific features I had seen on the way out, finding none. And then I realized what Number 12 had meant. On an out-and-back course, as athletes near the front of the race, we should have been meeting lots of slower racers head-on. And indeed we had been—until we hadn't. I stopped a second time to consider my options.

Already I had run twelve miles, give or take, at the fastest pace I felt I could sustain for 13.1 miles. In technical terms, this left me about a mile away from being toast. If my wrong turn had occurred where I now suspected it had, my present location was approximately two-and-a-half miles from the finish line, a distance that would surely turn me to burnt toast if I attempted it now.

Squinting ahead in the direction I'd been going, I spied what appeared to be a cluster of chain stores and restaurants. I began to walk toward them, and after ten or twelve minutes I came to a Carl's Jr., inside which I encountered a teenage girl sweeping a rag across table tops while flirting in a mixture of English and Spanish with a pair of young male loiterers. Her nametag identified her as Sabrina.

"Excuse me," I said.

Sabrina eyed me warily, as she had every right to do. I wore a skintight racing suit that left little to the imagination and an ankle-strapped timing chip that looked a lot like those house-arrest devices.

"Is that your boyfriend over there?" I asked her, gesturing toward the boy to whom she'd been giving the most attention, who wore a Kobe Bryant jersey and knee-length shorts.

Sabrina followed my finger.

"Yeah?" she said, the rising tone of her answer flipping it around into a question of her own: *And what's it to you?*

"Tell him I'll give him fifty bucks if he drives me back to my hotel. I was doing a triathlon," I said, flipping my race number, "and I got lost. I'm too tired to walk."

Sabrina held a quick conference in Spanish with her boyfriend, who then approached.

"I'm Juan," he said, giving me his right hand. "Where do you need to go?"

For the first time I noticed the braces on his teeth. He was seventeen, eighteen at the most. I followed Juan outside to a tricked-out 2006 Ford Mustang with aftermarket rims and paint. During the short drive to the hotel we talked about triathlons and muscle cars, nothing in between.

"Wait here," I told him at the hotel entrance. "I'll bring the money down."

Something appeared to be wrong with my right knee, which refused to unbend as I struggled to climb out of the low-slung vehicle. I took a cautious first step and collapsed against the Mustang's open door, an eruption of pain causing the injured joint (injured when? how?) to buckle.

"You okay, man?" Juan said.

A week later, the knee still hurt so much that I couldn't even ride my bike in its lowest gear. Enough was enough. I withdrew from Ironman Arizona, the fourth Ironman I had signed up for and failed to start because of injury.

To keep fit while I couldn't cycle, I ran every day, despite the touch-and-go state of my left Achilles tendon. Each run, predictably, was a little more painful than the last, and after a week I had no choice but to stop.

To keep fit while I couldn't cycle or run, I swam every day. This worked out okay until the muscles around my right shoulder blade began to give me trouble. Having no other exercise options to fall back on, I continued to visit the pool each morning until I could no longer lift my right arm overhead, at which point I had no choice but to give up swimming (and weights).

For the next two weeks, I was completely unable to exercise, unless you count walking Queenie, which I don't. During this period, because my showers had always come after workouts, I frequently forgot to bathe.

CHAPTER 14

MIND, BODY, WORLD

(Jailbreak Marathon)

FROM THE FINISH line of the Glass City Marathon I went straight to the beer tent and downed a pint of Glass City Glory (delicious) before hustling back to the hotel to shower and change. By noon, Nataki and I were seated on either side of a plastic tablecloth at a barbecue joint in west Toledo. The location had been recommended to us by the third member of our party, Dean, a local guy who had run the marathon as well and whose choice of cuisine was mildly ironic, Dean having recently lost 144 pounds by eating less of the crap we were about to stuff our faces with. But he'd also done it by running, and that's what I wanted to hear about.

"The ribs here are excellent," Dean offered as he studied a laminated menu and I, taking advantage of his preoccupation, admired his ZZ Top beard and tattoo sleeves.

"I'm not a big ribs guy, actually," I said, "and Nataki doesn't eat pork."

"Yeah, I get it," Dean said, patting his tummy. "Well, if red meat's out, the catfish fingers are also a good option."

"I don't eat catfish, either," Nataki said. "It's unclean."

Dean gave her a puzzled look. Unclean? What sort of diet was this lady on?

We let him wonder, but the answer was the Leviticus diet, better known as eating kosher—something Nataki had done off and on for years, though her latest return to it showed signs of permanence. Nataki's past flirtations with other diets—Jenny Craig, vegetarianism, the blood type thing—never lasted long, but with the God-backed Leviticus diet she had more motivation.

I wasn't always supportive of the whole kosher business, worrying that in the case of a non-Orthodox Jew with bipolar disorder it was more symptom than solution, but experience had taught me better. Four days before we sat down to lunch with Dean, back in Wilkes-Barre, we ordered lamb gyros at a hole-in-the-wall Greek place and brought them to our hotel to feast on. Unwrapping her sandwich, Nataki discovered that, although the cook had left off the feta cheese as she'd requested, she'd forgotten to ask him to hold the tzatziki sauce, which is made from yogurt, and Hebrew law forbids the consumption of meat and dairy together. Hungry, tired, and perhaps also tempted, Nataki went ahead and ate the gyro. That same evening, she suffered a minor "episode" (just a bit of grousing about how her family didn't respect her—something she hadn't believed when she woke up that morning and would no longer believe when she woke up the next morning), her first of our entire trip. I'd promised then to do my best to help her avoid future lapses, and I meant it.

"Were you fat as a kid?" I asked Dean after we'd placed our orders.

"Not at all," he said. "I played sports growing up: soccer, basketball, baseball. It wasn't until I hit sixteen and started driving that things changed. Exercise and sports went away, and I started driving everywhere. Then I went to college for photojournalism and I just wasn't liking school. The whole four-year college thing wasn't for me. So I spent a lot of time in my dorm, eating and watching TV, and that's when my weight really started to increase."

"Were you depressed?" I asked.

"It was just boredom, really," Dean said. "I had stopped going to class. Eventually, I went back home. I worked in a grocery store, in the produce department, which is funny because, other than potatoes, I ate no veggies whatsoever. So my weight just kept slowly growing."

Even today, post–weight loss, I had difficulty picturing Dean wearing an apron and stacking apples.

"Eventually, I took a job at the local Harley-Davidson dealership," he continued, "and that's what I've been doing for the last sixteen years. I met my wife, Mandy, at that dealership. We got married and bought a house and we both liked hanging around in front of the TV."

"And all this time you weren't exercising at all?" I asked, digging into a half-kosher plate of beef brisket and catfish fingers.

"No working out, no exercise, no anything," Dean said. "I did some yo-yo dieting, as people call it. Before our wedding I did Atkins and lost thirty pounds and then my tux didn't fit. My fiancé did the same thing and her dress wasn't fitting quite right. So we quit the diet and started eating everything so we could fit in our clothes. It was sad."

Sad but also funny, and we all laughed.

"Anyway, we got married and got very comfortable and very lazy," Dean said. "That got me to my heaviest weight, which was three hundred and seventeen pounds."

"Yikes!" I said. "And you're not exactly tall."

"Five seven," Dean said. "Here's my before-and-after."

He pulled out his phone and showed Nataki and me side-by-side images of a really fat guy who did not resemble the man before us and a much skinnier guy who did. I stole a glance at Nataki, concerned that Dean's sharing might make her feel like a "before" photo, but once again I'd underestimated the scope of her goodwill. Far from thinking of herself, she inspected the evidence of Dean's happy transformation with obvious pleasure.

"So I guess you want to know how I got from here to there," Dean said, pointing at the two photos.

"You guessed right," I said.

"Well, I'm the typical biker, right?" Dean said. "I ride my motor-cycle, I eat terrible food, I don't exercise. So, about four and a half or five years ago, I went to the doctor for a routine checkup and he did my blood work and called me back and brought me in and said I was basically one foot away from the cliff of full-blown diabetes. He said, 'I'll give you two months to make some changes and then you're going on medication.'"

"How old were you?"

"Let's see, I'm thirty-eight now," Dean said, "which would have made me thirty-four at the time. So I did what most people would probably do in that situation: nothing. I continued with my normal routine. I thought, 'Nah! It doesn't matter.'"

"Then what?" I asked.

"A month went by," Dean said, "and I thought to myself, 'Well, I'll get a gym membership and give it a try.' I signed up at a YMCA and did the ellipticals and the treadmills and the bicycles and the weights and nothing really caught on for me. I'd be on an elliptical machine for five minutes and I'd want to get off."

"That's pretty normal," I assured him.

"Anyway," Dean said, "the way the gym was set up, there was a big glass window, and on the other side there were basketball courts and tennis courts and stuff. And there was a track around the outside of all that. I would see people walking and running on the track and I was like, 'I'll give that a try.'"

"Smart move," I said.

"I went there and started jogging," Dean went on. "It was nine laps to a mile. I got about two laps done and I felt like I couldn't breathe anymore. My lungs were burning. But you know what? I also felt like I had gotten a real workout. You know what I mean?"

"I think I do," I said. "You're saying it was uncomfortable and yet at the same time it was exactly what you were looking for."

"Yeah," Dean said. "I felt like I was actually getting something out of what I was doing. I wasn't a mouse stuck on a wheel. So I took the next day off and then I went back and tried to beat what

I did the first time, even by one step if that's all I could do. Over the next few weeks, I got to half a mile, then a mile, and then two, and then three, and at that point I figured, 'I can do a 5K.' So in April 2013 I did a 5K and then the next week I did another one."

"They're highly addictive," I said, pushing my plate away.

"The other thing I noticed," Dean said, "was that my weight was starting to drop. I hadn't really changed much in my diet yet; I'd just started moving."

Having started moving, Dean couldn't stop, his weekly mileage, race distances, and competitive ambitions all rising as his weight continued to fall. The marathon he had just completed was his second, and by far the slower of the two, but only because an injury had compromised his recent training.

"It's interesting," I said, wiping my fingers with the moist towelette that had come with my food. "You told me that you got fat because you were lazy and you wanted to be comfortable. But there's nothing comfortable or lazy about running a marathon. Are you even the same person?"

"With all the other things I tried," Dean said, "all the fad diets, I didn't care if I failed. This time, I care if I fail. I've come so far now. It's the same thing in a race. Like, today, I'm at mile twenty-five and my knee starts hurting. I could have just walked to the finish, but I wanted to stick it out. I'd told my physical therapist beforehand, 'I don't care if I have to crawl to the finish line. I'm finishing this damn race.' I had all kinds of excuses. I didn't care. I was going to finish."

....

Two nights later we were in Chicago, where I led a group run from a Fleet Feet store and then gave a short talk. While I spoke my eyes kept being drawn to a poster on the shop's back wall that bore the slogan "Running changes everything." I felt an almost irresistible urge to steal it. When the event wrapped up, I went out for pizza and beers with my old college buddies Tim and Dan, who lived in the city. I staggered into Nataki's and my hotel room at 1:00 A.M., and was woken by Queenie's tongue at 5:00 A.M. (I swear to God I could set my watch by her).

We had chosen our lodgings on the criteria of pet friendliness and cost, but they had the added virtue of standing at the south end of Lakeshore Drive. After breakfast, we took a family stroll on the waterfront. Nataki walked with her chin lifted, her eyes half closed, and the corners of her lips turned up as we made our slow way along a path thick with joggers, our faces warmed by pale sunlight and fanned by a soft breeze perfumed with a faint tang of marine vegetation. Envious of the joggers, I told Nataki I fancied a run of my own.

"If you like, you can come back out with Queenie and walk some more while I'm doing my thing," I said.

"That's okay," she said. "I think I'll have a nap instead."

Nataki had woken from a nine-hour sleep less than three hours ago. Ah, the medicated life.

"I won't be gone long," I said. "One hour, eight miles."

"I don't know where you get all that discipline," Nataki said.

"It's not discipline, as you well know," I said. "It's dependency."

Those eight miles were indeed drug-like, the pleasures of fresh air and sunshine somehow magnified by my exertion. On the current of these sensations, my thoughts drifted back to a book I'd read recently, titled *The Nature Fix: Why Nature Makes Us Happier, Healthier, and More Creative*. According to author Florence Williams, when people place themselves in pleasant natural environments, the brain slips into an alpha-wave state that not only feels good but also *does* good inside us. Alas, most people today don't spend a lot of time in pleasant natural environments, and there's evidence that this loss is harming our mental and physical health.

Running counters the "epidemic dislocation from the outdoors," as Williams calls it, by drawing folks back into nature, transporting them from desk chairs and recliners to parks and trails. While many of the physical and mental benefits of running are intrinsic to the activity, other benefits have more to do with its service as a vehicle for reconnecting people with the environment.

There's a reason the human menstrual cycle is exactly the same length as the lunar cycle. We don't just *need* nature, we *are* nature, and we forget this at our peril. A human running in the woods is like an eagle gliding on a thermal draft or a bass leaping into the air after a fly—a creature at one with its proper home, and happy for it.

Even foul-weather running is enjoyable in its way, as I was reminded three days later in Madison, Wisconsin. Arriving in a light drizzle, we checked in to another pets-stay-free budget hotel, where Nataki immediately set about researching places to dine while I handled my own first priority of posting a social media callout for local running partners. Within minutes Nataki had settled on a nearby Chili's and I'd gotten a reply from Patrick, a professional triathlete and coach who offered to meet up the next morning at Colectivo Coffee on Monroe Street. A drilling rain fell as I drove there, bogging down traffic and causing me to arrive a few minutes late. Patrick stood just inside the door with his friend Nick, another local triathlete.

"Am I overdressed?" I asked them, eyeing their shorts and light jackets. I had swaddled myself in multiple layers.

Patrick replied with a joke about Wisconsin weather, and we left the cozy coffeehouse to begin a circuit of the Arboretum Loop, a popular Madison running route. As the continuing downpour soaked my hair, the styling gel I had unwisely applied earlier seeped into my eyes and stung them terribly, but I told myself that at least I wasn't stuck inside on a treadmill as I'd been the day before in Gurnee, Illinois, where Nataki and I stayed at a hotel that, although cheap and pet friendly, was located in an area of busy streets and no sidewalks that I judged unsafe for outdoor exercise.

Patrick and Nick asked me lots of questions about my search for the magic of the marathon, and I asked them about their lives. Nick, it turned out, had a heck of a story to share, and our conversation continued after the run, back at Colectivo. A Wisconsin native, Nick was a star wrestler throughout high school and into college, until a major shoulder injury brought his grappling days to an abrupt end at age nineteen. The next year was lost to depression and weight gain, but fate threw Nick a lifeline on a random Saturday in July 2000, when another wasted afternoon of apathetic channel surfing became something else entirely the moment Nick chanced upon some old footage of the 1989 Ironman World Championship. Curiosity turned to awe, awe to inspiration as Nick watched forty-nine-year-old Dick Hoyt tow and push his adult son Rick, who had cerebral palsy, through the entire 140.6-mile race.

"I said to myself, 'If that's what they can do, I can get off my fat ass and do some work,'" Nick told me.

That work began the next day, with two laps in the college pool, a perfect parallel to the two-lap limit Dean encountered in the first run of his weight-loss project. A couple of years later, Nick finished Ironman Florida, and he was still racing triathlons in 2012, when he and his wife Nicole's second child, Ellery, arrived prematurely after suffering a stroke in utero. Ellery spent the first two weeks of her postnatal existence in an incubator, where she was diagnosed with cerebral palsy.

Their lives would never be the same. Ellery would never walk, talk, or feed herself. Every meal she ever ate would have to be blended and administered through a tube. She would undergo multiple surgeries and be on as many as twelve medications at once. Three or four times a week, *every* week, the family would find themselves in doctor's offices for checkups, feeding therapy, physical therapy, occupational therapy, and other care. The medical bills would be staggering, the wrangling with insurance companies unending. Long-distance travel would be next to impossible. A specially equipped van would have to be purchased and a custom home built—a home Ellery would in all likelihood never leave.

In the beginning, Nick tried to keep up with his triathlon training, but the joy had gone out of it. His next race went poorly, and the one after that was even worse. He began to talk about quitting the sport. It was his sister Whitney who snapped him out of the funk, supplying her big brother with a whole new purpose for chasing finish lines by reminding him that it wasn't the *winner* of the 1989 Ironman who had inspired him to become a triathlete but a father who, out of love, towed and pushed his son—a son afflicted with the very same disease Ellery had—for fourteen and a half hours in tropical heat and humidity.

Nick did his first triathlon with Ellery in 2016, when she was four. It wasn't the famous Hawaii Ironman but a sprint race of about one-tenth the distance in Pardeeville, Wisconsin. Just like Dick Hoyt, however, Nick towed and pushed his child through it with all the love he had. Ellery shrieked with joy as she felt the wind in her face and the bumps in the road. When they came to the finish line, Nick pulled his daughter out of the wheelchair and strapped on her walking braces, allowing her to complete the challenge on her own feet, and she did so with a gaping grin directed straight up at her father, a smile that was captured in a photograph Nick showed me, passing his phone across the table. A thousand words couldn't describe its power.

What does it say that perhaps the greatest experience so far in the life of a little girl whom fate denied the full use of her body was racing a triathlon? I chewed on this question on the drive back to the hotel. All children, I reflected, are born a bit like Ellery—lacking the ability to do much with their bodies. But as healthy children grow and develop, their repertoire of physical skills expands tremendously, and they take great delight in this process. Sometimes it's hard work. See how determinedly babies struggle to acquire the ability to walk. They don't seem to mind straining against the outrage of their physical limits.

Pulling against these striving instincts, though, is another set of deeply ingrained drives that steer us away from all forms of discomfort and toward pleasure—a desire to feel the cosseting warmth of the heated bucket seat, the buzz of caffeine, the fillip of the text message received, the mouth explosion of the fast food burger bite, the arousal of the swimsuit issue, the rush of the action movie explosion, and to numb everything else, most especially effort. These instincts, perhaps more than any others in us, have shaped the arc of history. Automobiles, video games, microwave popcorn, and combine harvesters are all products of the will to make life easier and more pleasurable that have changed the way we live. The sum effect of these changes is a modern human whose mind is disconnected from his body in much the same way his mind *and* body are cut off from the natural world, as Dean ("very comfortable and very lazy") was before he discovered running.

Indeed, if running is the best fix for our epidemic dislocation from the outdoors, it is also the most dependable cure for this widespread mind-body disconnect. (Walking works pretty well, too, Nataki would submit.) Running reawakens our drive to see what our bodies can do, to challenge and push back our physical limits. At the same time, it reverses the perverse side effects of the pursuit of comfort and pleasure, which does to bodies like Dean's (and to Nick's during his briefer fat phase) something not unlike what cerebral palsy does to bodies like Ellery's.

Imagine how this must look to Ellery. She would probably give just about anything to be able to do a triathlon without help, yet millions of people born with the precious gift of perfect health willingly give away the ability to do stuff with their arms and legs. Running enables those of us who realize our mistake to reclaim our bodies and restore the mind-body connection—and affords the Nicks of the world the opportunity to *be* the arms and legs for the Ellerys.

Back at the hotel I found Nataki sitting on the bed with her journal, not a formal diary but more of a thought book in which she jotted down ideas worth saving.

"What have you been up to, Kitty?" I asked.

"Oh, me and Queenie just been hanging," she said.

"Did you make it down to the fitness room?" (Nataki had said she might do so before I left.)

"I didn't have the energy," she confessed.

I said nothing more, confident that Nataki *would* have had the energy to walk for thirty minutes or so on one of the hotel's two crappy treadmills if, instead of leaving her behind to run with Patrick and Nick, I had chosen to stay and exercise with her. At home in Oakdale, Nataki was always up for our morning constitutional, and in fine weather she would gladly go back outside with me in the evening for a leisurely bike ride, fully appreciating both the movement and the exposure. But when I traveled alone for business or racing, she tended to stay in the house, unable to muster the same oomph.

As I stripped off my wet running clothes and ran a hot shower, it occurred to me that one of my responsibilities to my wife was not entirely unlike one of Nick's responsibilities to his daughter.

....

My encounter with Nick took place on a Thursday. Two mornings later, just after sunrise, I parked the Fun Mobile in a deserted gravel lot at the Waushara County Fairgrounds in Wautoma, Wisconsin, site of the Jailbreak Marathon—number seven. Wearing a hat and gloves I'd picked up in Wichita, I stepped into yet another thirty-five-degree prerace chill to hunt down my number, targeting a distant pair of figures struggling to erect an inflatable start/finish arch, a tableau that struck me as vaguely parodic of the famous flag planting on Iwo Jima. It was from one of these two Packers fans (their hats gave them away) that I learned I had gotten the start time wrong—hence the empty parking lot. A full hour passed before my fellow racers began to arrive.

There weren't many of them. The Jailbreak Marathon is a small event—so small that the entire field of participants was able to fit inside an open-fronted sheet-metal structure (used for livestock auctions on fair dates) that served as its staging area. Portable heaters filled the space with a cozy warmth that we cleaved to until the literal last minute, and even the requisite performance of the national anthem took place there. The local warbler who sang it delivered a strangled wrong note on "glare," a bit of bathos that seemed to me in perfect keeping with the homely nature of the overall operation. At last the race director led us out to the start line on the fairgrounds' narrow access road, where final instructions were delivered.

"Here's what's going to happen," he said in a Wisconsin accent that sounded like a spoof of a Wisconsin accent. "I'm going to go like this: 'FIVE, four, three, two, one'—and then you're going to hear a horn. Ready? TEN . . ."

By biting my lip, I had been able to avoid committing the small treason of laughing during "The Star-Spangled Banner," but when I made eye contact now with the runner standing next to me, we both cracked up.

"Gotta love small marathons!" I said.

The horn sounded and we rolled out, buoyed by the cheers of several. A guy wearing a neon-green shirt unnervingly similar to my own rushed to the front. Seeming surprised to find himself in this position, he swiveled his head around to the runners behind.

"Does anybody know the way?"

This question was spoken with some urgency, as we were quickly approaching Fair Street, where the access road ended and an important choice awaited: left or right. Receiving only shrugs in answer to his appeal for guidance, our uncertain leader swiveled his head forward again and shouted out to a policeman stationed at the approaching intersection.

"Which way?"

"Left!" said the cop, reinforcing the directive with an emphatic, baseball umpire type of gesture.

We went left. I passed a few runners, moving into second place, and then drew a bead on Green Shirt. On the road ahead a splotch of red materialized, sharpening into the form of an upside-down painted number 26 as I approached. An empty moment followed—left foot, right foot. Then I wondered: *Did I just pass the twenty-six-mile mark of a marathon I've only started?*

In front of me, Green Shirt came upon a couple of women who were jogging in our direction, warming up for the half marathon that would begin in half an hour.

"You're going the wrong way!" one of them called out.

"He said go left!" Green Shirt objected.

I made a split-second decision to continue also, swayed by my recollection of the traffic cop's confident signal. Behind me, a short debate occurred among the runners I'd recently overtaken. Whatever decision they came to was lost in the wind, but five seconds of silence and a quick look back confirmed that they had turned around, and I now did the same. Casting my eyes up the road, I saw not a soul between our small pack and the traffic cop whose colossal fuckup appeared to have been corrected quickly, so that only the swiftest few runners were misdirected. As for Green Shirt, I like to think he just kept on running the wrong way and is still going even now.

When I reached the official 1-mile mark, I had already—according to my watch—run 1.8 miles. This meant I would cover 27 miles before I reached the finish line, and I would have to adjust my effort accordingly. The difference between 26.2 miles and 27.0 miles is 3 percent. I therefore reduced my subjective effort level by what felt like 3 percent. If you've been running as long as I have and gotten to know your body as well as you do in the course of completing some 10,000-plus workouts and nearly two hundred races, this is possible.

An aid station came into view ahead, operated by a gaggle of teens. Two drink options were available: water and Gatorade (Cool Blue flavor). I called out for Gatorade and was given a cup of water. Huh.

In the third official mile, fourth actual mile, I reeled in the only runner left in sight, having overhauled the rest of the field already. When I pulled even with her, I noticed that she was the woman I'd shared a laugh with on the start line.

"Are you the leader?" I asked.

"Nope. *You* are," she grumbled.

Another aid station appeared, its operators standing idly behind a cup-laden table like a bunch of neighborhood kids running a lemonade stand. Not taking any chances, I asked for "the blue stuff." Nobody moved. "Blue stuff!" I pleaded, now steps away from the table. The volunteers gave me the same bland stare I'd gotten from a herd of grazing cows a few minutes earlier. Left to choose between stopping and going thirsty, I stopped, making a show of patiently selecting the choicest-looking cup, gulping its contents with exaggerated relish, and swiping the back of my hand across my lips. *Aaaaah!*

"Gotta love small marathons!" I yelled as I ran on.

The next aid station was abandoned—just a well-stocked table standing unattended at the tailgate of a big pickup truck. I stopped a second time, quaffed a serving of Gatorade, and had just started moving again (not so easily as before) when a blushing young couple scrambled out of the cab, the girl hastily adjusting a bra strap. By this point I couldn't wait to see what lay ahead. Blue-lipped volunteers shrugging and saying, *sorry, but we just ran out*? Overgrown farm lads folding their arms and demanding ten bucks a cup?

By twenty-one miles, nothing was funny anymore. All nonessential brain activity had ceased, starved of resources. The task of maintaining a steady rate of forward progress against mounting fatigue now demanded total concentration, a pinhole focus that excluded every distraction, even self-awareness. My mind was reduced to the operation of my body, the world to an extension thereof. The wind in my face became the breath in my lungs. The heat of my pistoning muscles diffused into the day, cooling me, warming it. The pavement beneath me seemed an active conspirator in my progress. Half the energy that goes into a runner's propulsion, physics tells us, comes from the ground—an equal and opposite reaction to the force of impact. I felt this helpful rebound as I streamed through central Wisconsin farm country, coupled to the land as harmoniously as the men who worked the bean fields on either side of me.

Psychologists call this phenomenon transient hypofrontality, denoting a short-term suppression of activity in the brain's executive control centers that is experienced as an enjoyable state of total absorption in some goal-directed task. Others call it flow, and runners call it the runner's high. But research suggests the runner's high is a special kind of flow. In a series of studies that I'd come across earlier in my journey, German sports psychologist Oliver Stoll observed that runners exhibit transient hypofrontality only when their effort level is very high, which is to say, when they are suffering. In other activities, things like surfing and gaming, flow is *fun*—the playful exercise of a skill. But in a hard run there is no ball, no melody, only struggle. To feel the runner's high is to find enjoyment in this struggle, comfort in discomfort.

I could have coasted the last few miles—my latest backward glance revealing no potential threats to my first marathon victory in thirty-nine tries (give or take)—but I kept pressing, having set an arbitrary goal to finish the race in less than three hours despite the extra distance. When I hit 26.2 miles in 2:54:34, I knew it was going to be close, and when I made the last turn and spied the official race clock in the distance ahead, I realized that nothing short of an all-out sprint would deliver me to my meaningless goal. Teeth bared, I dashed toward the line, hope fading by the irrecoverable second until I hit the timing mat at 3:00:00.

A double-whammy of dizziness and nausea struck me the moment I stopped. I keened sideways a few paces, clearing space for half-marathoners finishing behind me and then doubling over to gag up a trickle of blue stuff, an invisible race volunteer slipping the champion's medal around my neck as I held this defeated pose. Gathering myself, I rose up smiling, not about the medal but about my scorched esophagus and throbbing calves, welcome signs of a body well tested—an acquired taste, to be sure, but like many acquired tastes, superior to most easy gratifications.

Back at the hotel, I sat in a hot tub with Nataki for twenty minutes before taking her out for a reward meal at the Hilltop

Pub and Grill, conveniently located next door. I ordered the tequila barbecue burger with beer-battered fries, Nataki something kosher.

Pleasure is contextual, heightened by contrast. A hot tub soak never feels better, a burger and fries never taste better, than after a marathon.

CHAPTER 15

CONQUERING HARD

IN THE STILLEST hour of a clear, cold Saturday in December 2009, Nataki gave up on sleep, threw back the bedcovers, and crept out of her sister Tayna's apartment in Antioch, where she'd been encamped for the past nine months. Eight hours later, she walked into the two-bedroom condominium in San Diego's Mira Mesa neighborhood that I'd been moldering in since her dramatic departure in the spring. Nataki's arrival, though early, was not unexpected. In the weeks after our weekend rendezvous in Las Vegas, our nightly phone conversations had been drama-free—no dark suspicions in her words, no lingering bitterness in mine—and the better we got along at five hundred miles' distance, the more we both yearned to live again like a normal married couple. It was time.

To celebrate our latest fresh start, we dressed up and made a reservation at one of our favorite downtown eateries. As always on such occasions, we took the better car, Glamour Puss, and I drove. We were cruising south on Interstate 5, listening to the local old-school R&B station Nataki had left the radio tuned to, when the DJ spun Al Green's "Let's Stay Together," and I found myself listening to the familiar lyrics with new ears, glancing sidelong at Nataki's profile once or twice to see if the relevance of the Reverend's musical message to our present situation had registered with her. She seemed lost in thought.

"'Let's Stay Together,'" I prompted. "How appropriate."

"Yeah," Nataki replied dreamily. "Al Green."

We listened to the second verse.

"I just remembered something," Nataki said. "Didn't his wife come after him with a frying pan?"

"I think it was his girlfriend," I said. "Caught him in the bathtub."

We lapsed back into silence, but then a single pulse of laughter, a rogue guffaw, burst through my lips.

"Hit him upside the head with an iron skillet!" Nataki said, the words tumbling from her.

I cracked up. Nataki lost it. We howled together with cathartic abandon, our blended hysterics (my shrieking falsetto layered atop her percussive "Ha! Ha! Ha!") communicating many things: remembrance, forgiveness, solidarity, hope. It was the kind of laughing jag you give yourself over to, whole minutes passing as our noisemaking tapered slowly from wails to chuckles to sighs. But the tickle soon came back, one stray giggle from me setting off another round of tearful merriment.

We parked in a public garage and walked two blocks to the restaurant, holding hands. A well-dressed cat daddy driving an immaculately detailed Cadillac Escalade slowed to a crawl alongside us and leaned toward the passenger window, ogling Nataki.

"Now *that's* what I'm talkin' about!" he rapped. "You want a real man to take you out tonight, baby girl?"

"You've still got it, Kitty," I said, squeezing her.

Over appetizers, our conversation turned serious, as it was bound to have done sooner or later. We revisited the choking incident that had precipitated our separation, and for the first time I told Nataki about Queenie's and my night of near homelessness and the risky Spiderman stunt I'd had to pull to rescue us from our predicament.

"I had no idea," Nataki said, dropping her eyes to her lap. "I'm sorry that happened. I'm embarrassed and ashamed. I promise, I'll never do nothing like that again."

"I've heard that before," I grumbled.

"This time it's different," she insisted. "I know I'm bipolar. I know I need my medicine. I'm not going to be stupid no more."

"Well, that's good," I said, softening.

"I've learned a lot since I've been away," Nataki said. "At first I was all broken up inside, but now I feel much stronger. I realized all my life I've been trying to find happiness in a man. I was always looking for someone to take care of me, maybe because I didn't get everything I needed from my dad. I even tried to do that with God. But now I realize I have to be happy in myself, because I love myself. No man can do that. Not even you. I want to be with you, Matthew, but I don't need you no more. I can take care of myself."

"I'm really glad to hear you say that," I said.

Our entrees appeared: sea bass for Nataki, scallops for me.

"What about you?" Nataki asked. "Have you learned anything?"

"Not really," I said. "I knew before you left that things would probably be okay if you got on track with your medication, and that's still what I believe."

A shadow passed across Nataki's face.

"But don't you think you could've done something different?" she asked.

"Sure, I could have done some things differently," I said, "but let's not kid ourselves—you would have had those episodes regardless."

"I know I wasn't myself," Nataki said. "But I think it was also more than that. There was a communication issue. I felt like you wasn't listening to me."

"I didn't drive you to attack me, if that's what you're suggesting," I said.

"No, I shouldn't have ever done that. But I was frustrated. You were so impatient. I felt as though you was always watching me and saying, 'I see the signs! You're going to get sick again!' But I *was* taking my medication. You put so much pressure on me. Maybe if you wasn't so impatient . . . "

I stopped chewing. With sudden, brutal clarity I saw the truth, a truth now so glaringly obvious that my prior blindness to it was as shaming as the thing itself. I *had* been impatient with Nataki, and for no other reason than pure selfishness. Eight years too late, I realized I really was that poor narcissistic bastard whose girlfriend made him saw his bike in half on national television. It was as if my soul had been dragged in front of a mirror, forced to see the reflected reality that the thing I hated most about Nataki's illness was not that it tormented her, nor even that it put my life at risk, but that it stole my attention away from its favorite object: me. *Just be quiet, take your medicine, and don't do anything disruptive so I can go back to focusing on myself.* This was the message my style of supporting Nataki—heavy on advice, light on encouragement— had sent her. People (her family, mine, the few friends I confided in) gave me credit for hanging in there with Nataki, but was hanging in there enough? Casting my mind back over the years, I saw so many moments when the word of encouragement I hadn't spoken would have helped the woman I loved more than the word of advice I had.

My half-chewed shellfish turned to ashes on my tongue. It was a struggle to speak.

"I will try to be more patient with you," I said.

"Thank you," Nataki whispered.

....

If only it was so simple. Despite Nataki's continuing compliance with her treatment, the next year was up and down, putting a final nail in the coffin of my slow-to-die belief that all she had to do to remain stable was obey the doctor. It was evident now that her mental state was governed not so much by what she took or didn't take but by the vagaries of her disease. At each low point, her psychiatrist (a new one—number six since her initial diagnosis) tweaked her meds in search of the magic formula that would put the suffering behind us once and for all. If a few good weeks followed an adjustment, our hopes rose, only to be dashed by another downswing.

Then, in the spring of 2011, it appeared we might have found the magic at last. Nataki had a good day, which became a good week, a good month, two good months. Almost before we knew it she was in a groove, walking a thin line high above the Pit of Mania on one side and the Abyss of Side Effects on the other. Energetic, happy, and forward facing, she codesigned a collection of handbags and sold them online under names like Furlicious and Urban Safari. We hooked back up with our old musician friend Alejandro and wrote and recorded a bunch of new songs together, including our consensus favorite, "Heaven Can Wait":

> *Heaven can wait*
> *I'm gonna enjoy my life*
> *Heaven can wait*
> *I'm gonna make the most of my time*
> *Heaven can wait while I do God's work*
> *He had to have a reason to put me on earth*
> *It's gonna be great, but heaven can wait for now.*

Three good months, six, eleven. I began to think we were home free. But then Nataki started getting into altercations on the roadways and bringing vagrants home to bathe and eat—classic red-flag behaviors. In January 2012, she took another go at throttling me and earned her fifth stay in a mental hospital.

Running was a lifeline for me during this period. More than just an escape from the messy reality of my life, more than stress-relieving time alone, running fundamentally altered my perspective on bad days and hard times. When I had a big race in front of me and I felt my body growing stronger in response to training, I was equal to life's struggles in a way I just wasn't otherwise. By some strange psychobiological alchemy, this stoic form of play steeled me for tests that bore no resemblance whatsoever to a track workout.

Nataki seemed to recognize this and was more accepting of my devotion to exercise than she'd been in the past. There were still occasions when she wanted us to go for a picnic and I wanted to run twenty miles, but she understood that running made me strong not just for myself but also for her, and more often than not she gave me permission to run. At the same time, I had become more inclined to postpone the run and do the picnic, having reached the conclusion that The Person I Want to Be was brave, yes, but also not an egocentric prick.

Nataki's permission would have done me little good, of course, if I was injured and physically unable to run twenty miles. But the Achilles tendon injury that had thwarted my preparations for Ironman Arizona in 2009 had finally healed up (more or less), and, now forty years old, I hungered for one last opportunity to achieve a marathon performance that fulfilled my true potential before the aging process diminished my potential any further. I set my sights on the Los Angeles Marathon, in preparing for which I applied every lesson I had learned from my many past failures. For starters, I greatly reduced my running mileage and spent more time doing low-impact activities like steep uphill treadmill walking. To further reduce the risk of injury, I waited until six weeks before the race to add speed work to my training. And, perhaps most important, I rested instead of plowing ahead whenever the wrong kind of pain announced itself in a muscle, bone, or joint.

When the big day arrived, I felt confident and ready, though troubled somewhat by a new sore spot on the right side of my pelvis. At the usual ungodly hour, I left a mouth-breathing Nataki in the Sheraton Grand Los Angeles and boarded a chartered bus that transported me and a few dozen other runners to the parking lot at Dodger Stadium, where I set about my well-practiced routine of stretching, using the bathroom, popping caffeine pills, and warming up.

My projected finish time put me in Corral A, reserved for the fastest 1,000 runners in the field of 23,000. Access to this prime bit of real estate was managed like the entrance to a trendy Beverly

Hills nightspot, burly Teamsters checking race numbers and admitting participants one by one from a line that was so long it had a turn in it. At half past six, a full thirty minutes before the official start time, admission was cut off with scores of runners still waiting, myself among them. A wave of groans passed from the head of the queue to the tail as news of our exclusion spread. When it got to me I flipped out, crashing the gate and pleading with the head gorilla to make an exception for me on the bullshit grounds that I had potential prize money on the line.

"Not my decision, bro," the gorilla said.

"So what am I supposed to do now?" I asked.

"Go to the back," he said, pointing in the direction of Corral E, where the slowest runners stood packed together like cattle.

My mouth fell open. I had nightmares just like this, dreams of absurd race-day fiascos that I always woke up from smiling, knowing they could never happen in real life. Now here I was, very much awake and not chuckling. What to do? The best runner in the world couldn't run a sub-2:40 marathon, as I hoped to do, if he started behind 23,000 slower runners. There was no point in even trying. I might as well just salvage the day by jogging back to the hotel and enjoying a relaxing Sunday in the city with Nataki.

But then I thought of something. My timing chip would not activate until I crossed the start line. If I waited until everyone else had cleared out, I could begin alone, and by the time I caught up with the masses they would be sufficiently spread out that I could pass through them like a slalom skier swishing between gates, and just maybe still achieve my goal.

I watched the start of the race from the sidelines, unsure if my plan was daffy or brilliant. It took a full forty minutes for the last few participants, most of them walkers, to pass over the timing mat that put them officially on the clock. I continued to wait until every last one of them had disappeared from sight, and then I started running, baffling the few non-runners still lingering about.

Before I'd even left the stadium grounds, I ran smack into an impenetrable jam of creeping humanity. Not the way I'd imagined it. I tried everything I could think of to force my way through the gridlock—juking like a tailback, using the sidewalk, calling out warnings—but the juking cost energy, the sidewalk was a minefield, and my warnings had a tendency to startle people *into* my path rather than out of it.

Worse, my sore groin did not approve of the unfamiliar gridiron running style I'd adopted, making its objections known through a slow crescendo of discomfort that intensified from an ominous warm feeling in the first mile to an alarming shredding sensation at mile seven. At this point, I realized two things: (1) I had absolutely no hope of surviving all the way to the finish line in Santa Monica, and (2) every step I took from here on would take me one step farther away from the hotel where Nataki, now probably enjoying a nice room-service breakfast, as I'd encouraged her to do, awaited me.

At the next intersection, I made an abrupt left turn, again baffling spectators, and winced my way to the Sheraton by dead reckoning, returning to find Nataki nibbling the last bites of her meal.

"You're back early," she said. "How did it go?"

"Add it to the pile," I said.

....

In May 2012, Nataki and I moved back to Oakdale. There were two reasons for this relocation, our eleventh as a couple. One was the loss of my job at Competitor Group, which left us needing to reduce our overhead. Reoccupying the home we'd been renting out at a loss for four years was the obvious way to achieve this objective. The other reason was Nataki's declaration, made around the same time, that San Diego was cursed.

Maybe so. But if San Diego was cursed, Oakdale was too. After the move, Nataki entered a lengthy period of being consistently *not quite right*—able to function in the world but caught in a fixed mood of sour aggrievedness. She spoke often about "cutting ties" and did so in a variety of ways—closing her Facebook account, changing her cell phone number, shutting herself inside the house. Even the church became a source of vexation, Nataki often complaining that it was now "all about money." The big problems of the world—war, poverty, disease—weighed on her personally, as though God had quit the throne and handed her his staff, saying, "Here, you deal with it."

This fraught equilibrium was in some ways even worse than Nataki's many past nosedives toward full-blown psychosis, for, as awful as these were, the crash landings they led to at least brought about legal and medical interventions that created an opportunity to try something different. I began to think that any change in her current so-so mental state, either for better or for worse, was preferable to more of the same.

As they say, be careful what you wish for. On a Friday morning in the autumn of 2013, apropos of nothing, Nataki stood up from our living room sofa, raised her computer overhead, and hurled it to the floor, destroying it. I had a clear view of this random act of self-victimizing vandalism from my office. Never wholly surprised by anything anymore, I didn't flinch. Behind my poker face and unchanged posture, however, neuronal sirens wailed and hormonal first responders mobilized, readying the muscular defenses for flight or battle.

"Let's go for a walk," I said.

Since the move, Nataki and I had taken up the habit of walking two miles together (with Queenie) every morning. This daily ritual was one of the little ways I was trying to do better, and it had the side benefit of teaching me that a little exertion sometimes took the edge off Nataki's agitation—and also that if violence did occur, I was safer outdoors than in. Nataki accepted my invitation to take some fresh air, but within minutes of our setting out on the bike path that encircles our development she was raining fists to the sides of my head. Using my forearms as shields, I stood my ground, hoping she would tire herself out before she knocked me silly. A cracking blow to my left cheekbone caused me to rethink this strategy. I took off like a buckshot stag, zigzagging through the neighborhood to frustrate pursuit while summoning Oakdale's Finest with my phone.

The dispatcher asked for Nataki's current whereabouts. To ascertain them, I made my way to a gap in a border wall at the end of our cul-de-sac that afforded an oblique view of the house. I hadn't been there ten seconds when the garage door slid open and our beleaguered Meep Meep backed out. I reported this information to the dispatcher and then continued to narrate as Nataki drove off with such ferocity that the car itself seemed angry. I began to look around for a hiding place. Finding none, I hustled in the direction that help would most likely come from, a broad road that intersected with our block's main cross street at a traffic circle.

Nataki came screeching into the roundabout, spotted me easily, and took aim. I froze in disbelief as the car crossed into the oncoming traffic lane, hit the curb, and continued its deadly approach on the sidewalk. I leaped behind the only protection available, a wispy sapling whose trunk was scarcely thicker than my wrist. Behind me stood a wall too high to scale. The car roared to within inches of my navel before skidding to a halt. Through the windshield I saw a familiar stranger, her face molten with hate. The car reversed hard, gashing deep divots into the grass verge, and came at me again. A passing motorist slowed to rubberneck but did not stop to render aid.

After a third aborted attempt to pin me to the wall, Nataki executed a savage 180 and roared back to the roundabout, where she raced around and around like a clown-car driver negotiating a tiny circus track, nearly T-boning a neighbor who rolled through on an errand for milk or tampons or whatever. Not a moment too soon, a police SUV came into view. I leapt and waved like a man on the roof of a burning building. Having gained the officer's attention, I pointed frantically at the revolving Honda, which just then was breaking its orbit of the traffic circle and finding a new target in the police vehicle itself, screaming down the center of the road with one pair of wheels on either side of the double yellow.

Fifty feet from collision, the cop slammed his brakes. Nataki, thank God, did the same. The cop scrambled out of his SUV and took a few cautious steps in the suspect's direction. Nataki, meanwhile, exploded out of the Meep Meep and charged the cop, screaming, "Shoot me! Go ahead!"

You don't know for sure that you would give your life for a person until you have the opportunity. I rushed at the policeman from his right flank, whether intending to tackle him or to get between him and Nataki, I couldn't say; there was no thought involved.

"No!" I screamed, my voice cracking.

Under attack from two sides, the officer gripped his sidearm with his right hand as a warning to me while extending his left palm toward Nataki.

"Stop!" he bellowed at both of us.

Something about the stentorian authority with which this command was uttered seemed to reach Nataki, and she gave up her kamikaze advance, permitting me to do the same.

"I'm not going to shoot you," the cop added in a different tone. "I don't like shooting people."

Nataki submitted docilely to being cuffed and stuffed while several more of our neighbors, their motorized transit from one side of the roundabout to the other stalled by our salacious performance, looked on with undisguised schadenfreude. The policeman transferred Nataki's keys to me, and I drove the Meep Meep home, feeling sorry for the poor thing, which had seen too much.

The county psychiatric hospital, our old haunt, had acquired new owners and management during our time away. Alas, it had not acquired a new standard of care. As before, Nataki was little more than warehoused there—fed, sheltered, and kept occupied for the legally mandated seventy-two hours and then released with no meaningful change in her treatment, hence no hope for change in her life outside.

And so it was that, a few weeks after her release, Nataki went off again, and at the worst possible time, when I was stark naked, drawing a warm bath after a chilly December bike ride. She accused me of plotting against her with our neighbors in some ill-defined way, discerning a malign secret code in a couple of my behavioral ticks.

"You be playing games," she snarled, jabbing a finger at my pink bare chest. "I know what you be up to with your [here she sniffed the first and second fingers of her left hand, as I often do after eating] and your [here she pulled at an eyebrow with the same digits, as is my habit when concentrating], but it ain't gonna work."

"Don't be silly," I said with forced breeziness. "That's just the puppet master spirit trying to control my body. You're not the only one he's after, you know."

This was a lie (as far as I knew), but tactically adroit. Deprived of the expected cue to escalate, Nataki cooled down a few degrees. Having gained an inch, I went for a mile. Using the same jocular tone, I ordered her to take off her own clothes and join me in the tub. To my great relief, she complied. We stepped into the steaming froth and sat down facing each other from opposite ends, our bent legs intertwined. A second later, Nataki's hands were around my neck.

I'd seen this movie so many times before that I made no immediate effort to pry Nataki's talons from my throat. Instead I passively observed the situation from an upper balcony of my mind and wondered whether my wife really would kill me if I let her. When I felt the two sides of my esophagus come into contact with each other, I had my answer.

Instinct took over. I ripped Nataki's hands away from my bruised larynx and burst out of the bath, grabbing the cell phone I had prudently positioned on the tub's lip. Even with my life at stake, I just couldn't bring myself to streak cock-flapping through the neighborhood for help, so instead of dashing toward the staircase and escape I scrambled inside the water closet, slamming the door behind me and pasting my body against it. Then suddenly, Nataki's shoulders and fists were thundering against the flimsy rectangle of low-density composite wood, forcing it open an alarming inch or two with each manly blow.

My defensive efforts were compromised by the unavailability of my right arm, which was employed in the task of making my umpteenth 9-1-1 call. I was on the verge of success when an especially powerful thump to the door sent the phone flying out of my hand and tumbling in slow motion (it seemed) toward the toilet bowl. My heart stopped as I watched the device clank against the seat and rattle to the floor. I scooped it up, completed the call, and, like a quarterback barking out signals to his teammates amid the roar of a hostile stadium crowd, described the pickle I'd gotten myself into, every third word drowned out by Nataki's banging.

"Sir, you're going to have to speak more clearly," the dispatcher said.

"For fuck's sake!" I raved. "Just send the police! Is that clear enough?"

The pounding ceased abruptly. Wagering that Nataki had gone away only to fetch some form of battering instrument, I kept my full weight on the door. Soon I sensed her return. Then I smelled smoke. My body went cold with terror.

"Nataki!" I shouted. "Don't do it! This is your house too! Don't do it!"

"What's she doing?" the dispatcher asked.

"She's started a fire!" I yelled.

Nataki said nothing in response to my continued pleading. The stench (why did it smell like singed hair?) grew stronger. The dispatcher kept asking me what was going on.

"I don't know!" I said.

Again I sensed that Nataki was no longer outside the door. Perhaps she had fled the burning house. If so, I prayed she had at least taken Queenie.

"The police are there," the dispatcher said.

"They're inside?"

"They have your wife in custody. You're safe."

I opened the door and peered out cautiously. Nothing. I passed through the bathroom and saw the charred remains of a lambskin rug that normally rested before the fireplace in the master retreat, now soaking face-down in bathwater. Nataki had put out the very fire she'd started. I died a little then, as I did each time I caught another flashing glimpse of the real Nataki resisting with all she had the insurgent forces that sought to control her.

I slipped on a pair of pajama pants and crept downstairs, where I found a policeman standing in the kitchen, scribbling calmly on a notepad, his partner having already led Nataki outside. Turning in the direction he faced, I was jolted by the sight of a lurid orange stain covering nearly half the family room carpet in a wild snaking pattern. Observing my reaction, the cop silently pointed toward the kitchen island, upon which sat an empty bottle of Sriracha.

This one was a real head-scratcher.

Christmas must be peak season for incidents of this sort, for the county psychiatric hospital had no free beds—an inconvenience that, in retrospect, I consider a blessing in disguise, possibly more. After some calling around, Nataki was transported to a facility in Fremont, some ninety minutes away, where we'd lived briefly after her first involuntary confinement. Per routine, I drove there the next evening for visiting hours. Both outside and inside, this institution had the same depressingly Soviet look and feel as every other psychiatric hospital I'd had the misfortune to inspect. There are cancer treatment centers as comfortable and lavish as a beachside resort, addiction-recovery clinics so posh they make you almost wish you were addicted to something. But mental wards are universally low budget and dismal.

I checked in, made my way to D Ward, where adult patients were kept, and announced myself at the reception desk.

"Your wife is in Room 215," said the smiling young Indian woman who sat behind it.

I found Nataki's quarters at the end of a long hall. Empty. I returned to the front desk.

"She's not there," I said.

"Oh, she may be with Dr. Khan," the receptionist said.

This was another bit of luck. I had come in the hope of gaining an audience with whoever was put in charge of Nataki's treatment.

"Perfect! Nataki wanted me to sit in on that," I lied. "Which office is Dr. Khan's?"

The receptionist gestured. I hastened to the door indicated, gave it two quick raps with a knuckle, and opened it uninvited. Nataki was there, seated in a plastic chair against the near wall, facing the interior. The doctor, a jowly man in his midsixties, sat in a reclining desk chair on wheels, facing Nataki—and me. His basset-hound eyes widened as I entered.

"Sorry to barge in like this," I said. "I'm Nataki's husband." (The doctor's eyes widened further.) "I was hoping I could maybe join you."

"I don't want him here," Nataki said. "He's the enemy."

"Listen," I said, still addressing Dr. Khan. "Let me just say one thing. Nataki has been hospitalized seven times since 2004. Seven. Something's got to change. We're chasing our tails. There must be a different option we can try—a stronger drug, a combination of drugs, I don't know. All I know is I was almost burned alive last night. Nataki nearly got herself shot—and not for the first time. You have no idea what we've lived through. Please help us. *Please.* We're losing hope."

My voice quavered as I spoke these last words. In the ensuing silence, Dr. Khan sat as still and silent as a statue. But there was a subtle slackening of his features, a glint in those hangdog eyes, that I very much wanted to interpret as a sign I had reached him. When he did speak, he said what he had to—that, naturally, any treatment he recommended would have to be based on a full evaluation, which had not yet been completed, yadda yadda. But I left the hospital feeling encouraged, thinking that, just maybe, somebody was finally listening.

Three days later, Nataki came home with a collection of new medications, stuff that had never been mentioned by any of the psychiatrists we'd dealt with previously. It didn't take long to discover why. Nataki's appetite became ferocious. She ate almost nonstop, packing so many meals and snacks into her waking hours that we often ran the dishwasher twice a day. And she craved all the worst crap: pork rinds, egg McMuffins, honeybuns, ramen noodles. It was as if her new medicines had been formulated for the express purpose of making her gain weight and they just happened to stabilize her mood and her thoughts as collateral outcomes.

Suddenly Nataki's past ten-pound medicine-induced bulk-ups seemed quaint. Her taut, athletic body expanded so rapidly under the caloric onslaught that the process was almost observable in real time, like watching a rubber raft inflate. Her weight literally doubled over the course of several months. But the drugs did in fact stabilize her mood and thoughts. Not every day was a good day, but her bad days weren't so bad anymore and she no longer had bad weeks and months. As vain as the next person, Nataki hated getting fat, but as she told me after stepping off the scale one day, "It's better to be fat and in your right mind than skinny and out of it."

Amen.

....

Around the same time Nataki achieved lasting mental stability, the groin injury that had taken me out of the LA Marathon in 2012 and that dogged me for two years afterward finally went away on its own, for no clear reason, like every other chronic injury I'd ever had. As usual, I took advantage of my restored health by stepping up my training and looking for races to do. But this time was different. With my hair graying and my testosterone levels declining, I had given up on chasing the perfect race, accepting the hard fact that it was just too late.

Far from triggering a midlife crisis, my abandonment of the quest that had defined the second act of my life as an endurance athlete freed me to experience running in different ways. Instead of numbers I chased adventure and discovery. I ran a marathon in a wildlife preserve in Kenya, sharing a racecourse with giraffes and zebras and African wild dogs. I participated in a couple of multiday team relay races, finding unexpected joy in the mixing of running and sleep deprivation. I even broke a vow and jumped aboard the ultramarathon bandwagon, running the American River 50-Miler in northern California (and getting lost one mile from the finish line, true to form).

Next up was the 2016 Lake Chabot Trail Run, a laid-back event in the San Francisco Bay Area that I did as a low-expectations lark, sort of like my first date with Nataki. My mind-set going into it was *the harder, the better,* and so I chose the longest option from a smorgasbord of distance offerings that ranged from five miles to fifty kilometers. The day before the race, Nataki and I boarded Queenie, drove seventy miles west to Castro Valley, checked in to a Holiday Inn, and went out for Thai food. In the morning, I kissed Nataki's untroubled brow and drove a short distance to Lake Chabot Regional Park, where at eight thirty a hatted gentleman with a passing resemblance to Mike Rowe of *Dirty Jobs* fame raised an air horn overhead as 299 pairs of eyes watched him.

I felt utterly calm, my once-crippling prerace anxiety a fading memory. The thing that cured me, it turned out, was not any particular technique but simple repetition. Like an actor with extreme stage fright who finds a remedy in his five-hundredth performance, I just kept doing the thing I feared until it was too damn familiar to be scary anymore. Also, by this point in my life, I had survived worse traumas than the pain of endurance racing. And, again, I had my new attitude—I was racing for thrills, not to purge ancient regrets.

The horn blared, and I set off at about the same pace I might have chosen for an easy solo run on any old Wednesday at home. After some initial jockeying I found myself behind fifteen or twenty faster starters. (Okay, it was seventeen—I counted.) Some of these runners, surely, were contesting the lesser distances, but it was impossible to know for sure. All of that would sort itself out in due time. Sticking to my plan, I made no effort to move forward, covering the relatively flat, paved first mile of what was advertised as a mostly off road and murderously hilly course in a nose-breathing 7:44. A few hundred meters farther on, we veered right and plunged into the woods, kicking up dust on a wide dirt path that canted steeply upward. I found a happy medium between slowing down to keep my effort steady and keeping my pace steady at the cost of greater effort, and the result was that I picked off a handful of the seventeen on the way to the top.

A jarring descent down the hill's precipitous backside brought us to a split. A lead group of six runners, who'd evidently chosen the five-mile distance, stayed on the Cameron Loop, which curved to the left, back in the direction we'd come from, as the rest of us made a hard right and rattled over a narrow wooden footbridge that dumped us onto the Live Oak Trail. Almost immediately, we began another ascent. Up and up we went on a rutted track that afforded no view of a summit that just *had* to be around the next bend but never was. A handful of the runners still ahead of me were reduced to a walk. Among those who kept running was a wiry man close to sixty who spoke as I glided past his left shoulder.

"This is a lot harder than last year!" he said almost cheerfully. I laughed politely, unsure what he meant. Had the course changed or had he?

At last I reached the top, where I came upon a small drink station staffed by a couple of volunteers who seemed mildly put out by my failure to pause and partake, but I had plenty of raspberry flavored Tailwind left in my hand flask and a target in front of me, a tall figure running shirtless in long-sleeve weather. My eyes were still on this runner's exposed back when, about a mile farther on, a runner who looked almost young enough to be my son came prancing toward me with the grace of a gazelle, having already reached the turnaround point at 6.55 miles (or one half of a half marathon) and begun the inbound portion of lap one. I acknowledged him with a small wave and was ignored so utterly that I ran on half-doubting he'd even seen me.

Shirtless Guy proved far more sociable when I caught him shortly after he and I circled the traffic cone that marked the turnaround.

"Are you in the half or the fifty?" he asked.

"The fifty," I said, wondering how he knew I wasn't entered in the 30K or the marathon. Then again, I was equally certain the gazelle ahead of us was also running the 50K. Call it a runner's sixth sense.

Running down the big hill was as challenging as coming up it had been, but in an entirely different way. If ascending it was a grind (lungs clawing for air, calves straining against gravity), descending it just plain *hurt* (toes jamming into the fronts of my shoes, thighs clenching like fingers gripping armrests on a nose-diving passenger plane to keep my knees from buckling). By the time I reached the bottom, I had arrived at the conclusion that running downhill was in fact worse than going up, only to change my mind after I crossed the footbridge and started up the hill that led back to the bike path.

I met the gazelle a second time on my approach to the start/finish area, his lead having expanded to more than two minutes. Once again he displayed an almost superstitious-seeming refusal to acknowledge my existence, which did not bother me. Some runners just turn into cyborgs when the gun goes off.

The big hill was both taller and steeper the second time around—I was sure of it. I understood now what that older guy had meant when he said the race was harder this year. About halfway up I encountered a photographer crouching behind a bulky Nikon, who informed me as he snapped my picture that the leader was only thirty seconds ahead and struggling. I had my doubts, given how he'd looked just fifteen minutes earlier, but when I came around the next bend, there he was. The now inevitable dethroning occurred just before the turnaround, where I mumbled a word of encouragement as I claimed first place. Expecting no response, I got none.

At the big hill I made the unhappy discovery that my legs were destroyed—so damaged by prior descents that I could no longer control my speed, rumbling down the fissured trail like a runaway eighteen-wheeler, brakes shot, one false foot-plant away from a high ankle sprain. At the bottom I hazarded a look back, hoping to not see the gazelle but unsurprised that I did. Cyborgs don't go down easy.

I crossed the footbridge a fourth time and began to ascend the wooded Cameron Loop hill. A miniature devil appeared on my left shoulder (at least that's how I remember it) and whispered in my ear, tempting me to walk. Even champion ultrarunners take tactical walk breaks on tough climbs, but this was only my second ultra and I remained steeped in the norms of road racing, where walking is surrender. To avoid this embarrassment, I slowed my running pace to the point where it would have been faster to swallow my pride and walk. Realizing this, I went ahead and walked, but walking felt so *wrong*, so close to cheating, little different from turning around before the turnaround cone just because nobody's looking, that after a few dozen hurried paces and another fearful glance backward (no sign of the gazelle, but I was in the trees now and couldn't see far) I resumed running.

The ensuing descent deposited me once more on the paved path—the part of the course most conducive to fast running. My brain told my legs to speed up, and my legs did nothing. It was like turning the key in the ignition switch of a car with a bad alternator. Suddenly I felt as if I had neither slept nor eaten in two days. The devil appeared again on my left shoulder, pitching a new idea. I was one mile away from the start/finish area, and also a mile away from completing a full marathon. To finish out the fifty-kilometer distance I had signed up for, I would have to turn around and run the five-mile loop that others had chosen as their full race distance. But if I crossed the finish line instead (the devil pointed out), I would be the winner of the marathon *and* I would also be out of my misery. Not a bad bargain. Sure, I would hate myself a little for doing less than I'd planned to, but I was miserable, and (the devil reminded me) I wasn't running to prove anything any-more but for giggles. The decision was made: I would bail out.

It was now past eleven o'clock in the morning. The day had warmed and the path was crowded with joggers and hikers and dog walkers and capering kids. I threaded my way between them, calling out the occasional feeble heads-up, drawing curious second looks from those who noticed the race number pinned to my shirt. I came around a curve and spied my destination. My deliverance.

Suddenly my vision turned inward. A series of images flashed before my mind's eye, reeling backward in time. I saw myself aban-doning the 2012 Los Angeles Marathon with a groin injury, quit-ting the 2009 Magic Mountain Man Triathlon after getting lost a mile from the finish line, abandoning the same year's Orange County Marathon at the halfway point, walking at mile twenty-three of the same year's Boston Marathon, scratching from the 2002 Boston Marathon with a knee injury, walking parts of the 2000 Long Beach Marathon, tearing off my race number in disgust at mile nineteen of the 1999 California International Marathon, and finally, but also firstly, intentionally missing the start of the 1988 Hanover Invitational boys' 3200 meters.

My vision swung outward again. Fifty feet ahead of me stood a ramshackle finish arch hanging over a grassy area to the left of the path and linked to it via a makeshift chute fashioned from metal stakes and plastic rope flags. Twenty feet closer, in the center of the path, sat the traffic cone that marked the turnaround.

This is the second and final call . . .

I circled the cone and kept running.

Despite the spontaneity of my decision to continue, I had the presence of mind to glance at my watch when I made the turn: 3:28:51. When the gazelle passed me coming the other way, gri-macing, looking as though he were running in prison shackles, I checked it again: 3:29:35. I had ninety seconds on him.

Five miles to go.

In training, I regarded this distance as so trivial that it wasn't even worth the bother of lacing up my running shoes for; seven miles was my minimum. Now the same distance seemed galactic, unfathomable. I checked my watch obsessively, convinced by the Jupiter-gravity heaviness of my body and my glacially slow approach toward the joggers and hikers and dog walkers and capering kids before me that I was losing speed, but in fact I wasn't. Yet.

One last hill: 0.64 miles long, 240 feet high. It might as well have been El Capitan for all the hope I had of getting over it. But, as I began to slog my way up, I felt an unexpected unburdening, a slight but difference-making buoying, like a weight-room spotter's gentle assistive push on that last rep, and it was then I knew I was going to make it.

The final mile of the Lake Chabot Trail Run 50K was as hard as any mile I have ever run, but I relished it, because at long last I was conquering hard—not coasting to easy victory or succumbing to my suffering as I had so many times in the past but *suffering with the certainty of victory*, and it felt as good as I had always believed it would, good in a way there's no word for, a secret-menu joy that many people don't even know exists: the sublime pleasure of defeating pain—of mastering self.

When I crossed the finish line, not a soul was present. A few race-related persons milled about the general vicinity, but no clapping spectators lined the chute, no local journalist jotted down my name and hometown, no smiling race volunteer greeted me with a bottle of water or a finisher's medal. The moment I stopped, I experienced an urgent need to vomit, but nothing came up. I wandered about dazedly, not sure what to do with myself. When the gazelle finished he shook my hand graciously and we had a nice friendly chat.

Eager to get back to Nataki, I dragged my erstwhile adversary to the popup tent where we had received our number bibs in the dark several hours earlier to see about our awards. I got a coffee mug for winning the 50K and a medal for winning the men's forty-five to forty-nine age group. Mitch (as I now knew him) got a medal for winning the men's thirty to thirty-four age group. We shook hands again and I hobbled toward the parking lot.

Inside Glamour Puss 2 (Nataki's year-old Tesla), I stared vacantly out the windshield for a minute or two before dropping my forehead to the steering wheel, as though I were the lone survivor of some terrible disaster and the initial shock had just worn off. So this was what redemption felt like: Relief. A great big spiritual exhalation. An invisible load set down and left behind. The sweet emancipation of letting go. For once my body, my mind, and my luck had held up on the same day, and the experience changed everything, redefining all that came before. Every failure, every mishap now seemed necessary to this final outcome, all stepping-stones to *here*.

Perhaps I could have lived the second half of my life in perfect peace without this experience, but I am immeasurably grateful that I won't have to. They say it's the journey that matters, not the destination, and that's mostly true. My long pursuit of full and final athletic redemption served the purpose of making me a stronger person even without delivering a single race performance that I was wholly satisfied with. But there is something to be said for actually getting where you want to go. I am confident now that for the rest of my days I will not recall the shame of the 1988 Hanover Invitational without also remembering its bookend, the 2016 Lake Chabot Trail Run.

Book end.

Indeed, if the story of my life begins on the day I discovered I was a coward, it concludes here, on the day I put a final dagger in that inner coward. We tell our stories—all of us, in one way or another—to make sense of our lives. Nataki says everything happens for a reason, but I say we find reasons for everything that happens. It is our nature to narrativize. And yet, as I unstuck my forehead from the steering wheel of Glamour Puss 2 and began the short drive back to the hotel, my life sure seemed to make sense in a way that was foreordained, not contrived in hindsight.

When I was nineteen years old and not running I read a novel by John Irving about a New Hampshire boy, Owen Meany, whose obsessive rehearsal of an odd sequence of basketball moves turned

out much later to have been unconscious preparation for his heroic thwarting of a terroristic bombing (at the cost of his own life).
It was a pretty good book overall, but as I read it I had a hard time
suspending disbelief. And yet how different is my own story, about
a New Hampshire boy, pet-named Booby, whose personal quest to
"conquer hard" on the racecourse turned out to be just the sort of
training he needed to not quit on the woman he loved, even if it
meant going down with her?

The precise official distance of the marathon—twenty-six
miles, 385 yards—converted to decimal form and rounded to the
nearest hundredth, is 26.22 miles. My precise age when I met
Nataki—twenty-six years, eighty-two days—converted to decimal
form and rounded to the nearest hundredth, is 26.22 years. You
can't make this shit up!

For a long time I thought I needed to find courage through
running for my own sake. And I did. But what I *really* needed
courage for, I discovered, was *life*, and for Nataki especially. The
part of my story that seems uncanny to me even today is this last
part—that only after I let go of the dream of the perfect race
and began to do the little things for Nataki, not just the One Big
Thing, was I rewarded with the athletic experience I had desired
for so long. How else can this almost-too-perfect denouement be
interpreted but as a kind of fate-authored lesson, a providential
reinforcement of the life priorities I had arrived at by encountering, exploring, and becoming The Person I Want to Be—through
running?

But if the story of my life does end here, what about the rest
of my actual life? Nataki and I are not old. God willing, we have
many years ahead of us. As I arrived back at the hotel, pulling into
the same parking space I had pulled out of before dawn, I found
myself looking to the future in a way I hadn't dared to do for a
very long time. I saw a new story beginning, for me and for us, a
story where we got to choose what happened a little more than
we had the first time.

In our room I found Nataki sitting placidly on the edge of the bed, wrapped in a plush bathrobe and watching a local morning show. Seeing her, I shivered with déjà vu, not because this moment seemed to have happened before but because it *had* happened before, so many times.

"How did it go?" Nataki asked.

"I won," I said.

"Really? Did you get any money?"

Two years earlier, I had come home from a local 5K with a crisp one-hundred-dollar bill—the only cash prize I had ever claimed at a race. Ever since then, Nataki, to whom I'd handed over that prize, had lived in perennial hope of a second lucky strike.

"I got a coffee mug and a medal," I said.

I showered and dressed, and we checked out of the hotel. We had plans for a night on the town in San Francisco with friends, so instead of heading east toward Oakdale we went farther west on Highway 580. Approaching the Bay Bridge, I broke a companionable silence.

"You know how we've always talked about driving cross-country together?" I asked.

We had. Early in our relationship, I regaled Nataki with stories of the month-long journey from Pennsylvania to California my brothers and I had undertaken in 1995, straining to convey the exquisite freedom I had felt throughout it—and not again since. Nataki liked the sound of this, of breaking out and hitting the open road, and as our lives merged it became our shared dream to bust loose one day and see America together, a dream we foretasted by visiting RV sales lots to shop for the perfect vehicle. But the thing itself was always deferred, never actively planned for. Any traveling we did, save for the occasional family gathering, centered on my racing or my work (or both). As the years went by, the dream's symbolism evolved—what began as an exciting promise of adventure morphing over time into a desperate hope for escape. And by 2016, it was on the brink of passing over from dream to fantasy.

Our RV sales lot visits continued, but they had become an empty ritual, a "Next year in Jerusalem" kind of thing.

"Yes, of course," Nataki answered.

"Well," I said, "I think I've figured out a way to make it happen."

"Let me guess. You're going to run a bunch of marathons."

CHAPTER 16

PURSUIT OF HAPPINESS

(Eugene Marathon)

HEARING MY NAME, I froze, awkwardly, my body halfway inside a portable toilet, one in a row of such shelters lining the edge of a soccer field on the campus of the University of Oregon, where I'd come to pick up my Eugene Marathon number bib. Peeking around the edge of the open door, I identified the source of the greeting as a young man with heavily inked bare arms who had just emerged from a plastic privy three or four doors down from mine. I pretended to know the gentleman and stepped toward him with my right arm extended.

"Jay," he prompted, seeing through my act. "I was at your event the other day in Salem."

It all came back to me. His name was in fact J—just the letter, we'd had a whole conversation about it—and I'd signed a book for him at Gallagher Fitness Resources, where I had spoken the previous night, a nontraditional but pleasant enough way to observe my forty-sixth birthday. I remembered too that J would be running tomorrow's Eugene Half Marathon while I ran the full marathon

261

as the eighth and final event in my search for the magic of the marathon. In an effort to make up for having failed to recognize him, I told J that if memory served, he hoped to complete his race in an hour and thirty-five minutes or less.

"That's right," he said. "How about you? What are you shooting for?"

"I'd like to run under 2:50," I said. "I haven't done that in a long time, and the fitness is definitely there. I'm just not sure how much my body has left at this point."

I had set this goal immediately after the Jailbreak Marathon in Wisconsin, glad at that point to have survived my seventh marathon in as many weeks but also tired of holding myself back (if only a little) to save something for the next marathon, a restraint that felt unnatural and stifling to me, like a seven-footer not allowing himself to dunk the ball. With no ninth marathon to preserve my legs for, I looked forward to Eugene as a reward for my prior discipline—the dessert, as it were, to the brussels sprouts of running just to finish. And it was then, naturally, that my body decided to suddenly fall apart.

It wasn't the running that did me in, oddly, but the driving. The three days that followed Jailbreak were the longest travel days of the whole adventure—a 2,000-mile haul. On the first day, Nataki and I ran smack into a blizzard just west of St. Cloud (on the first of May, for God's sake). I drove half the freeway speed limit with a death grip on the steering wheel, jackknifed big rigs and spun-out cars scattered everywhere. This continued for a couple of hours, fraying my nerves to the point where I began to think about stopping somewhere to ride out the rest of it. But then, approaching Fargo, we passed abruptly from total whiteout to blue sky and sunshine, as though we'd emerged from some sort of theme park storm tunnel. We marveled at the small miracle for some time before either of us spoke.

"I hope it stays like this," Nataki said eventually.

"Sunny, you mean?" I asked.

"No, I mean our relationship. We've been so peaceful on this trip. I hope it stays like this when we're back home."

"Me too," I said, reaching for Nataki's hand.

Feeling her eyes on me, I turned my head and met her gaze, and held it, recklessly, indulging fully in one of those deep and tender soul stares that happened so often, so naturally, in the early days of our romance.

In that moment I regretted nothing, nothing at all. Not the whimpering demise of my high school running career. Not the phone call I made to Nataki on July 29, 1997, to request a second date. Not the heartbreaks and frustrations of my adult racing career. Not even Nataki's illness, the 9-1-1 calls, my attempt to end my life. Because without all of that, there was no *this*.

"Do you ever wish I was a runner?" Nataki asked later in the drive, one of a handful of zinger questions she pops on me seemingly randomly every now and again.

"How many times have you asked me that?" I asked.

"Tell me again," Nataki demanded in her coaxing little girl's voice.

"No, never," I said. "I'm actually very glad you're not a runner. It's good that we're different. Running is both my hobby and my job. I wouldn't want my life to be one-dimensional. *Something* in me knew what it was doing when it wouldn't let me let you go."

Nataki nodded and smiled as though hearing these words for the first time.

"What about you, Kitty?" I asked. "Do you ever wish I *wasn't* a runner?"

"I used to, but not anymore," Nataki answered with her usual directness. "All I ever wanted was for you to be the best Booby you can be."

"Well," I said, chuckling, "I guess that makes two of us."

We spent the following night in Missoula. In the morning, Queenie roused me right on schedule with an assault of nuzzling. Her lolling tongue and wagging tail seemed vaguely taunting as she dragged me stiff-kneed and bed-headed out into the freezer of springtime Montana to take her sweet time doing her business. Nine hours later, I parked the Fun Mobile, now spattered in dead flies, at a trailhead in Vancouver, Washington, stripped off my outer layer of clothes, and without so much as touching my toes, began running in an atmospheric stew of eighty-two-degree heat and 75 percent humidity. In hindsight, I find it incredible that I failed to anticipate the disaster that ensued. My plan had been to warm up with an easy mile and then run out the balance of an hour at 6:15 per mile—a touch below my goal pace for Eugene. Under different circumstances this would have been fairly easy, but as it was I felt as I might have felt if I had attempted the same workout on the morning of New Year's Day 1999, when I woke up next to Nataki hungover and flu stricken having shat the bed during the night. After thirty-seven minutes, I bailed out, my confidence rubble.

Sean's house, where Nataki and I were to crash before moving on to Salem and Eugene, lay just over a mile from the trailhead. When Nataki and I got there, my brother informed me that he had locked his keys in his car at a lodge in Skamania, fifty miles away, and he needed me to drive him out there to meet a locksmith. He might as well have answered the door with a kick to the balls. We returned from the mission to a darkened house, our wives having long since gone to bed. Next thing I knew, Queenie's tongue was on the back of my neck.

My body felt no better three days later in Eugene, where, after my encounter with J at the expo, I received a running tour of a section of the marathon course from Tracy, a runner I'd coached for the past couple of years and Nataki's and my local hostess. I wasn't injured or sick or otherwise diagnosable, as far as I knew; I just seemed to be not very good at running anymore. Discouraged, I told Tracy she might want to reconsider coming out to cheer me on the next morning, as there might be little to cheer for. She reminded me that a lot could change in a day.

"I've taught you well, grasshopper," I said, affecting a Japanese accent.

In this particular instance, however, a day changed nothing, and when I started my prerace jog on Agate Street the next morning my legs acted like a pair of unwilling St. Bernards being leash-dragged to the vet's office. Having loosened up as best I could, I stashed my sweats in a gear check bag and bid Godspeed to Josh, who had lost ten pounds since Modesto and improved his sleep and overall well-being with the help of a prescription for Ambien. He hoped to achieve a modest redemption on this day by covering the whole 26.2 miles without walking a step.

At 7:04 A.M., the limbering effect of my warm-up having fully reversed itself within the cramped confines of Corral A, professional runner and actress Alexi Pappas—whose debut feature film, *Tracktown*, would open the following week—was introduced as the official starter of the 2017 Eugene Marathon.

"Enjoy your fitness!" she chirped before delivering the start instructions. For some reason the suggestion caught my funny bone ("Enjoy the ride!" said the hangman), and I laughed out loud, drawing disapproving looks from a few of my fellow runners.

The gun cracked and the crowd of mostly 3:30 marathoners surrounding me took off at a 2:30 pace. I picked my way through the carnage as, one by one, they lost momentum over the first couple of miles. Around 2.5 miles I spotted Tracy and her spouse, Martha. They shouted encouragement and I gave them a thumbs-up.

Tracy came to running late in life, but she possessed a youthful passion for the sport, having found in it an outlet for a competitive side she'd never known she had. As her coach I often struggled to hold Tracy back. She always wanted to do more, and the training plan I had just created for her included double runs on some days, an extraordinary commitment for a fifty-one-year-old professional financial planner. We had gone over the plan the previous evening as she and Martha and Nataki and I sat around the dining room table with plates of homemade strawberry shortcake before us, our discussion of intervals and target paces spinning out toward loftier planes, perhaps owing to the presence of our significant others.

"I guess you could say it's selfish," Tracy said at one point in reference to her training. "But I think a little selfishness can be a good thing. I've always been a very giving and considerate person. Running has forced me to prioritize my own needs."

"That can put a strain on a relationship," I said with a nod in Nataki's direction. "I speak from experience."

"It *has* had an impact on Martha," Tracy conceded. "The more I train, the more running creeps into every aspect of our lives. I'm more demanding in setting our bedtime and wake-up alarms, more insistent on what and when we eat. Many of our vacations are planned around races and training runs. I spend our money on not only shoes, gear, and races but also on massages, physical therapy, supplements, books, and coaching."

I now glanced at Martha, half-expecting her to make a mood-lightening joke, but she just sat there in silent interest.

"I knew this change would be good for me," Tracy went on. "But what surprised me was what a positive impact it had on my relationship with Martha. Our dynamic changed. We became more balanced. We had a healthy struggle to get what we each needed. Martha had something to push back on. She didn't always have the pressure to be the one to make decisions for me to go along with. We spent more time pursuing our own individual interests. We had new things to share with each other when we came back together. It allowed her to give something to me that I really wanted."

"Aw, that's beautiful!" Nataki said, repeating the words she'd spoken to me in New Mexico when I called her from the race-course to share Jim Simpson and Betty Wailes's hookup story.

Eight weeks on the road certainly hadn't diminished our capacity to be inspired by happy older couples (Tracy had a decade on Nataki, Martha five years more). But perhaps we now depended a bit less on outside sources of hope than we had before.

Tracy abruptly put down her fork, stood up, and left the room, raising an index finger to indicate she'd be right back. When she returned, she handed me a single sheet of office paper that contained the following text:

> When you're a competitive runner in training you are constantly in a process of ascending. . . . It's not something that most human beings would give a moment of consideration to, that it is actually possible to be living for years in a state of constant betterment. To consider that you are better today than you were yesterday or a year ago, and that you will be better still tomorrow or next week or at tournament time your senior year. That if you're doing it right you are an organism constantly evolving toward some agreed-upon approximation of excellence. Wouldn't that at least be one definition of a spiritual state?
>
> —From *Again to Carthage*, by John L. Parker Jr.

I gave the passage a quick glance and passed it back to Tracy, whose eyes widened with surprise and incipient hurt.

"Did you even read it?" she asked.

"I didn't have to," I smiled. "I have it memorized."

At 6.5 miles I saw Tracy and Martha a second time, and though I probably looked unchanged to them (same black half-tights and top, same race number), I had become a completely different runner on the inside and was now coasting through an effortless 6:15 mile and feeling as though I weighed eighty-nine pounds, had grown a third lung, and had pogo sticks for legs. When I least expected it, fate had gifted me with one of those magical days when one's very best body shows up to answer the gun, an unexplained phenomenon I had experienced exactly twice before in twenty-six years of running. All I had to do now was not fuck it up—and with almost twenty miles of running left ahead of me, there was plenty of time for that. One way to waste the opportunity would be to get too greedy, but when I completed mile nine—the hardest of the race, with a whopper of a hill—in 6:28, or smack on 2:49 marathon pace, I decided to go for 2:48, damn the torpedoes.

By this point attrition had whittled my company down to a handful of men, all of them very young, extremely fit-looking, and biomechanically perfect—and a plurality of whom wore University of Oregon uniforms. Nearly a quarter century removed from my own college days, I felt more than a little self-conscious among these bucks. And yet, one by one, they fell off a pace that remained easy for me until I found myself alone with just one fit young guy with perfect form in a University of Oregon uniform.

A large digital clock stood at the halfway mark, the number 1:24:29 flashing on its face as I passed it. Doubling this figure in my head, I came up with 2:48:58. Eek! All I had to do now was repeat what I had just done—on legs that had done it once already.

Over the next several miles, my rival and I did not so much run together as take turns chasing each other. Always focused more internally than externally during races, I paid little attention to my yo-yoing companion, concentrating instead on time and pace. Fatigue had begun to scramble my computational faculties, but I was fairly certain I would need to reach the twenty-mile mark at or before 2:09:00 to remain on track toward my new goal. I got there at 2:08:43—which was good—but no longer did I seem to weigh eighty-nine pounds or have three lungs or pogo sticks for legs. The struggle bus had come for me, a bit earlier than I would have liked, and I began to doubt my ability to hold my present pace the rest of the way. Sure enough, I ran mile twenty-one in 6:33, my slowest split since the first.

"Damn it!" I said aloud, startling my young opponent, who just happened to be passing me at that very moment and might have thought, *Jeez, this old dude sure hates to lose!*

Studies indicate that people never try harder than when their goal is within reach, but *barely*. This was where I found myself twenty-four miles into the Eugene Marathon, a slow but steady loss of momentum over the preceding four miles having erased my earlier cushion, an involuntary slackening that even the predatory frisson of finally ridding myself of my collegiate challenger couldn't halt. I felt as though I were running in a riptide, everything but my will pulling in the wrong direction. Numbers meant nothing to me anymore. All I knew was that I had no margin to falter, and that any chance I had of squeaking under 2:49 demanded that I run the remaining distance as a kind of seppuku.

This is where you want to be, I told myself. *You live for this.*

I call these lifelines: little mantras that come to me spontaneously in the crisis moments of races—attempts by The Person I Want to Be to gain my weaker side's acceptance of the pain I am inflicting on myself. Manipulative? Sure. But in an honest way, because the words don't help if they're not true—and this case was no exception. With two miles to go in the 2017 Eugene Marathon, I *was* where I wanted to be. I *did* live for (among other things) the challenge of mastering the suffering of endurance racing. Not even the tiniest part of me resisted my choice to press toward the finish line with all I had, whatever the price. My legs felt as dead and the rest of my body as bled-out as they ever had in any marathon, but these feelings, which had so overwhelmed me in the past, no longer bothered me in the slightest—instead they seemed familiar, right, and necessary. I was indeed enjoying my fitness.

A lone runner came into view ahead of me, another fluid stripling clad in a Ducks singlet. I now told myself that if I could overtake him before the finish, I would hit my time—maybe true, maybe not, but in this case helpful regardless. As I went after him, I felt my face contort into the beastly grimace I had seen in some of my recent race photos, an expression so very unlike the one I wear in many of my old high school race photos, in which I look like a person who is being tortured. In these newer images, I looked like the torturer.

The race ended with a half-circuit on the track at famous Hayward Field. The moment I stepped onto its spongy red surface and checked my watch, I knew I had fallen short. Nevertheless, I ran hard to the finish line, crossing at 2:49:14. Another disappointment.

"Woohoo!" I shouted, pumping a fist.

Or maybe not. As I bowed to receive my medal and tottered toward the recovery area, I went back over the race in my mind.

What could I have done better? I considered the elements of race execution—nutrition, tactics, self-talk, grit, pacing—probing for mistakes, finding none. I had run every single mile within twelve seconds of my average pace for the full distance, closing with my second-fastest mile. The inescapable conclusion was that, in my fortieth attempt at the distance (give or take), I had finally pulled off a perfect marathon.

After retrieving my sweats from the gear check tent, I walked back to the course and found my sisters-in-law, Josh's wife Jennifer and Sean's wife Jocelyn, and my nephews, Caleb, Luca, and Dax. (Nataki had stayed back at Tracy and Martha's house to make sure Queenie didn't get into something and then poop all over the place, as she'd done in Dori's home.) After a brief conference, we agreed to watch Josh finish from trackside and were soon there, tittering at the race announcer's droll commentary.

"Here comes David Elsbernd from Salem, Oregon, our state capital," he said, and everybody clapped for David.

Twenty-five seconds passed.

"Finishing now is Steve Ashe from Sacramento, California, and that's the capital of *that* state!" the announcer said, in a what-are-the-odds sort of way.

Another four seconds passed.

"Next we have Leslie Barclay from Austin, Texas—and that's the capital of THAT state!" he roared, beside himself with amazement.

Several minutes went by before Josh's impossible-to-miss neon-lime shirt appeared at the far side of the track. My elder brother looked as though he were running against an actual physical wall. When he came closer, I saw that his face had begun to melt into his neck—or so it appeared. A streak of blood was visible on his jersey, descending from the right nipple. My heart swelled with pride.

Josh crossed the finish line at 3:58:36—about thirty-six minutes shy of the time needed to claim a Boston Marathon race number. But he'd beaten his Modesto Marathon time by almost fifteen minutes and avoided walking, and, most important, he'd finished the race with a melted face and a bloody nipple.

....

Nataki and I (and Queenie) returned home the following afternoon. I took the next four days off from running—which is not to say I didn't exercise. On our first full day in Oakdale, I pumped air into the tires of my bike, oiled the chain, and hopped onto the saddle for a one-hour ride. Eighteen minutes in, just after I ran a stop sign, I was pulled over by a motorcycle cop, a squat man in blue who produced a notepad and pen as he approached me.

"What's so funny?" he asked, catching a smile I couldn't suppress despite my best efforts.

"Oh, nothing," I said. "Only that I drove my car almost 10,000 miles in the last seven weeks. Yep. Went clear across the country and back. And you know what? I didn't get a single moving violation. Not even a parking ticket. Came home yesterday. Decided to go for a bike ride. And now . . . "

The policeman's face was unreadable, giving no indication he'd even heard me, let alone appreciated the irony I found so amusing. But he put away his notepad.

"Because I've had no prior contact with you, I'm just going to issue you a written warning," he said magnanimously.

No prior contact? I wondered about that. I'd had my share of interaction with the local constabulary. Indeed, this guy looked a lot like the fleshy patrolman who had told Nataki she looked "calm enough" as she sat on the roof of the Meep Meep in the middle of the road, just a few blocks from our present location. In any case, I felt reasonably confident that I would have no *future* encounters with this particular badge-wearer, at least none of the 9-1-1 type. But then again, who really knew? One of the worst mistakes you can make in a marathon is to expect to keep feeling great when you're feeling great—to stop bracing for the worst. I won't make this mistake in my life. There will be more bad days, I know. Days of loss and grief, if not of trauma and violence. I don't want to face these days. But when they come, I want to face them like a marathoner.

I ran three more stop signs on the way back to the house, which I entered through the garage, hearing Nataki before I saw her, sitting in the family room with her phone to her ear. My first thought was that she was on a conference call with the "Prophet," as she calls him—an East Coast minister who specializes in a form of Christian fortune-telling and to whom Nataki tithes a substantial portion of her monthly Social Security check. When she started taking these calls a couple of years after her last hospitalization, alarm bells rang inside my head. But then I thought, *Why stress out over this? She's obviously doing well. She's managing her health and well-being successfully on every level. Just back off and trust her.* So I did, and it became evident that there was indeed nothing to be alarmed about. As with the Leviticus diet, Nataki benefitted from her relationship with the Prophet regardless of whether I understood it, and what fun would it be to fully understand your soul mate anyway? As I passed through the kitchen toward the stairs, though, I remembered that Nataki rarely speaks—as she was now doing—when she's on the line with the Prophet.

"I discovered something different in humanity that I had never seen before," I overheard, "and it made me happy."

It required no further deductive effort on my part to guess that Nataki was in fact talking to Tayna about our trip, and specifically about the people we had met along the way. It appeared that she, too, had soaked up a bit of the marathon's magic, and this made *me* happy.

Three days later I treated myself to a two-hour run. I felt a bit creaky at first, but after a couple of miles I loosened up and found a good groove and my thoughts floated away from the cloudless, seventy-two-degree afternoon around me. Before long, my brain was in full alpha-wave mode as I thought about all I had experienced and learned over the preceding eight weeks.

So. Had I found the magic?

This much was clear: the magic of the marathon is no single thing. It has many dimensions, and it works on individual runners in different ways. Beginning with Josh in Modesto and continuing with Jim Simpson in New Mexico and James and Robbie in Kansas and Michelle and her dad in Virginia and Rome and Mike in Boston and John in Pennsylvania and Dean and Lisa in Ohio and Nick in Wisconsin and Tracy in Eugene, I had witnessed the marathon's power to do everything from nurture the ability to fail with poise to teach a deeper empathy. But as I looped around Fred Myers Park in the neighboring town of Riverbank and headed home, it struck me that, for all the diversity I had seen in people's reasons for running marathons, *all* of these folks were happier as runners than they had been as non-runners.

The one thing *everyone* wants is to be happy. We seek happiness in all we do, however misguidedly at times. The most obvious way to go after happiness is to satisfy our worldly wants: to get the house we want, the spouse we want, the food we want, the social media recognition we want. But this way never succeeds. None of us can create a world in which we have everything we want and nothing bad happens. Disappointment, pain, and hardship are inescapable.

The other way to chase happiness is to change not the world we occupy but ourselves. In my experience, the happiest men and women are those who have become, or are becoming, the persons they want to be. The folks among us who have consciously *chosen* themselves possess more strength and harbor less fear than do those who have everything they want (for now), and it is strength and fearlessness, not luck, that we need to face life's unpleasant parts.

To become the person you want to be, you must first define that person and then you must work hard to close the gap between your current and best selves. This work may take a variety of forms, but in my experience none is more effective than running marathons. In the pain of a marathon we learn who we are, discovering within ourselves both the weaknesses and flaws that hold us back and the strengths and virtues that drive us forward, which are different in each of us. To the extent that we keep going, finishing today's race and trying again tomorrow, we actively choose our strengths and virtues and reject our flaws and weaknesses. Over time, the good things in us grow as the bad things shrink, a process not unlike building muscle and burning fat. It is simply impossible to become a better person in one's own estimation through such a process and not at the same time become a happier person.

The eight weeks I spent in search of the magic of the marathon with Nataki were the happiest weeks of my life. I was living the way I want to live: adventuring, running, writing, meeting people, and spending time with the person I love more than any other, who, in her own way, was also having the experience of a lifetime. But the main source of the happiness I felt in those dreamlike days was something I carried inside: a peace, a confidence, and a lightness of being that came from knowing who I was and what I was made of, and from recognizing that I was on a path toward becoming The Person I Want to Be. It was not *luck* that made this possible. *Endurance* made it possible, a never-quit mentality that I needed for Nataki and that I honed by coming back to the marathon again and again until I mastered it.

As to where Nataki's own, even greater, endurance came from, she says God, whereas I say faith, so we agree on that much at least.

I turned left off Crane Road and onto the bike path on which Nataki had pummeled my head with her fists four years before, on our very worst of many bad days, neither of us knowing then how soon our best days would follow. A young woman appeared in the distance, jogging toward me. When we were close enough for eye contact, I smiled and she smiled back. No words were exchanged, no hand wave, only an implicit runner-to-runner wink that seemed to me to say, "It appears you've found the secret, and as you see, I've found it too. Don't ever stop."

The bike path deposited me at the foot of our block and I picked up my pace a little, feeling alive. Having completed the inbound part of the workout (as always) a little faster than the outbound part, I ran past our house, past the never-locked house Katie and Wes no longer lived in, all the way to the end of the cul-de-sac, until my watch showed two hours even and I was permitted to quit. Suddenly aware of my fatigue, I laced my fingers together on top of my head and walked in lazy circles, enjoying the slow slackening of my breath as a flag-snapping valley wind wicked the cooling sweat off my exposed arms and neck.

It was then that I remembered something Dori said to me as she and Nataki and Mike and I ate pasta together the evening before the Boston Marathon. Whip-smart and skeptical in the Socratic way, Dori couldn't help but point out the obvious flaw in the marathon as a metaphor for life.

"It seems to me that the difference between a marathon and life," Dori said, "is that when you're happy, you wish there were no finish line."

ACKNOWLEDGMENTS

Everyone whose name appears in this memoir has made a valuable contribution to it for which I am deeply grateful. In most cases, the nature and scope of the contribution is evident from the narrative context, but in the case of the greatest contributor of all, my wife, Nataki, I'm not so sure this rule holds. No words can express sufficiently my appreciation for the trust and generosity she has shown in permitting and encouraging me to tell our story from my perspective.

A great many people whose names do *not* appear in the pages of our story also played important roles in its telling, and I am equally grateful to these individuals. In particular I wish to thank my literary agent, Linda Konner, for her unwavering belief in this book and in me; Renee Sedliar, Miriam Riad, Amber Morris, and their book-loving colleagues at Da Capo, for their investments of passion and skill; Rob Klingensmith, Margot Moore, Lisa Shapiro, and the rest of the team at Hyland's, for their generous sponsorship of the Life Is a Marathon Project; the Treatment Advocacy Center, for partnering with me to increase awareness of the need for better treatment opportunities for people suffering from serious mental illness; my fellow memoirist Rebecca Walker, who offered valuable feedback on an early draft; my friend Teresa White, for encouragement; Teresa Touey and the other super commenters on the Life Is a Marathon Facebook page, for following my journey with Nataki (and Queenie) with such avid interest; and my fellow Haverfordian Elena Rocanelli Veale, for research.

Lastly, I gratefully acknowledge the following permission:

Untitled

Words and Music by Michael Nehra and Greg Giampa

Copyright (c) 1991 EMI Blackwood Music Inc. and Refried Music

All Rights Administered by Sony/ATV Music Publishing LLC, 424 Church Street, Suite 1200, Nashville, TN

37219

Reprinted by Permission of Hal Leonard LLC